Reflections on the Contemporary Law of the Sea

Publications on Ocean Development
Volume 71

A Series of Studies on
the International, Legal, Institutional and Policy Aspects
of Ocean Development

General Editors: Vaughan Lowe and Robin Churchill

The titles published in this series are listed at brill.nl/pood

Reflections on the Contemporary Law of the Sea

By
Helmut Tuerk

MARTINUS
NIJHOFF
PUBLISHERS

LEIDEN • BOSTON
2012

This book is printed on acid-free paper.

Library of Congress Cataloging-in-Publication Data

Tuerk, Helmut.
  Reflections on the contemporary law of the sea / by Helmut Tuerk.
    p. cm. — (Publications on ocean development, 0924–1922 ; v. 71)
  Includes bibliographical references and index.
  ISBN 978-90-04-21257-2 (hardback : alk. paper) 1. Law of the sea. I. Title.
  KZA1145.T84 2012
  341.4'5—dc23

                                                              2011037340

ISSN: 0924-1922
ISBN: 978 90 04 21257 2 (hardback)
ISBN: 978 90 04 21258 9 (e-book)

To my wife Monika

Contents

Foreword

The author is a judge of the International Tribunal for the Law of the Sea in Hamburg and served as its Vice-President from 2008 to 2011. For many years he was a member of the Austrian delegation to the Third United Nations Conference on the Law of the Sea and also represented his country at subsequent meetings and negotiations in that field. Opinions expressed in this book are personal and do not necessarily reflect those of the Tribunal as a whole.

The "Reflections on the Contemporary Law of the Sea" are essentially based on various articles by the author on law of the sea topics, describing the evolution of the law of the sea, the results of the Third United Nations Conference on the Law of the Sea and subsequent developments, in particular with respect to the increased rights of coastal States, the principle of the common heritage of mankind, the situation of landlocked States, the role of the International Tribunal for the Law of the Sea and the waning freedom of the seas, as well as current phenomena like the resurgence of piracy and terrorism at sea. The book also reflects personal experiences of the author at various negotiations in the field of the law of the sea. It does not purport to give a comprehensive overview over this entire, increasingly important area of international law.

The author wishes to express his sincere gratitude to Professor Wolfgang Mantl, University of Graz (Austria), for having had the idea for this book. Special thanks is due to those who have collaborated in this effort, interns at the United Nations Commission on International Trade Law (UNCITRAL) and, in particular, Ms. Szilvia Petkov and Ms. Vasiliki-Celia Liagkoura for their invaluable assistance and time dedicated to the editing and referencing of the book in its present form.

Chapter One

Introduction

The great oceans of the world – the Pacific, Atlantic, Indian and Arctic – constitute a single interconnected expanse, one continuous body of salt water that is the defining geographic feature of planet earth.[1] The oceans and their marginal seas – which cover almost 71% of the Earth's surface and constitute a vast area of communication, a source of living and non-living resources, and an important object of scientific research – have long been an indispensable arena for intercourse between human communities. Before the onset of air traffic and instantaneous communication, people, goods, and ideas travelled the world by ship. Today, even with advances in technology, seaborne commerce remains the linchpin of the global economy, as more than 90% of global trade is carried by sea.[2] In the development of humanity the oceans and seas have always played a significant role, not only as a means of communication and trade, but also as a most important source for satisfying nutritional needs. Since the beginning of the twentieth century, in view of an ever increasing world population, a growing necessity has arisen to exploit marine resources, whether living or non-living.[3]

The diversity of possible uses of marine spaces and resources continues to be further extended by technological progress. It was this development that made it increasingly urgent to lay down a new and universal legal order for the oceans and seas. A major motivation for the elaboration of a comprehensive convention on the law of the sea was the proposal by Malta in 1967 to declare the seabed and the ocean-floor beyond the limits of national jurisdiction the "common heritage of mankind", coupled with the – hitherto unfulfilled – expectation of substantial profits from deep seabed mining. It had, furthermore, become obvious that besides elaborating legal rules for the international seabed

---

[1] The White House, National Strategy for Maritime Security, at 1 (September 2005), available at: www.dhs.gov/xlibrary/assets/HSPD13_MaritimeSecurityStrategy.pdf (last visited 1 July 2011).

[2] R.N. Hass, *The National Interest and the Law of the Sea*, Foreword to S.G. Borgerson, Council on Foreign Relations, Council Special Report No. 46, at vii (May 2009), available at: www.cfr.org/content/publications/attachments/LawoftheSea_CSR46.pdf (last visited 1 July 2011).

[3] See H. Tuerk & G. Hafner, *The Landlocked Countries and the United Nations Convention on the Law of the Sea*, in: Essays on the New Law of the Sea, B. Vukas (ed.), at 58 (1985).

area, the traditional law of the sea needed revision based upon a new consensus of the international community.[4]

At the Third United Nations Conference on the Law of the Sea, which lasted from 1973 to 1982, traditional law of the sea issues thus played an equally important role as the implementation of the concept of the common heritage of mankind with respect to the seabed beyond the limits of national jurisdiction. In defining these limits, a majority of coastal States was pitted against the landlocked and geographically disadvantaged States which could only lose from an extension of coastal States' rights and jurisdiction over the seas. However, it soon became clear that these coastal States were not prepared to make any important sacrifices of what they considered as rightfully being or becoming theirs in favor of the idea of the common heritage of mankind. Continuous appeals for a "meaningful" common heritage did not meet with an appropriate response.

On 10 December 1982 the Third United Nations Conference on the Law of the Sea finally adopted the United Nations Convention on the Law of the Sea (UNCLOS)[5] as a "package deal" after years of protracted and arduous negotiations. The Convention, which provides a comprehensive legal framework to regulate all ocean space, its uses and resources, was opened for signature on the same day and entered into force on 16 November 1994. As of 1 July 2011, 161 States and the European Union were parties to UNCLOS, which is slowly moving towards universal adherence.[6] It is to be noted that the practice of States not yet bound by the Convention largely follows its provisions.

UNCLOS is a legal instrument of paramount importance for the entire international community. It is based on the fundamental premise that all the problems of the oceans are closely interrelated and need to be considered as a whole. The Convention has thus rightly been called a "Constitution for the Oceans"[7] and the most significant legal instrument of the twentieth century. UNCLOS tries to strike a careful balance between the rights of the coastal States and

---

[4] See also D. Anderson, *The Development of the Modern Law of the Sea*, in: Modern Law of the Sea: Selected Essays, at 12 (2008).

[5] United Nations Convention on the Law of the Sea, 10 December 1982, 1833 UNTS 3 (hereinafter referred to as UNCLOS), available at: www.un.org/Depts/los/convention_agreements/texts/unclos/unclos_e.pdf (last visited 1 July 2011).

[6] See status of the Convention at: www.un.org/Depts/los/reference_files/chronological_lists_of_ratifications.htm (last visited 1 July 2011).

[7] T.T.B. Koh, *A Constitution for the Oceans, Remarks made by the President of the Third United Nations Conference on the Law of the Sea*, in: Official Text of the United Nations Convention on the Law of the Sea with Annexes and Index, at xxxiii (1983); see also R.R. Churchill, *10 Years of the UN Convention on the Law of the Sea – Towards a Global Ocean Regime? A General Appraisal*, 48 German Yearbook of International Law, at 84 (2005).

the freedoms enjoyed by all States, whether coastal or landlocked. Nevertheless, the pendulum has clearly swung from *mare liberum* to *mare clausum* by the recognition of substantial sovereign rights and jurisdiction of coastal States over the most valuable areas of the seas. At the same time, the Convention has put a certain halt – at least from a territorial point of view, much less from a functional one – to a continual extension of national jurisdiction over the seas;[8] such "creeping jurisdiction" had been plaguing the international community during the preceding decades.[9]

Since its entry into force, UNCLOS has undoubtedly played a major role in bringing order to the oceans, in particular by laying down a clear and universal framework of coastal State maritime jurisdiction.[10] Although far from perfect, it nevertheless represents a common denominator for the divergent interests with respect to the sea of all States, whether coastal or landlocked.[11] It has to be borne in mind that by its very nature, the Convention could only be a framework treaty to be implemented in several areas at a national as well as an international level. Thus, for instance, modern domestic anti-piracy legislation is required, certain rights of landlocked States need implementation at a bilateral or regional level and also multilateral implementation agreements are necessary, such agreements already having been adopted with respect to fisheries[12] and illicit traffic in narcotic drugs.[13]

It should also be mentioned that a large number of international agreements relating to specific maritime aspects have been elaborated by United Nations specialized agencies, in particular the International Maritime Organization (IMO), but also by the Food and Agricultural Organization (FAO) and the International Labour Organization (ILO). The international community further had to take into account new phenomena that were virtually inexistent at the

---

[8] S. Kaye, *Freedom of Navigation in a Post 9/11 World: Security and Creeping Jurisdiction*, in: The Law of the Sea – Progress and Prospects, D. Freestone, R. Barnes & D.M. Ong (eds.), at 347–348 (2006).

[9] See also E. Franckx, *The 200-mile limit: Between Creeping Jurisdiction and Creeping Common Heritage?*, 39 George Washington International Law Review, at 467 (2007).

[10] Churchill, *10 Years of UNCLOS* (note 7), at 115.

[11] H. Tuerk, *The Landlocked States and the Law of the Sea*, 40/1 Revue Belge de Droit International, at 92 (2007).

[12] Agreement for the Implementation of the Provisions of the United Nations Convention on the Law of the Sea of 10 December 1982 relating to the Conservation and Management of Straddling Fish Stocks and Highly Migratory Fish Stocks, 4 August 1995, 2167 UNTS 3 (hereinafter referred to as the Fish Stocks Agreement), available at: www.un.org/depts/los/convention_agreements/convention_overview_fish_stocks.htm (last visited 1 July 2011).

[13] United Nations Convention against Illicit Traffic in Narcotic Drugs and Psychotropic Substances, 20 December 1988, 1582 UNTS 95, available at: treaties.un.org/doc/Publication/UNTS/Volume%201582/volume-1582-I-27627-English.pdf (last visited 1 July 2011).

time of the elaboration of UNCLOS, such as the problem of terrorism at sea, and to agree on pertinent legal rules.[14] In addition, gaps in the Convention have been and will be filled by jurisprudence, in particular with respect to the delimitation of maritime zones between States with opposite or adjacent coasts. This is facilitated by a comprehensive and innovative system for the settlement of disputes, including the newly created International Tribunal for the Law of the Sea (ITLOS).

---

[14] See in particular the Convention for the Suppression of Unlawful Acts Against the Safety of Maritime Navigation, 10 March 1988, 1678 UNTS 221 (hereinafter referred to as the SUA Convention), available at: www.imo.org/About/Conventions/StatusOfConventions/Documents/Status%20-%202011.pdf (last visited 1 July 2011).

Chapter Two

The Development of the Modern Law of the Sea[15]

A. *The Historic Evolution of the Law of the Sea*

Ever since humankind managed to venture out onto the seas, the freedom of this seemingly limitless space was challenged by domination from the land. As it has been so aptly put by a distinguished international lawyer, the sea has always been battered by two opposing winds: *"le vent du large, qui souffle vers la terre, est celui de la liberté; le vent de la terre vers le large est porteur des souverainetés."*[16]

Many of the principal features of the international law of the sea have been formed by the interplay between these two opposing forces – later referred to as the doctrines of *"mare liberum"* and *"mare clausum"*.[17] The ascendancy of one doctrine over the other during any particular historical period has tended to reflect the interests of the predominant powers of the day[18] – also a striking example of political expediency constituting the basis for the development of customary international law.

The dispute over who controls the oceans may date back to the days when the Egyptians first plied the seas in papyrus rafts.[19] As the ancient Greeks were among the first in recorded history to explore the Mediterranean all the way to the Straits of Gibraltar – not enough is known about the feats of the

---

[15] For this chapter see in particular H. Tuerk, *The Waning Freedom of the Seas*, in: L'évolution et l'état actuel du droit international de la mer, Mélanges de droit de la mer offerts à Daniel Vignes, R. Casado Raigon & G. Cataldi (eds.), at 907–936 (2009).

[16] R-J. Dupuy, *La mer sous compétence nationale*, in: *Traité du Nouveau Droit de la Mer*, R-J. Dupuy & D. Vignes (eds.), at 219 (1985).

[17] See T.T.B. Koh, *The Origins of the 1982 Convention on the Law of the Sea*, 29/1 Malaya Law Review, at 2 (1987); see also Anderson, *Modern Law of the Sea* (note 4), at 3,4; see further R. Rayfuse & R. Warner, *Securing a Sustainable Future for the Oceans Beyond National Jurisdiction: The Legal Basis for an Integrated Cross-Sectoral Regime for High Seas Governance for the 21st Century*, 23/3 The International Journal of Marine and Coastal Law, at 400 (2008).

[18] E.D. Brown, *Freedom of the High Seas Versus the Common Heritage of Mankind: Fundamental Principles in Conflict*, 20 San Diego Law Review, at 521 (1982–1983).

[19] The United Nations Convention on the Law of the Sea – A historical perspective, available at: www.un.org/Depts/los/convention_agreements/convention_historical_perspective.htm (last visited 1 July 2011).

Phoenicians – it is not surprising that Greek rulers were the first to proclaim themselves rulers of the sea. According to Herodotus, Minos, the semi-legendary King of Crete, declared himself emperor of the Hellenic Sea.[20] During the Hellenistic period, the Island of Rhodes became the chief naval power not only in the Aegean Sea but also in a large part of the Mediterranean. The principle of freedom of navigation was a recognized rule in the maritime code of Rhodes and it was the Rhodian fleet that successfully upheld it against the Byzantine Emperors.[21] Although that principle had clearly been accepted in Roman law under the legal formula according to which the sea is "*res communis*", it fell into disregard after the disintegration of the Roman Empire.[22]

With the discovery of new territories far beyond the shores of Europe by Spain and Portugal in the late fifteenth century these two powers asserted that the sea was capable of being subject to dominion and sovereignty, Spain claiming exclusive dominion over the Pacific Ocean and the Gulf of Mexico, Portugal over the Atlantic Ocean, South of Morocco, and the Indian Ocean. In 1493, Pope Alexander VI promulgated a Papal Bull "*Inter Caetera*" under which the ocean space and territories discovered west of a line drawn down the Atlantic Ocean would belong to Spain and those to the East to Portugal. The two countries in 1494 concluded a bilateral treaty at Tordesillas (Spain) in line with the Papal Bull.[23] The doctrine of *mare clausum* had thus been unequivocally expressed by the major maritime powers of the time. These monopolistic ambitions were protested against by the then rising naval powers of England and Holland, adhering to the doctrine of *mare liberum* by underlining that the sea was incapable of appropriation as it was a *res communis*, belonging to all nations.[24]

The latter position was elaborated and reinforced in 1609 when the Dutch lawyer Hugo Grotius published his famous treatise "Mare Liberum", also influenced by Spanish theologians as well as perhaps by ancient Asian traditions of unobstructed freedom of commercial shipping and international maritime trade.[25] According to Grotius, nobody can claim dominion or exclusive fisheries rights on the high seas, or an exclusive right of navigation. The sea is under no one's dominion except God's; it cannot by its very nature be appropriated; it is common to all, and its use, by the general consent of mankind, is common,

---

[20] L.B. Sohn, *The Greek Contribution to the Development of the International Law of the Sea*, in: Greece and the Law of the Sea, T.C. Kariotis (ed.), at 3 (1997).

[21] Id., at 4.

[22] R.P. Anand, *Freedom of the Seas, Past, Present and Future*, in: Law of the Sea, H. Caminos (ed.), at 216–217 (2001).

[23] Koh, *The Origins of the 1982 Convention on the Law of the Sea* (note 17), at 1.

[24] Id., at 2.

[25] See also Anand, *Freedom of the Seas* (note 22), at 216–217.

and what belongs to all cannot be appropriated by one; nor can prescription or custom justify any claim of the kind, because no one has the power to grant a privilege adverse to mankind in general.[26]

Grotius' approach to the freedom of the seas is essentially based upon the conceptualization of the sea as *res communis* and accordingly not subject to territorial appropriation. Although the expression *res communis* implies common property, the concept can also be seen as essentially a negative one. *Res communis* may in fact also be interpreted as *res nullius*, for, unless there is a structure to administer common property, it is something which may be used by everyone in the same manner and can therefore also be considered as belonging to no one.[27]

As Britain had, in the meantime, moved away from the position of *mare liberum* to that of *mare clausum*, legal scholars sought to refute the Grotian thesis, the most important being John Selden with his book "Mare Clausum sive De Dominio Maris" published in 1635.[28] Selden admits that to prohibit innocent navigation would be contrary to the dictates of humanity, but in his view permitting such navigation does not derogate from the dominion of the sea – it is comparable to the free passage on a road across another's land – and cannot always be claimed as a right. He rejects the argument that the sea cannot be appropriated, pointing to rivers, lakes, and springs as examples. He also denies that the sea is inexhaustible and maintains that its usage – e.g. fishing, navigation, commerce and the extraction of pearls and corals and the like – by others, may diminish its abundance and prejudice its use by its owner.[29]

In this battle of doctrines, Selden at first seemed to be the victor, as all European powers followed his advice to try to control as much ocean as their power would permit. It was, however, the Grotian concept of freedom of the seas that gradually attracted general support and became a principle of customary international law.[30] This doctrine was peacefully accepted because freedom of the sea in essence meant freedom of navigation and the sea in itself was not seen as a repository of resources and a source of economic wealth. The principle of non-appropriation of the seas only had the effect that coastal States were not entitled to intercept foreign ships on grounds that they were entering

---

[26] See Koh, *The Origins of the 1982 Convention on the Law of the Sea* (note 17), at 22, quoting R. Lapidoth, *Freedom of Navigation – its Legal History and its Normative Basis*, 6 *Journal of Maritime Law and Commerce*, at 261–268 (1975).

[27] A. Blanco-Bazán, *Freedom of Navigation – an outdated concept?*, Lecture given at the Summer Academy at ITLOS, 17 August 2007, at 1 (on file with author).

[28] See also Anand, *Freedom of the Seas* (note 22), at 220.

[29] See Koh, *The Origins of the 1982 Convention on the Law of the Sea* (note 17), at 3, quoting R. Lapidoth (note 26).

[30] Anderson, *Modern Law of the Sea* (note 4), at 5.

appropriated territory. The law of the sea was only the law of the flag States on board ships; there was no law governing ocean spaces as such.[31]

The only activity of exploitation of sea resources known at Grotius's time, namely fishing, was never understood as an exploitation implying appropriation of territory under the concept of coastal State jurisdiction. By its very nature, fishing was an activity exclusively to be carried out by fishermen of coastal States. The notion of foreign vessels coming from far away to fish in sea areas historically exploited by coastal fishermen was unthinkable until a few decades ago. Neither the technology nor the economic rationale existed to justify a fleet crossing overseas distances in order to appropriate fish stocks traditionally serving as the source of nourishment and to engage in related economic activities; this only made sense for local fishermen.[32] Furthermore, the living resources of the seas were considered to be in such abundance that their exploitation – at least from a certain distance from the shore – did not give rise to concern by coastal States and any exploitation of the seabed was by definition regarded as an impossible task.[33]

Although the balance between *mare clausum* and *mare liberum* had clearly tilted in the latter's favor, this doctrine was not carried to its extreme logical conclusion, namely, that no part of the sea is susceptible of being placed under coastal State jurisdiction. Such a conclusion would have been a practical absurdity, for States have a vital interest in the protection of their laws, their security, and as the case may be their neutrality in times of war, within a strip of the seas adjacent to their coasts.[34] Thus, neither the doctrine of *mare liberum* nor that of *mare clausum* could apply to the total exclusion of the other: a balance had to be struck between them. The initial balance was established in the seventeenth century, minimizing national authority by essentially limiting national rights and jurisdictions over the oceans to a narrow belt of sea adjacent to a nation's coastline – in general three nautical miles, based on the so-called "cannon shot" rule –,[35] thus maximizing the extent of the high seas and its freedoms.[36]

---

[31] Blanco-Bazán, *Freedom of Navigation* (note 27), at 2.

[32] Id., at 4.

[33] Id., at 2.

[34] See Koh, *The Origins of the 1982 Convention on the Law of the Sea* (note 17), at 3, quoting L.C. Caflisch, *The Doctrine of 'Mare Clausum' and the Third United Nations Conference on the Law of the Sea*, in: International Relations in a Changing World, R. Blackhurst et al. (eds.), at 201 (1977).

[35] See UNCLOS – A historical perspective (note 19), at 6.

[36] Anderson, *Modern Law of the Sea* (note 4), at 6.

B. *The Twentieth Century Challenge to the Freedom of the Seas*

The balance in favor of the doctrine of *mare liberum* was not really challenged until the twentieth century when the world witnessed a major shift towards national authority and the consequential diminution of the extent of the high seas, coupled with an attenuation of its freedoms.[37] This was prompted by the growing realization – based on scientific research and technological progress – of the enormous resources and the great economic potential of the seas, growing concern over the toll taken on coastal fish stocks by long-distance fishing fleets and over the danger of pollution and wastes from transport ships and oil tankers carrying noxious cargoes which threatened coastal communities and all forms of ocean life.[38] Thus, a process was set into motion that gradually led to a transition of the law of the sea from what has been called a "law of movement" to a "law of territory and appropriation".[39]

Ironically, the first major challenge to the freedom-of-the-seas doctrine came from the power that has the utmost interest in maintaining it – the United States of America. In September 1945, President Harry S. Truman, responding in part to pressure from domestic oil interests, issued a Proclamation[40] unilaterally extending United States jurisdiction over all natural resources on that nation's "continental shelf" which was described as generally extending to the point where the waters reached a depth of six hundred feet or two hundred meters isobath.[41] A second Truman Proclamation concerned fisheries off U.S. coasts which, however, did not advance jurisdictional claims to the waters over the continental shelf, calling instead for the establishment of conservation zones in parts of the high seas contiguous to the coasts of the United States territorial

---

[37] Id.

[38] UNCLOS – A historical perspective (note 19), at 1.

[39] See Dupuy, *La mer sous compétence nationale* (note 16), at 219–220; see also Anand, *Freedom of the Seas* (note 22), at 225.

[40] Presidential Proclamation Nr. 2667, *Policy of the United States with Respect to the Natural Resources of the Subsoil and Seabed of the Continental Shelf*, 28 September 1945, 10 Federal Register 12, 303 (1945); see also UNCLOS – A historical perspective (note 19), at 1; see further Anand, *Freedom of the Seas* (note 22), at 221. The view has also been put forth that the Treaty relating to the Submarine Areas of the Gulf of Paria of 1942 between the United Kingdom and Venezuela (Société des Nations – Recueil des Traités No. 4829) could be deemed the impetus from which the modern concept of the continental shelf emerged; see A.A. Lucky, The Contribution of Trinidad and Tobago in the development of the Regime of the Continental Shelf, International Symposium on Scientific and Legal Aspects of the Regime of the Continental Shelf and the Area, Beijing, 28–29 May 2010, at 5 (on file with author).

[41] See reference by Koh, *The Origins of the 1982 Convention on the Law of the Sea* (note 17), to the Press Release accompanying the Truman Proclamation, at 1.

sea by means of agreements with those States whose subjects traditionally fished in the areas in question.[42]

This Truman Doctrine was not only not challenged by other States but on the contrary used as a basis for emulating and even exceeding the U.S. claims. Mexico issued a similar proclamation one month after the United States. A year later, Argentina claimed an "Epicontinental Sea", comprising not only sovereignty over the continental shelf, but also over the water column above. Between 1946 and 1957, ten other States claimed sovereignty over their continental shelves and the superjacent waters. Within that period five Latin American countries declared 200 nautical mile limits for exclusive fishing rights. In the Santiago Declaration of 1952, Chile, Ecuador and Peru proclaimed sovereignty and exclusive jurisdiction over the sea up to a minimum distance of 200 nautical miles from their coasts.[43] Soon after the Second World War, Egypt, Ethiopia, Saudi-Arabia, Libya, Venezuela and some Eastern European countries had departed from the traditional 3-mile limit by claiming a 12-mile territorial sea – which had already been claimed by Russia since 1927.[44]

This movement was said to be prompted by increased nutritional needs of coastal State populations, in particular the concern by developing countries that long-distance fishing fleets of industrialized countries would exhaust the fishing grounds off their shores, increasing energy needs and coastal States' desire to protect their national security as well as their marine scientific knowledge, perceived as a national wealth.[45] This tendency resulted in establishing a continental shelf regime and led to the unilateral extension of the breadth of the territorial sea by coastal States as well as the claim for an exclusive fisheries or economic zone. While the doctrine of the continental shelf was quickly accepted into international law, no general agreement on the breadth of the territorial sea was in sight.[46]

In 1956, the International Law Commission (ILC), entrusted by the UN General Assembly with the progressive development of international law and its codification, submitted a draft convention to the General Assembly in which the Commission recognized that international practice was not uniform regarding the delimitation of the territorial sea, but also considered that international

---

[42] Presidential Proclamation Nr. 2668, *Policy of the United States with Respect to Coastal Fisheries in Certain Areas of the High Seas*, 28 September, 1945, 10 Fed. Reg. 12, 303 (1945); see also Anderson, *Modern Law of the Sea* (note 4), at 8.

[43] Koh, *The Origins of the 1982 Convention on the Law of the Sea* (note 17), at 10; see also X. Hinrichs, *Die Ausschließliche Wirtschaftszone und die Praxis der lateinamerikanischen Staaten*, at 41 (1997).

[44] UNCLOS – A historical perspective (note 19), at 2, see also Koh, *The Origins of the 1982 Convention on the Law of the Sea* (note 17), at 11.

[45] G. Hafner, *The 'land-locked' viewpoint*, 5 Marine Policy, at 281 (1981).

[46] See also Tuerk, *Waning Freedom of the Seas* (note 15), at 911.

law did not permit its extension beyond 12 nautical miles. The ILC proposed that the breadth of the territorial sea be fixed by an international conference.[47]

The First United Nations Conference on the Law of the Sea of 1958 was confronted with a wide variety of proposals on the limit of the territorial sea, ranging from three to 200 nautical miles, none of which obtained the necessary two-thirds majority.[48] At the Second UN Conference on the Law of the Sea in 1960 a proposal for a six mile territorial sea plus a six mile fisheries zone beyond failed by only one vote to secure adoption by a two-thirds majority. This proved to be a turning point for the future development of the law of the sea.[49] Although the four 1958 Geneva Conventions – on the Territorial Sea and the Contiguous Zone,[50] on Fishing and Conservation of the Living Resources of the High Seas,[51] on the High Seas[52] and on the Continental Shelf[53] – all entered into force, they, however, failed to gain the necessary widespread acceptance. In the following years these Conventions were to an important extent overtaken by State practice. It also turned out that it had been a major mistake, not to be repeated in the future, to split the law of the sea into four different legal instruments from which States could pick and choose.

In retrospect, it has become quite clear that one of the most important decisions taken at the 1958 Conference related to the continental shelf. The respective Convention in fact nationalized the most valuable areas of the seabed to the detriment of States without long coastlines or with off-shore areas not offering any realistic possibility for exploitation in any foreseeable future. An important and, as later developments would show, irrevocable step was thus taken to distribute most of the mineral riches of the oceans among a relatively limited number of States, without any regard to the interests and needs which States in a less advantageous geographical position, including landlocked countries, might have in this regard.[54] The Convention on the Continental Shelf furthermore

---

[47] Koh, *The Origins of the 1982 Convention on the Law of the Sea* (note 17), at 12.

[48] Id.

[49] See Anderson, *Modern Law of the Sea* (note 4), at 8–10.

[50] 1958 Geneva Convention on the Territorial Sea and the Contiguous Zone, 29 April 1958, 516 UNTS 205, available at: untreaty.un.org/ilc/texts/instruments/english/conventions/8_1_1958_territorial_sea.pdf (last visited 1 July 2011).

[51] 1958 Geneva Convention on Fishing and Conservation of the Living Resources of the High Seas, 29 April 1958, 559 UNTS 285, available at: untreaty.un.org/ilc/texts/instruments/english/conventions/8_1_1958_fishing.pdf (last visited 1 July 2011).

[52] 1958 Geneva Convention on the High Seas, 29 April 1958, 450 UNTS 11, available at: untreaty.un.org/ilc/texts/instruments/english/conventions/8_1_1958_high_seas.pdf (last visited 1 July 2011).

[53] 1958 Geneva Convention on the Continental Shelf, 29 April 1958, 499 UNTS 311, available at: untreaty.un.org/ilc/texts/instruments/english/conventions/8_1_1958_continental_shelf.pdf (last visited 1 July 2011).

[54] Tuerk, *Landlocked States* (note 11), at 97.

suffered from a fundamental weakness by defining the outer limits of the continental shelf in terms of depth – 200 meters isobath – as well as exploitability. These two criteria in practice proved unsatisfactory in view of technological advances. The rapid movement of the offshore oil and gas industry into deeper and remoter waters had not been anticipated in 1958.[55]

Moreover, it has rightly been pointed out that, the Convention on Fishing and Conservation of the Living Resources of the High Seas failed to provide a solution to the allocation and attendant conservation problem that arises when exploitation of a stock by multiple users approaches or exceeds its sustainable yield. This increasing threat prompted political pressure on coastal States to find ways to protect local fishing industries facing foreign competition for a limited resource. That mounting pressure in no small measure contributed to the claims to control the sea up to 200 nautical miles and even beyond.[56]

By the mid-1960's, the major maritime powers and the majority of coastal States both felt a need for a new legal order for the oceans. The maritime powers needed a new consensus regarding the rules of ocean law compatible with the mobility, flexibility and credibility of a routine global deployment of forces, thus in particular with respect to their strategic interest in unimpeded passage through and over straits used for international navigation. Most coastal States wanted a new legal order to ratify the unilateral claims which they had made for oceanic jurisdiction, oceanic resources, for the protection of the marine environment, and for their security.[57]

At the same time, the composition of the international community was changing as a result of former colonial territories attaining independence. These newly-independent States had interests similar to those of the Latin American countries and pressure for wider limits of national jurisdiction therefore continued to grow. The quest for an extension of sovereign rights by coastal States was also strengthened by the International Court of Justice (ICJ) when it decided in 1969 in the North Sea Continental Shelf Cases that customary law required the application of the concept of "natural prolongation" with respect to the continental shelf. This expression was also used to underpin claims to an ever-wider continental shelf, especially as new technology permitted the industry to advance into deeper waters, although it was employed by the Court to justify the appurtenance of the continental shelf to the coastal States and not to clarify its outer limit.[58] Already in 1951, the Court in its decision in the

[55] See Anderson, *Modern Law of the Sea* (note 4), at 10.
[56] B.H. Oxman, *The Territorial Temptation: A Siren Song at Sea*, 100 American Journal of International Law, at 833 (2006).
[57] See Koh, *The Origins of the 1982 Convention on the Law of the Sea* (note 17), at 16.
[58] B. Kwiatkowska, *Creeping Jurisdiction beyond 200 Miles in the Light of the 1982 Law of the Sea Convention and State Practice*, 22 /2 Ocean Development and International Law, at 157 (1991).

Anglo-Norwegian Fisheries Case had indirectly contributed to an extension of coastal State jurisdiction beyond the then prevailing limits by permitting the use of straight base lines for measuring the breadth of the territorial sea, when justified by special geographic circumstances.[59]

The opportunity to build a new consensus on the law of the sea arose in 1967 when the then Ambassador of Malta to the United Nations, Arvid Pardo, drew the attention of the world to the immense resources of the seabed and ocean floor beyond the limits of national jurisdiction and proposed that such resources be declared the "common heritage of mankind", not subject to national appropriation, and reserved exclusively for peaceful purposes.[60] In 1970 the UN General Assembly decided to hold the Third United Nations Conference on the Law of the Sea and also unanimously adopted the Declaration of Principles on the Seabed and the Ocean Floor Beyond the Limits of National Jurisdiction, based on the Maltese proposal,[61] which constituted an important basis for the future Convention on the Law of the Sea.

Besides elaborating rules for the international seabed area, the need for a revision of the traditional law of the sea was underlined by the fact that at the start of the Conference at the end of 1973, the States that maintained the traditional claims to a three-mile territorial sea numbered a mere 25.[62] By then, 66 countries had claimed a 12-mile territorial sea limit, 15 others claimed between 4 and 10 miles, and one remaining major group of eight States claimed 200 nautical miles. Furthermore, two important groups of developing countries adopted Declarations calling for the creation of zones of national jurisdiction extending to 200 nautical miles. These were the Yaoundé Declaration of the African States concerning the Exclusive Economic Zone and the Santo Domingo Declaration concerning the Patrimonial Sea drawn up by a group of Latin American and Caribbean States. Although both Declarations provided for a substantial extension of coastal States rights, they retained the freedom of navigation.[63]

The stage had thus been set for the most significant changes to the law of the sea since the times of Grotius.[64] It has rightly been pointed out that the old

---

[59] Fisheries (United Kingdom v. Norway), Judgment, 18 December 1951, ICJ Reports 1951, at 116; see also Dupuy, La mer sous compétence nationale (note 16), at 233.

[60] Koh, *The Origins of the 1982 Convention on the Law of the Sea* (note 17), at 16; see also Anand, *Freedom of the Seas* (note 22), at 228.

[61] UN General Assembly Res. 2749 (XXV) of 17 December 1970, Declaration of Principles Governing the Seabed and the Ocean Floor, and Subsoil Thereof, Beyond the Limits of National Jurisdiction; see also Anderson, *Modern Law of the Sea* (note 4), at 12.

[62] See UNCLOS – A historical perspective (note 19), at 5.

[63] See also Anderson, *Modern Law of the Sea* (note 4), at 13.

[64] S. Bateman, D.R. Rothwell & D. VanderZwaag, *Navigational Rights and Freedoms in the New Millennium: Dealing with 20th Century Controversies and 21st Century Challenges*, in: Navigational Rights and Freedoms and the New Law of the Sea, D.R. Rothwell & S. Bateman (eds.), at 314 (2000).

legal order of the seas collapsed under the weight of three causes: the progress of technology, the failure of the traditional law to deal adequately with the concerns of coastal States regarding the utilization of oceanic resources, and the emergence of a large number of developing countries.[65]

C. *The 1982 United Nations Convention on the Law of the Sea (UNCLOS)*

With respect to the high seas, UNCLOS in Part VII essentially retained the provisions of the respective 1958 Convention,[66] declaring the high seas to be open to all States, whether coastal or landlocked, reiterating the invalidity of claims of sovereignty over the high seas, and confirming the exclusive jurisdiction of the flag State over its ships.[67] The legal status of the high seas is characterized by the total prevalence of the principle of freedom. It is a zone of "no sovereignty", neither territorial nor functional, open to common use by all States. The doctrine of *mare clausum* is thus clearly negated.[68] It has been stated that the high seas can be described neither as *res nullius*, because they are not susceptible to appropriation, nor as *res communis omnium*, because they do not fall under the condominium of the international community. They are, in fact a good equally accessible and open to all States. Accordingly, the basic rule of the high seas is that every State can make free use of that maritime space within the limits of equality of freedom for other States and with due regard to their interests.[69]

Article 87(1) of UNCLOS sets forth a non-exhaustive list of freedoms of the high seas, both for coastal and landlocked States, which are to be exercised not only under the conditions laid down by the Convention, but also by other rules of international law. While the freedoms of navigation and overflight are not qualified by any specific limitations, the freedoms to lay submarine cables and pipelines, to construct artificial islands and other installations permitted under international law, of fishing, and of scientific research, are subject to other provisions of the Convention.

---

[65] See Koh, *The Origins of the 1982 Convention on the Law of the Sea* (note 17), at 14.

[66] 1958 Geneva Convention on the High Seas (note 52).

[67] Arts. 87(1), 89 and 92 UNCLOS.

[68] D. Anderson, *Freedom of the High Seas in the Modern Law of the Sea*, in: The Law of the Sea – Progress and Prospects, D. Freestone, R. Barnes & D.M. Ong, (eds.), at 331 (2006).

[69] J.C. Lupinacci, *The Legal Status of the Exclusive Economic Zone in the 1982 Convention on the Law of the Sea*, quoting Jiménez de Aréchaga, in: The Exclusive Economic Zone, A Latin American Perspective, F. Orrego Vicuña (ed.), at 107 (1984).

The freedom of navigation provides vessels of any State with the right to traverse the high seas with minimal interference from any other State,[70] a key exception being the right of visit under certain well-defined circumstances. Article 110 UNCLOS sets out four instances where warships may exercise a right of visit against a foreign-flagged vessel: piracy, slavery, unlawful broadcasting, and where suspicions as to the nationality of the vessel arise. It has been pointed out that these exceptions to flag State authority and the freedom of the high seas have resulted from "globally-shared needs and troubles, especially in modern times".[71] There are furthermore limited instances where a State may prescribe and enforce certain measures against foreign vessels for the management and conservation of fisheries or the protection of the marine environment.[72] A ship is to sail under the flag of one State only and there must be a genuine link between that State and the ship. Exceptions to the exclusive jurisdiction of the flag State are limited to those expressly provided for by treaty.[73] Warships and ships owned or operated by a State and used only on government non-commercial service are entitled to complete immunity from the jurisdiction of any State other than the flag State when on the high seas.[74] As a result, third-state rights against foreign warships on the high seas are virtually non-existent. Instead, an attempt to exercise law enforcement jurisdiction against a foreign warship could be tantamount to a threat or use of force against a sovereign instrumentality of a foreign State.[75]

The right to fish the high seas has long been considered a constituent element of the freedom of the seas, the wealth of aquatic resources having been assumed to be an unlimited gift of nature. However, with increased knowledge and dynamic development of fisheries it was realized that these resources, although renewable, are not infinite and need to be properly managed.[76] According to Article 116 UNCLOS, the right to fish the high seas is therefore subject to certain limitations and conditions. It is, in particular, qualified by the provisions on the protection and preservation of the living resources, including the duty

---

[70] N. Klein, *The Right of Visit and the 2005 Protocol on the Suppression of Unlawful Acts against the Safety of Maritime Navigation*, 35 Denver Journal of International Law and Policy, at 295 (2006–2007).

[71] J.L. Jesus, *Protection of Foreign Ships against Piracy and Terrorism at Sea – Legal Aspects*, 18/3 The International Journal of Marine and Coastal Law, at 373 (2003).

[72] See Art. 73, respectively Art. 220 UNCLOS.

[73] Art. 91 (1) UNCLOS.

[74] Art. 95, 96 UNCLOS.

[75] B.H. Oxman, *The Regime of Warships under the United Nations Convention on the Law of the Sea*, 24 Virginia Journal of International Law, at 815 (1984).

[76] See Code of Conduct for Responsible Fisheries, Food and Agriculture Organization of the United Nations (FAO), Preface (1995), available at: www.fao.org/docrep/005/v9878e/v9878e00.HTM (last visited: 1 July 2011).

to cooperate with other States in the adoption of conservation measures, and by other relevant treaty obligations.[77]

As already described, the trend towards a 12-mile territorial sea, which had emerged by the late 1960s, had rapidly been gaining momentum and that distance, measured from the normal baseline along the low-water mark, or from straight baselines enclosing internal or archipelagic waters, was finally enshrined in Article 3 UNCLOS as a maximum limit. Within that limit, coastal States are in principle free to enforce any law, regulate any use and exploit any resource. At the same time, the right of "innocent passage" – defined as passage "not prejudicial to the peace, good order or security of the coastal State",[78] which had long since formed part of customary international law, was confirmed in Article 17 UNCLOS for ships of all States, whether coastal or landlocked. Whether this right also applies to warships in an unqualified manner is, however, not undisputed.[79] Although the prevalent view based on the Convention – which does not distinguish between categories of ships – is that it does, and that the passage of warships through the territorial sea does not require prior notification of the coastal State, or even gaining that State's prior permission, a substantial number of coastal States insist on such a requirement.[80] In any case, as before, submarines must navigate on the surface and show their flag and there is also no right of overflight.[81] With respect to innocent passage, UNCLOS did not substantially change the previously existing law – even John Selden had recognized such a right.

---

[77] Arts 116–120 UNCLOS; see also G.D. Pendleton, *State Responsibility and the High Seas Marine Environment: A Legal Theory for the Protection of Seamounts in the Global Commons*, 14 Pacific Rim Law and Policy Journal, at 501 (2005).

[78] See Arts. 15–19 UNCLOS.

[79] Kaye, *Freedom of Navigation Post 9/11* (note 8), at 349; see also id S. Davidson, *The Law of the Sea and Freedom of Navigation in Asia Pacific*, in: International Law Issues in the South Pacific, J. Leane & B. Van Tigerstrom (eds.), at 141 (2005); see further B. Vukas, *The Law of the Sea, Selected Writings*, Chapter 10: The New Law of the Sea and Navigation: A View from the Mediterranean, at 135–142 (2004).

[80] The Commander's Handbook on the Law of Naval Operations of the United States Department of the Navy lists 27 States that require prior permission for passage through the territorial sea and 12 that require prior notification – see Z. Keyuan, *Law of the Sea Issues between the United States and East Asian States*, 39/1 Ocean Development and International Law, at 70 (2008), citing I. Shearer, *Military Activities in the Exclusive Economic Zone: The Case of Aereal Surveillance*, 17 Ocean Yearbook, at 552 (2003); see also J.A. Roach & R.N. Smith, *United States Responses to Excessive Maritime Claims* (2nd ed.), Chapter 2, at 23–24 (1996); see also Kaye, *Freedom of Navigation Post 9/11* (note 8), at 349; see further S. Bateman, *Security and the Law of the Sea in East Asia, Navigational Regimes and Exclusive Economic Zones*, in: The Law of the Sea – Progress and Prospects, D. Freestone, R. Barnes & D.M. Ong (eds.), at 369 (2006).

[81] Id., Bateman, at 367; see also Art. 20 UNCLOS.

The delimitation of the territorial sea between States the coasts of which are opposite or adjacent to each other is dealt with by Article 15 UNCLOS which is essentially based on Article 12 of the respective 1958 Geneva Convention. Where such a situation occurs, neither State is entitled, failing agreement between them to the contrary, to extend its territorial sea beyond the median line. This provision does not apply in the presence of historical title or other special circumstances which may justify or necessitate some other method of delimitation.[82] It is worth noting that this Article contains no provisions regarding provisional arrangements in case of a dispute or its settlement.[83]

UNCLOS in Article 33, furthermore, provides for the possibility of an extension of the contiguous zone – which is no longer said to be a zone of the high seas – to a maximum of 24 nautical miles instead of previously 12 miles.[84] In that zone, a coastal State may exercise the control necessary to prevent or punish infringement of its customs, fiscal, immigration or sanitary laws and regulations within its territory or territorial sea.[85] Quite a number of States have, however, asserted rights beyond the enumeration contained in the Convention, in particular, regarding security jurisdiction.[86]

The extension of the limits of the territorial sea placed more than one hundred straits used for international navigation under national sovereignty, including strategic passages such as the Strait of Gibraltar, the Strait of Malacca, the Strait of Hormuz and Bab el Mandeb.[87] The Convention therefore, as a corollary to this extension, introduced the novel concept of "transit passage",[88] maintaining the right to unimpeded navigation and overflight with respect to such straits by allowing ships, aircraft, and submarines to transit through, over, and under such straits and their approaches.[89] Ships and aircraft in transit passage must, however, observe international regulations on navigational safety, civilian air-traffic control and prohibition of vessel-source pollution and the conditions to proceed without delay and without stopping, except in distress situations,

---

[82] See United Nations Convention on the Law of the Sea, 1982, A Commentary, Vol. II, S.N. Nandan and S. Rosenne (Volume Editors), N.R. Grandy (Assistant Editor), (hereinafter referred to as Virginia Commentary), at 132, 136 (1993).

[83] Id., at 143.

[84] See 1958 Geneva Convention on the Territorial Sea and the Contiguous Zone (note 50), Art. 24.

[85] Art. 33 (1) UNCLOS.

[86] See also Roach & Smith, *US Responses to Excessive Maritime Claims* (note 80), Chapter 6, at 166–171; see further Kaye, *Freedom of Navigation Post 9/11* (note 8), at 353.

[87] See also UNCLOS – A historical perspective (note 19), at 6.

[88] See Art. 37– 41 UNCLOS.

[89] Statement of Admiral Patrick M. Walsh, US Navy, Vice Chief of Naval Operations, Statement Before the Senate Committee on Foreign Relations Hearing on the Law of the Sea Convention, 27 September 2007 (on file with author), at 4.

and to refrain from any threat or use of force against the coastal States. In all matters other than such transient navigation, straits are to be considered part of the territorial sea of the coastal State.[90]

UNCLOS in Part IV further contains a new concept in international law: that of the archipelagic State – a State that is constituted wholly by one or more archipelagoes, a group of closely spaced islands.[91] This innovation seems to have also been inspired by the opinion of the ICJ regarding the permissibility of applying the system of straight baselines. For archipelagic States, the territorial sea is a 12-mile zone extending from a line drawn by joining the outermost points of the outermost islands of the group that are in close proximity to each other. The waters between the islands are declared archipelagic waters, which are under national sovereignty.[92] Archipelagic states are, however, obliged to respect existing submarine cables laid by other States, and ships of all States enjoy the right of innocent passage. Furthermore, all ships and aircraft enjoy the right of "archipelagic sea lanes passage," akin to transit passage, in sea lanes and air routes designated by an archipelagic State for "the purpose of continuous, expeditious and unobstructed transit." The designation of such sea lanes by the coastal State in both cases of passage requires approval by the IMO.

The exercise of the rights of transit passage and archipelagic sea lanes passage has, in practice, given rise to certain problems of interpretation as these rights of passage are to be exercised by ships and aircraft in the "normal mode".[93] While it is generally accepted that the "normal mode" of transit for submarines is submerged – which under certain circumstances may lead to safety risks – it seems sometimes rather difficult to determine the "normal mode" in the case of aircraft.[94] There is also continuing disagreement between the maritime powers and the archipelagic States over the appropriate locations and regimes for archipelagic sea lanes passage.[95] An open question is whether there should be some form of "burden sharing" between the coastal States concerned and transiting States with respect to measures required for ensuring the safety of passage.[96]

An entirely new concept in international law to which Part V of UNCLOS is devoted is the exclusive economic zone (EEZ). In that zone with a maximum

---

[90] UNCLOS – A historical perspective (note 19), at 6. While according to Article 25(3) UNCLOS a coastal State may for security reasons temporarily suspend the innocent passage of foreign ships in specified areas of its territorial sea, transit passage is non-suspendable.

[91] Id., at 7; Art. 46 UNCLOS.

[92] UNCLOS – A historical perspective (note 19), at 6.

[93] See Arts 39 (1) (c) and 53 (3) UNCLOS.

[94] Bateman, *Security and the Law of the Sea in East Asia* (note 80), at 377–378; see also T.T.B. Koh, *The Territorial Sea, Contiguous Zone, Straits and Archipelagoes under the 1982 Convention on the Law of the Sea*, 29/2 Malaya Law Review, at 183 (1987).

[95] Davidson, *Law of the Sea and Freedom of Navigation in Asia Pacific* (note 79), at 139.

[96] See Bateman, *Security and the Law of the Sea in East Asia* (note 80), at 371–372.

limit of 200 nautical miles from the baselines from which the breadth of the territorial seas is measured,[97] the coastal State has sovereign rights for the purpose of exploring and exploiting, conserving and managing all natural resources and also with respect to other economic activities. Moreover, it has jurisdiction regarding the establishment and use of artificial islands, installations and structures, marine scientific research, the protection and preservation of the marine environment, as well as other rights and duties provided for in the Convention.[98] It is important to note that the provisions of UNCLOS relating to the high seas – Articles 88 to 115 – and other pertinent rules of international law continue to apply to the EEZ in so far as they are not incompatible with it.[99] As with respect to the high seas, the use of this language makes it clear that the Convention is not the only source of law in relation to the use of that zone.[100] All States, whether coastal or landlocked, enjoy the high seas freedoms of navigation and overflight and of laying submarine cables and pipelines, and other internationally lawful uses of the sea related to these freedoms, such as those associated with the operation of ships, aircraft and submarine cables and pipelines, and compatible with the other provisions of UNCLOS.[101] In contrast, several of the basic freedoms of the high seas have disappeared, in particular the freedom of fishing, other freedoms relating to the exploration and exploitation of resources, and the freedom of marine scientific research.[102]

The EEZ has a *sui generis* legal status constituting a compromise between sovereignty of the coastal State and freedom for all States. It is a zone not of territorial, but of functional sovereignty;[103] it does not form part of the territorial sea nor of the high seas, nor can it be assimilated to either maritime space.[104] The rights and jurisdiction of the coastal State and the rights and freedoms of other States are governed by the relevant provisions of the Convention. In exercising their rights and duties in the EEZ, coastal States are required to

---

[97] Art. 57 UNCLOS.

[98] Art. 56 UNCLOS.

[99] Art. 58 (2) UNCLOS.

[100] See Arts. 87 (1) and 58 (2) UNCLOS.

[101] Art. 58 (1) UNCLOS.

[102] Lupinacci, *The Legal Status of the EEZ under UNCLOS* (note 69), at 100.

[103] See B. Kwiatkowska, *The 200 Mile Exclusive Economic Zone in the New Law of the Sea*, at 4–5 (1989).

[104] J. Castañeda, *Negotiations on the Exclusive Economic Zone at the Third United Nations Conference on the Law of the Sea – a reprint by the Government of Mexico in commemoration of the 20th Anniversary of the United Nations Convention on the Law of the Sea*, December 9–10, 2002, at 48, first published in: Essays in International Law in Honour of Judge Manfred Lachs, J. Makarczyk (ed.), at 621 (1984); see also C-G. Hasselmann, *Die Freiheit der Handelsschiffahrt: eine Analyse der UN-Seerechtskonvention*, at 107 (1987).

have due regard to the rights and duties of other States, and vice versa.[105] This emphasis also on State duties is a remarkable characteristic of the new law of the sea, reflected throughout the text of UNCLOS.[106]

Coastal States have two types of rights in the EEZ: sovereign rights that are directly resource related, and jurisdictional rights that are intimately linked to the exploration, exploitation and protection of resources. It would therefore not seem legitimate for a coastal State to restrict navigational rights in that zone unless such rights interfered with its ability to explore, exploit or protect its resources.[107] Article 73(1) UNCLOS allows coastal States to stop and search any fishing vessel suspected of violating its laws governing resource exploitation in its EEZ. This provision appears to grant the power to coastal States to expect every foreign fishing vessel to identify itself and explain its intentions whenever it enters such a zone, even if the vessel is only transiting on its way to distant fishing grounds.[108] Furthermore, the jurisdiction of the coastal State regarding the protection and preservation of the marine environment may raise questions about the extent to which interference with navigational rights to achieve this end is justified.[109] In this context, there is potential disagreement over the transportation of hazardous materials through the EEZ. In any case, there is no indication in UNCLOS of any restrictions that can be placed on navigation in that area based upon the nature of the cargo.[110]

The controversies during the negotiations leading to UNCLOS regarding military activities in the EEZ persist in state practice. The basic problem is a matter of interpretation as to whether military activities are included in the freedoms of navigation, of overflight and other internationally lawful uses of the sea under the Convention. Some coastal States claim that other States cannot carry out military activities in or over their EEZs without their consent, and have sought to apply restrictions on navigation and overflight in these zones that are not accepted by those States.[111] The opposing view, obviously held by major maritime powers, is that the regime of the EEZ does not permit the coastal State to limit traditional non-resource related, high seas activities in that area. Such activities may in their view include task force maneuvering, flight operations, military exercises, telecommunications and space activities, intel-

---

[105] Bateman, *Security and the Law of the Sea in East Asia* (note 80), at 379; see Arts. 56 (2) and 58 (3) UNCLOS.

[106] Kwiatkowska, *The 200 Miles EEZ* (note 103), at 6.

[107] Davidson, *Law of the Sea and Freedom of Navigation in Asia Pacific* (note 79), at 144.

[108] J.M. Van Dyke, *The disappearing right to navigational freedom in the exclusive economic zone*, 29/2 Marine Policy, at 108 (2005).

[109] Kaye, *Freedom of Navigation Post 9/11* (note 8), at 361; see also Davidson, *Law of the Sea and Freedom of Navigation in Asia Pacific* (note 79), at 129; see further Art. 220 UNCLOS.

[110] Id., Kaye at 361; see also id. Davidson, at 146–149.

[111] Bateman, *Security and the Law of the Sea in East Asia* (note 80), at 380.

ligence and surveillance activities, marine data collection and weapons' testing and firing.[112]

The concept of the continental shelf as enshrined in the respective 1958 Geneva Convention was basically retained by UNCLOS: attempts, in particular by the landlocked and geographically disadvantaged States, to subsume it under that of the EEZ had failed. At the same time, however, that concept was substantially broadened and is now subject to a twofold definition: on the one hand, the customary notion of the continental shelf is applied to the entire continental margin, comprising the shelf, the slope and the rise; on the other hand, that notion was extended to 200 nautical miles, even where no geological shelf exists.[113] The existing sovereign rights of the coastal States over the continental shelf for the purpose of exploiting it and exploring its natural resources were confirmed by Article 77 UNCLOS. These resources are defined as mineral and other non-living resources of the seabed and subsoil together with living organisms belonging to sedentary species. The rights enjoyed by the coastal States in the EEZ with respect to artificial islands, installations and structures also apply to the continental shelf.[114]

As under the previous legal regime, the rights of the coastal States over the continental shelf do not affect the legal status of the superjacent waters or of the air space above those waters.[115] The exercise of these rights must furthermore not infringe upon, or result in any unjustified interference with, navigation and other rights and freedoms of other States as provided for in the Convention.[116] The right of all States to lay submarine cables and pipelines on the continental shelf is maintained.[117] It is, however, accompanied by conditions which render it "a regulated right" that can hardly any longer be considered a freedom.[118] The requirement of consent by the coastal State regarding the delineation of the course for the laying of pipelines appears to stress the fact that the course may not be delineated if no agreement exists.

An essential innovation relating to the continental shelf concerns its more precise delimitation which was indispensable in view of the seabed and its resources beyond the limits of national jurisdiction, having been declared the

---

[112] Id.

[113] See Art. 76 (1) UNCLOS; see also: Kwiatkowska, *Creeping Jurisdiction* (note 58), at 154; see further A.G. Oude Elferink, *Article 76 of the LOSC on the Definition of the Continental Shelf: Questions Concerning its Interpretation from a Legal Perspective*, 21/3 The International Journal of Marine and Coastal Law, at 275 (2006).

[114] Art. 80 UNCLOS.

[115] Art. 78 (1) UNCLOS.

[116] Art. 78 (2) UNCLOS.

[117] Art. 79 UNCLOS.

[118] See J.F. Pulvenis, *Le plateau continental, définition et régime*, in: Traité du nouveau droit de la mer, R.J. Dupuy & D. Vignes, (eds.), at 328 (1985).

"common heritage of mankind". According to Article 76 UNCLOS, the outer limit of the continental shelf may be set beyond 200 nautical miles at a maximum distance of up to 350 nautical miles from the baselines from which the breadth of the territorial sea is measured, or up to 100 nautical miles from the 2,500 meter isobath, which is a line connecting the depth of 2,500 meters.[119] As coastal States may choose which method of delineation is in their best interests, there is not even an absolute limit of 350 nautical miles from the baselines regarding sovereign rights of these States over the continental shelf.[120] In this connection, divergent opinions may well arise, in particular, as to the distinction between "submarine ridges" to which the 350 nautical miles limit applies and "submarine elevations", that are natural components of the continental margin, to which it does not.[121] It should also be borne in mind that some of the scientific terms used in UNCLOS may no longer correspond to the present situation as scientific knowledge about the nature and extent of the continental margin has greatly evolved from its original definition.[122]

Where a coastal State intends to establish the outer limits of its continental shelf beyond 200 nautical miles, it is obliged to submit the particulars of such limits to the Commission on the Limits of the Continental Shelf set up under Annex II to UNCLOS, at the latest within ten years of the entry into force of the Convention for that State.[123] The members of the Commission, 21 experts in the field of geology, geophysics and hydrology,[124] are elected for a term of five

---

[119] See Art. 76 (5) UNCLOS. A coastal State has two possibilities to establish the outer edge of the continental margin wherever it extends beyond 200 nautical miles from the baselines: either by a line delineated by reference to the outermost fixed points at each of which the thickness of sedimentary rocks is at least 1 per cent of the shortest distance from such point to the foot of the continental slope (the Gardiner or Irish Formula), or a line delineated by reference to fixed points not more than 60 nautical miles from the foot of the continental slope (Hedberg Formula); see Art. 76 (4) (a) UNCLOS.

[120] See also B. Kunoy, *The Rise of the Sun: Legal Arguments in Outer Continental Margin Delimitations*, 53/2 Netherlands International Law Review, at 247–272 (2006).

[121] See Art. 76 (6) UNCLOS; see also: S.V. Suarez, *The Outer Limits of the Continental Shelf, Legal Aspects of their Establishment*, at 247 (2008); see further Oude Elferink, *Article 76 UNCLOS on the Definition of the Continental Shelf* (note 113), at 297–307.

[122] R. Lagoni, *Festlandsockel und Ausschließliche Wirtschaftszone*, in: Handbuch des Seerechts, W. Graf Vitzthum (ed.), at 197 (2006); see also C. Carleton, *Article 76 of the UN Convention on the Law of the Sea – Implementation Problems from the Technical Perspective*, 21/3 The International Journal of Marine and Coastal Law, at 307 (2006).

[123] See Annex II, Art. 4 UNCLOS. The Eighteenth Meeting of States Parties in 2008 decided that this time limit is also being met by submitting only indicative preliminary information concerning the outer limit of the continental shelf beyond 200 nautical miles. See document SPLOS/183 of 24 June 2008, available at: www.un.org/Depts/los/meeting_states_parties/documents/splos_183e_advance.pdf (last visited 1 July 2011).

[124] See Art. 76 (8) and Annex II to UNCLOS.

years by the States parties to UNCLOS.[125] The limits of the shelf as established by a coastal State, however, only become "final and binding" – with respect to all States parties to the Convention and the International Seabed Authority (ISA) – if adopted "on the basis" of recommendations by the Commission, the broad mandate of which is thus "to act as a watchdog to prevent excessive coastal State claims".[126] The term "on the basis" with respect to these recommendations was chosen by the negotiators at the Conference on the Law of the Sea in order to allow the coastal State some flexibility in their implementation. The question arises whether any State party could challenge the limits set with the argument that the provisions of UNCLOS had not been correctly applied or that the limits were based on insufficient or flawed scientific data.[127]

Articles 74 and 83 UNCLOS address the delimitation of the EEZ and the continental shelf between overlapping claims of States with opposite or adjacent coasts. The fundamental norm is that, in order to "achieve an equitable solution" the delimitation between those States shall be effected by agreement on the basis of international law as referred to in Article 38 of the Statute of the ICJ.[128] If no agreement can be reached within a reasonable period of time, the States concerned shall resort to the dispute settlement procedure provided for in Part XV of the Convention. Pending agreement between the States in dispute, they shall make every effort to enter into provisional arrangements of a practical nature and, during this transitional period, not to jeopardize or hamper the reaching of final agreement.[129] These provisions are the outcome of protracted negotiations between two approaches: should delimitation should be effected by the application of the median line or equidistance line, coupled with an exception for special circumstances, or should it involve a stronger assertion of equitable principles. It was, however, recognized that delimitation by agreement is the most satisfactory way of resolving issues arising from overlapping claims.[130]

While the aforementioned provisions with respect to delimitation are substantively the same, they also reflect the fact that the regimes of the EEZ and of the continental shelf developed separately, are addressed in different parts of the Convention and have not been fully harmonized. Although the continental

---

[125] See Annex II, Art. 2(1) UNCLOS.

[126] L.D.M. Nelson, *The Continental Shelf: Interplay of Law and Science*, in: Liber Amicorum Judge Shigeru Oda, N. Ando et al. (eds.), at 1237 (2002).

[127] See also A. Cavnar, *Accountability and the Commission on the Limits of the Continental Shelf: Deciding Who Owns the Ocean Floor*, 42/3 Cornell International Law Journal, at 8–9 (2009); see further R. Wolfrum, *The Delimitation of the Outer Continental Shelf: Procedural Considerations*, in: Le procès international – Liber amicorum Jean-Pierre Cot, R. Badinter (Président du Comité d'Honneur), at 349–366 (2009).

[128] See Virginia Commentary, Vol. II (note 82), at 800, 952.

[129] Art. 74 (2) (3), 83 (2) (3) UNCLOS.

[130] See Virginia Commentary, Vol. II (note 82), at 801.

shelf may on the basis of geology extend beyond 200 nautical miles, both regimes apply within that zone, and to that extent they overlap.[131] State practice has, with very few exceptions, overwhelmingly resorted to the establishment of single maritime boundary lines, a practice that has been endorsed by courts and tribunals.[132]

As the progressive degradation of the marine environment had become a matter of increasing concern for the international community as a whole, UNCLOS in Part XII contains detailed rules regarding its protection and preservation. Article 192 for the first time in treaty form established the general obligation of all States "to protect and preserve the marine environment". The requirement for States to balance their "sovereign rights to exploit their natural resources pursuant to their environmental policies" with that basic duty is an important innovation.[133] Regarding pollution from ships, UNCLOS gives priority to international rules and standards, in the case of the remaining sources, i.e. land-based sources, seabed activities and dumping, priority is accorded to national legislation and other measures taken by States. Moreover, while the principles and rules related to seabed activities and dumping apply to both the EEZ and the continental shelf, those concerning coastal State competence with regard to pollution from ships apply only to the former.

Article 218 UNCLOS provides for enforcement by port States, granting them the right to undertake investigations and institute proceedings against foreign vessels for violation of applicable international antipollution rules and standards committed beyond their jurisdictional waters.[134] The most potent provision in favor of coastal State authority seems to be Article 220 (3)–(6), which authorizes coastal States to obtain the identification of and to conduct search of commercial vessels in their EEZ, if there are "clear grounds" for believing that a vessel is violating international pollution standards.[135]

Article 234 UNCLOS contains a special provision on ice-covered areas giving coastal States the right to adopt and enforce non-discriminatory laws and regulations for the prevention, reduction and control of marine pollution from vessels in such areas within the limits of the EEZ. This Article is thus directed at preserving the fragile ecology of ice-covered areas, it does not, however, apply to warships and others vessels entitled to sovereign immunity.[136] The

---

[131] B. Oxman, *The Barbados/Trinidad and Tobago Arbitration Award of 2006*, B. Macmahon (Series Editor), T.M.C. Asser Press, at 2, 3 (2009).

[132] Id., at 3, referring to an observation by the Tribunal in the Barbados/Trinidad and Tobago Arbitration.

[133] Kwiatkowska, *The 200 Miles EEZ* (note 103), at 162, 163.

[134] See also id., at 169, 170.

[135] Van Dyke, *The disappearing right to navigational freedom in the EEZ* (note 108), at 109.

[136] J. Kraska, *The Law of the Sea Convention and the Northwest Passage*, 22/2 The International Journal of Marine and Coastal Law, at 274 (2007).

question may be asked as to what will happen to that provision if the ice should disappear – would it then become obsolete and with it special rights granted there under to the coastal States concerned with respect to the protection of the environment.[137]

Prior to the respective 1958 Geneva Convention, which established a consent regime regarding research activities on the continental shelf, there were no global instruments regulating the conduct of marine scientific research in that area. UNCLOS has retained the basic principle of consent by coastal States for research on the continental shelf and extended that principle also to the EEZ. The provisions on marine scientific research – dealt with in Part XIII of UNCLOS – were considerably expanded, adding general principles as well as detailed rules governing its conduct.[138] The negotiators at the Conference on the Law of the Sea, however, specifically rejected a proposed definition of marine scientific research on the grounds that it was unnecessary.[139] Article 238 UNCLOS affirms the right of all States and competent international organizations to conduct marine scientific research subject to the rights and duties of other States as provided in the Convention, to be carried out exclusively for peaceful purposes and without unjustifiably interfering with other legitimate uses of the sea. According to Article 241, marine scientific research activities shall not, however, constitute the legal basis for any claim to any part of the marine environment or its resources.

The consent required by coastal States regarding marine scientific research in the EEZ and on the continental shelf must not be delayed or denied unreasonably. Consent may be withheld in certain circumstances, *inter alia*, if the research is of direct significance for the exploration and exploitation of natural resources,[140] whether living or non-living. In case of such research the coastal State may also require prior agreement for making internationally available the research results of a project.[141] States and competent international organizations intending to undertake marine scientific research in the EEZ or on the continental shelf have to provide information to the coastal State and to comply with certain conditions, including to allow the coastal State to participate in the marine science project, if it so desires.[142]

---

[137] H. Tuerk, *The Arctic and the Modern Law of the Sea*, in: Governing Ocean Resources, Essays in Tribute to Judge Choon-Ho Park, J.H. Paik, J. Van Dyke and S. Lee (eds.), Brill/Martinus Nijhoff Publishers, Leiden/Boston, (forthcoming in 2012).

[138] See The Law of the Sea, National Legislation, Regulations and Supplementary Documents on Marine Scientific Research in Areas under National Jurisdiction, UN Office for Ocean Affairs and the Law of the Sea, at 1 (1989).

[139] P. Birnie, *Law of the Sea and Ocean Resources: Implications for Marine Scientific Research*, 10/2 International Journal of Marine and Coastal Law, at 241–242 (1995).

[140] Art. 246 UNCLOS.

[141] Art. 249 (2) UNCLOS.

[142] See Arts. 248, 249 (1) UNCLOS.

Opinions differ as to whether coastal State jurisdiction extends to activities in the EEZ such as hydrographic surveying and collection of other marine environmental data that is not resource-related or is not done for scientific purposes. While there is, as pointed out, a clear consent regime for marine scientific research, there is no specific provision for hydrographic surveying in the EEZ. Some coastal States require consent with respect to such surveys by other States, while the contrary opinion holds that hydrographic surveys in that area can be freely conducted.[143] A certain trend towards a consent regime seems, however, to be evolving.[144]

D. *The Extension of Coastal State Sovereignty and Jurisdiction*

The modern law of the sea enshrined in UNCLOS is thus characterized by a number of major changes in favor of coastal States compared to the traditional law. Through the extension of the territorial sea from the hitherto most widely recognized limit of three to twelve nautical miles, a larger area of the seas was placed under national sovereignty than ever before in history. At the same time, the contiguous zone with certain coastal States' rights was considerably extended. The new legal concept of the archipelagic State has rightly been called the "most remarkable explosion of sovereignties based on islands",[145] as it in fact nationalizes vast areas of the seas and constitutes one of the major potential limitations of the freedom of navigation.[146] This substantial extension of coastal States' rights and jurisdiction must, however, also be seen in connection with the right of innocent passage, transit passage and archipelagic sea lanes passage, which have been referred to as the "crown jewels of navigation and overflight".[147] These rights are vital to the major maritime powers, as they ensure the global strategic mobility of their armed forces. Safeguarding them was thus a precondition for these powers to agree to the changes in the law of the sea in favor of coastal States.[148]

The creation of the EEZ was certainly one of the most revolutionary features of UNCLOS,[149] recognizing the right of coastal States to jurisdiction over the

---

[143] Bateman, *Security and the Law of the Sea in East Asia* (note 80), at 382.
[144] Id., at 384–385.
[145] Dupuy, *La mer sous compétence nationale* (note 16), at 237.
[146] See also Davidson, *Law of the Sea and Freedom of Navigation in Asia Pacific* (note 79), at 137.
[147] Statement of Admiral Patrick M. Walsh (note 89), at 4.
[148] See also Koh, *Territorial Sea, Contiguous Zone, Straits and Achipelagoes under UNCLOS* (note 94), at 176.
[149] G. Kullenberg, *The Exclusive Economic Zone: Some Perspectives*, 42/9 Ocean and Coastal Management, at 849 (1999).

resources of some 38 million square nautical miles of ocean space – a gener-
ous endowment indeed and a major inroad on the freedom of the seas.[150] The
EEZ represents a dramatic geographic and functional expansion of coastal State
jurisdiction – probably the largest transfer of resources to national jurisdiction
in history.[151] These zones cover about 8% of the surface of the Earth, 36% of
the surface of the seas, 25% of global primary productivity, and account for
almost 90% of fisheries – the same being true for many other marine resources.
It has also been estimated that 87% of the offshore hydrocarbon resources are
situated within 200 nautical miles and that the EEZs provide for about 43%
of the value of the world's "ecosystem services".[152] It must be emphasized that
the preservation of non-resource related high seas freedoms within that zone
was a *conditio sine qua non* for the acceptance of that concept not only by the
maritime powers, but also by many other States.[153]

The main argument for the creation of the EEZ was the need for protecting
the economic interests of developing States and, in particular, of coastal fishing
communities by allowing them to gain access to resources to which they previously might not have had a legitimate and undisputed claim.[154] The assumption that such zones would primarily be in the interest of developing countries,
however, turned out to be erroneous. On the contrary, the creation of the
EEZ has rather favored important industrialized countries: there is only one
developing State – Indonesia – among the seven States which together make
up for more than 40% of the world total of EEZs.[155] It has also been pointed
out that one of the practical effects of the establishment of such a zone was that
it gave free reign to domestic fishing fleets to harvest marine resources without
competition from global fleets. Rather than ensuring sound management and

---

[150] See also UNCLOS – A historical perspective (note 19), at 7.

[151] Kullenberg, *The Exclusive Economic Zone* (note 149), at 849.

[152] Id., at 850–851; "Ecosystem Services" are the processes by which the environment produces
resources that are often taken for granted, such as clean water, timber, and habitat for fisheries, and pollination of native and agricultural plants; see Ecological Society of America (ESA),
available at: esa.org.

[153] See also Brown, *Fundamental Principles in Conflict* (note 18), at 522; see also Vukas, *The New
Law of the Sea and Navigation* (note 79), at 148; see further I.A. Shearer, *The International
Tribunal for the Law of the Sea and its Potential for Resolving Navigation Disputes*, in: Navigational Rights and Freedoms and the New Law of the Sea, D.R. Rothwell & S. Bateman
(eds.), at 267–268.

[154] See also the Statement by Venezuelan President Carlos Andrés Pérez at the opening of the
Caracas Session of the Third United Nations Conference on the Law of the Sea, as quoted
by Anand, *Freedom of the Seas* (note 22), at 275.

[155] The other countries are: Australia, Canada, France, New Zealand, Russia and the United States;
see also Dupuy, *La mer sous compétence nationale* (note 16), at 247; see further UNCLOS – A
historical perspective (note 19), at 8.

better conservation of stocks, it often led to the phenomenon of accelerating depletion of fisheries.[156]

The fundamental problem with the EEZ regime lies in the need to maintain an appropriate balance between the rights and duties of the coastal State and those of other States. Attempts to swing this balance in favor of the States having declared such zones, if successful, would lead to a gradual assimilation of the EEZ with the territorial sea and would over time lead to a further substantial diminution of the freedoms of the seas.[157] Article 59 UNCLOS contains a very wise, but rather imprecise formula for the resolution of conflicts regarding the attribution of rights and jurisdictions in the EEZ, as such a "conflict should be resolved on the basis of equity and in the light of all the relevant circumstances, taking into account the respective importance of the interests involved to the parties as well as to the international community as a whole". This formula, however, still needs to prove its value in practice.

The broadening of the concept of the continental shelf so as to include the entire continental margin up to a distance of 350 nautical miles from the baselines, and in certain cases even beyond, and the creation of a legal continental shelf extending to 200 nautical miles signifies a further substantial extension of sovereign rights of coastal States over natural resources of the seabed. The so-called "broad-margin States" were thus able to gain recognition for their claims to vast areas of the seabed beyond the EEZ and, subject to certain qualifications, able to achieve their fundamental objectives at the expense of all other States.[158] If one adds to the area of the EEZ that of the continental shelf where it extends beyond 200 hundred nautical miles, an estimated 97% of offshore hydrocarbon resources fall under national jurisdiction.[159] It should also be pointed out that the negotiators at the Conference on the Law of the Sea were led to believe that no more than 30 to 35 States would be able to claim a continental shelf beyond 200 nautical miles.[160] At the present time, however, it seems that there may be about 80 such States with the consequence of further considerably diminishing

---

[156] See J.R. Rasband, J. Salzman & M. Squillace, *Natural Resources Law and Policy*, at 462, 468 (2004).

[157] See also Oxman, *The Territorial Temptation* (note 56), at 839.

[158] Tuerk, *Landlocked States* (note 11), at 106; see also S. Vasciannie, *Landlocked and Geographically Disadvantaged States and the Question of the Outer Limit of the Continental Shelf*, 58 British Yearbook of International Law, at 272 (1987).

[159] Id., Tuerk, at 104–105.

[160] See also G. Taft, *Applying the Law of the Sea Convention and the Role of the Scientific Community Relating to Establishing the Outer Limit of the Continental Shelf Where It Extends Beyond the 200 Mile Limit*, in: Law, Science & Ocean Management, R. Long, T.H. Heidar & J.N. Moore (eds.), at 470 (2007).

the area of the common heritage of mankind.[161] A certain price the broad-margin States had to pay for the recognition of their claims is the obligation according to Article 82 UNCLOS to make payments or contributions in kind for the exploitation of the non-living resources of the outer continental shelf to be distributed to the States parties to the Convention through the ISA.

The provisions of UNCLOS relating to marine-based pollution have brought remarkable changes to the environmental law of the sea existing prior to its adoption with direct implications for navigational and other communications freedoms in the vast areas encompassed by the EEZ and the continental shelf. The Convention has even been called "the strongest comprehensive environmental treaty now in existence or likely to emerge for quite some time".[162] The respective provisions attempt to strike a compromise between the major flag States advocating freedom of navigation as unrestricted as possible, and the coastal States aiming at the modification of this freedom by recognizing certain environmental powers of the coastal and port State.[163]

With respect to marine scientific research, as regulated by UNCLOS, it has been stated that the consent regime provides a balance between the coastal

---

[161] The Commission on the Limits of the Continental Shelf has so far received 56 submissions made by 48 coastal States and a further 45 preliminary indicative communications made by 29 States; see Table of the Submissions to the Commission on the Limits of the Continental Shelf, available at: www.un.org/Depts/los/clcs_new/commission_submissions.htm (last visited 1 July 2011); see also letter dated 5 May 2011, addressed to the President of the Twenty-first Meeting of States Parties by the Chairperson of the Commission, SPLOS/225, 5 May 2011. Hitherto, the Commission has adopted recommendations in respect of 14 submissions: Russia (not yet final) in 2002, Ireland (concerning Porcupine Abyssal Plain), Brazil (an amendment to the submission is still pending) in 2007, Australia, New Zealand in 2008, France, Ireland, Spain and the United Kingdom (joint submission in the area of the Celtic Sea and the Bay of Biscay) in 2009, Norway (in the North East Atlantic and the Arctic), Mexico (in respect of the Western polygon in the Gulf of Mexico), France (with respect to Guyana and New Caledonia) in 2009, Barbados, United Kingdom (with respect to Ascension Island) in 2010, Indonesia (in respect of the area North West of Sumatra), Mauritius and Seychelles (joint submission concerning the Mascarene Plateau region), and Suriname in 2011. In view of the heavy workload it may take a few decades until the Commission will be able to finally deal with all the submissions, unless it is converted from a part-time to a full-time body; see also www.un.org/Depts/los/clcs_new/clcs_workload.htm (last visited 1 July 2011). Using the information calculated from the submissions made thus far, including the preliminary information, the foreseeable area of the outer continental shelf amounts to approximately 30 million square km; this includes the area generated from Antarctic territory; see UNEP/GRID Arendal report, Continental Shelf – the Last Maritime Zone, at 16 (2009), available at: www.grida.no/_res/site/file/publications/Shelf_LastZone_scr.pdf (last visited 1 July 2011).

[162] Oxman, *The Territorial Temptation* (note 56), at 843; see also E.B. Weinstein, *The Impact of Regulation of Transport of Hazardous Waste on Freedom of Navigation*, 9 The International Journal of Marine and Coastal Law, at 168 (1994).

[163] Kwiatkowska, *The 200 Miles EEZ* (note 103), at 170.

State's rights and the rights of the international community – although the latter does not have any legal standing under general international law or the Convention.[164] In any case, the respective provisions of UNCLOS can operate to effectively remove approximately one-third of the ocean from independent scientific as well as environmental scrutiny.[165]

---

[164] See M. Gorina-Ysern, *An International Regime for Marine Scientific Research*, 9 Transnational Publishers, at 347 (2003).

[165] P.A. Verlaan, *Experimental activities that internationally perturb the marine environment: Implications for the marine environmental protection and marine scientific research provisions of the 1982 United Nations Convention of the Law of the Sea*, 31/2 Marine Policy, at 213 (2007).

Chapter Three

The Principle of the Common Heritage of Mankind[166]

A. *The Evolution of the Concept*

It has rightly been stated that the development of general concepts of international law reflects the spirit of a given historic period.[167] This is certainly also true of the "common heritage of mankind" which constitutes an essential element of UNCLOS, the difficult negotiations on the Convention having focused, to a large extent, on the implementation of that concept. The debates on a new law of the sea also inspired the incorporation of the common heritage principle into the "Moon Treaty".[168] That concept is to some degree further reflected in the legal framework for the protection of the environment of Antarctica where reference is made to "the interests of all mankind".[169] Its full application to that area would, however, at a minimum require the extinguishment of all national claims and the establishment of a more universal regime of administration and control.[170] Such a development does not, at least at present, seem to be in sight.

Already in 1830, Andrés Bello, poet, scholar, and international jurist in the Grotian mould from South America, wrote that things which could not be held by any nation without affecting the interests of other nations, were of the nature of "indivisible common patrimony". According to his view, there were areas of the planet which should be set apart in common for the use of all people, which

---

[166] For this chapter see in particular H. Tuerk, *The Idea of the Common Heritage of Mankind*, in: Serving the Rule of International Maritime Law, Essays in honour of Professor David Joseph Attard, N.A. Martinez Guttierrez (ed.), at 156–175 (2010).

[167] R. Wolfrum, *The Principle of the Common Heritage of Mankind*, 43 Zeitschrift für ausländisches öffentliches Recht und Völkerrecht, at 312 (1983).

[168] Agreement Governing the Activities of States on the Moon and other Celestial Bodies, 5 December 1979, 1363 UNTS 3.

[169] See Wolfrum, *The Principle of the Common Heritage of Mankind* (note 167), at 313; see also A.C. Kiss, *Conserving the Common Heritage of Mankind*, 39 Revista Juridica Universidad de Puerto Rico, at 774 (1990).

[170] G. Nicholson, *The Common Heritage of Mankind and Mining: An Analysis of the Law as to the High Seas, Outer Space, the Antarctic and World Heritage*, 6 New Zealand Journal of Environmental Law, at 192 (2002).

were not capable of being subject to claims of State sovereignty or ownership, but which were subject to certain defined rights of common use.[171] In the course of that century the sea began gradually to be seen as an important repository of resources, and seabed mining was proposed as early as 1876.[172] The idea that the exploitation of the resources of the oceans should also take account of the common interests of mankind, however, only gained ground in the twentieth century. In the course of the work of the League of Nations to promote the progressive codification of international law, the Argentine jurist José León Suárez in 1927 proposed that the living resources of the seas should be considered a "heritage of mankind".[173] In 1955, a member of the ILC, Georges Scelle, suggested the creation of a system of international concessions for the exploitation of the seabed, proposing in particular the establishment of a competent international organ within the framework of the United Nations.[174]

In the 1960's, there was a sudden surge of interest in the exploitation of the seabed based on studies that a wealth of resources existed on the deep seabed with the most common minerals being cobalt, copper, manganese and nickel, recoverable from both mineral nodules and mineral crusts. It was, *inter alia*, estimated that there are one and a half trillion tons of manganese nodules on the ocean floor containing these minerals.[175] At the same time, the idea gained ground that this "fortune on the seabed" should benefit mankind as a whole and not be left to the technologically advanced countries alone.[176] The drive towards an internationalization of the seabed was to a large extent also motivated by the attempt to call a halt to the creeping jurisdiction of coastal States with respect to the seas, a concern shared by many developing and developed countries.[177]

---

[171] Id., at 177–178.

[172] B.E. Heim, *Exploring the Last Frontiers for Mineral Resources: A Comparison of International Law Regarding the Deep Seabed, Outer Space and Antarctica*, 23 Vanderbilt Journal of Transnational Law, at 822 (1990–1991).

[173] T. Scovazzi, The *Seabed beyond the Limits of National Jurisdiction: General and Institutional Aspects*, in: The International Legal Regime of Areas beyond National Jurisdiction: Current and Future Developments A.G. Oude Elferink & E.J. Molenaar (eds.), at 43, footnote 2 (2010).

[174] See A-C. Kiss, *La notion de patrimoine commun de l'humanité*, 175-II Recueil des Cours, at 199 (1982).

[175] W. Wertenbaker, New York Times, August 1977 (on file with author), at 4; see also id., Kiss, at 197.

[176] See D. Cronan, *A Fortune on the Seabed*, UNESCO Courier, February 1986, at 8; see also A. Pardo & C.Q. Christol, *The Common Interest: Big Tension between the Whole and Parts*, in: The Structure and Process of International Law: Essays in Legal Philosophy, Doctrine and Theory, R. St. J. Macdonald & D.M. Johnston (eds.), at 653 (1986).

[177] See also E. Franckx, *The 200 Mile Limit: Between Creeping Jurisdiction and Creeping Common Heritage?*, 39/3 George Washington International Review, at 478 and footnote 49 (2007).

The year 1967 marked a breakthrough for the concept of the common heritage of mankind. The World Peace through Law Conference, referring to the high seas as "the common heritage of all mankind", recommended to the UN General Assembly to issue a proclamation declaring the bed of the sea to appertain to the United Nations, subject to its jurisdiction and control.[178] On 1 November 1967, Ambassador Arvid Pardo of Malta presented a Memorandum at the General Assembly which proposed that the seabed and the ocean floor beyond the limits of national jurisdiction be declared the "common heritage of mankind", not subject to national appropriation, and reserved exclusively for peaceful purposes.[179] This proposal was to be the basis for the concept of the common heritage of mankind being enshrined in international legal instruments and becoming a principle of international law.

As Ambassador Pardo subsequently stated, the objective of the Maltese proposal was to replace the principle of freedom of the seas by the principle of common heritage of mankind in order to preserve the greater part of ocean space as a commons accessible to the international community. International administration of the commons and management of its resources for the common good distinguished the principle of common heritage from the traditional principle of the high seas as *res communis*. The common heritage concept implied that it was open to use by the international community, but was not owned by it. It required a system of management in which all users had a right to share as well as an active sharing of benefits, reservation for peaceful purposes, insofar as politically achievable, and lastly reservation for future generations, and thus had environmental implications.[180]

In acting upon the Maltese proposal, the General Assembly in 1968 established the Committee on the Peaceful Uses of the Seabed and the Ocean Floor beyond the Limits of National Jurisdiction – the "Seabed Committee" – and a year later adopted the Deep Seabed Mining Moratorium Resolution[181] prohibiting the exploitation of the resources of the seabed beyond the limits of national jurisdiction and not recognizing any claim to any part of that area or its resources. The legally binding nature of the moratorium was, however,

---

[178] Wolfrum, *The Principle of the Common Heritage of Mankind* (note 167), at 315–316.

[179] Koh, *The Origins of the 1982 Convention on the Law of the Sea* (note 17), at 16; see also Nicholson, *The Common Heritage of Mankind and Mining* (note 170), at 180–181.

[180] L.F.E. Goldie, *A Note on some diverse meanings of 'The Common Heritage of Mankind'*, 10 Syracuse Journal of International Law and Commerce, at 87 (1983).

[181] UN General Assembly Res. 2574 (XXIV) of 15 December 1969, Question of the reservation exclusively for peaceful purposes of the sea-bed and the ocean floor, and the subsoil thereof, underlying the high seas beyond the limits of present national jurisdiction, and the use of their resources in the interests of mankind (Deep Seabed Mining Moratorium Resolution).

contested by industrialized countries.[182] The "Declaration of Principles Governing the Sea-Bed and the Ocean Floor and the Subsoil Thereof, Beyond the Limits of National Jurisdiction" of 1970[183] declared the respective area as well as its resources the "common heritage of mankind", not to be subject to appropriation by any means by States or persons and to be reserved exclusively for peaceful purposes. The exploration of the area and the exploitation of its resources were to be carried out for the benefit of mankind as a whole, irrespective of the geographical location of States, whether landlocked or coastal, and taking into particular consideration the interests and needs of the developing countries.

In a "Draft Ocean Space Treaty" of 1971, the Government of Malta suggested that the principle of common heritage be applied to ocean space as a whole, that is, to the surface of the sea, the water column, the seabed and its subsoil without regard to the jurisdictional status of any particular area. The application of the principle would, however, not be the same in areas within national jurisdiction as in areas outside thereof. In the former, the coastal States on behalf of mankind would exercise wide powers of resource management and regulation of uses, while the latter would be administered by "International Ocean Space Institutions" with wide functions.[184] The Maltese draft rejected "laissez-faire freedom" beyond national jurisdiction as well as "unfettered sovereignty" of the State within national jurisdiction.[185]

B. *UNCLOS and the Common Heritage of Mankind*

The negotiations regarding the common heritage of mankind at the Third United Nations Conference on the Law of the Sea were, above all, marked by intense debates between developing and developed States as to the meaning, the scope and the practical consequences of applying that principle to the deep seabed. The Maltese proposal to also include living resources of the seas in the concept was not retained as it was considered unrealistic.[186] Some major elements of Part XI of the Convention dealing with the international

---

[182] See Goldie, *Diverse meanings of 'The Common Heritage of Mankind'* (note 180), at 94–97; see also E. Guntrip, *The Common Heritage of Mankind: An Adequate Regime for Managing the Deep Seabed?*, 4/2 Melbourne Journal of International Law, at 382 (2003).

[183] UN General Assembly Res. 2749 (XXV) (note 61).

[184] Draft Ocean Space Treaty, Working Paper submitted by Malta, UN doc. A/AC.138/53 (1971); see also Pardo & Christol, *The Common Interest* (note 176), at 654.

[185] Id., Draft Ocean Space Treaty, at 6.

[186] See also Pardo & Christol, *The Common Interest* (note 176), at 655; see further Franckx, *The 200 Mile Limit* (note 177), at 486; see also Scovazzi, *The Seabed beyond the Limits of National Jurisdiction* (note 173), at 3.

seabed "Area", that is the seabed and ocean floor and subsoil thereof beyond the limits of national jurisdiction, had remained controversial throughout the Conference – as they favored developing, over developed, countries and did not follow a market–oriented approach. As a result, UNCLOS was not approved by consensus, the United States, *inter alia*, voting against it, and important industrialized countries only adhering to it until these provisions had undergone a substantial change.

The core provision of Part XI is Article 136 declaring the "Area" and its resources the "common heritage of mankind". The introduction of the term "mankind" combined with the word "heritage" indicates that the interests of future generations have to be respected in making use of the international commons.[187] The States parties to the Convention further agreed that there shall be no amendments to the basic principle set forth in that Article and that they shall not be party to any agreement in derogation thereof.[188]

According to Article 137 no claim or exercise of sovereignty or sovereign rights over any part of the "Area" or its resources nor appropriation by any State, natural or juridical person shall be recognized. It is to be recalled that already the 1958 Geneva Convention on the High Seas prohibits any occupation of the high seas, including the respective seabed.[189] The aforementioned provision, however, goes one important step further by enshrining the principle of non-recognition of any such claim or appropriation, the latter also being valid for private persons. The prohibition of occupation and appropriation has thus been given a legal status the effect of which is similar to that of *jus cogens*. Moreover, that provision constitutes an obligation of all States and not only of the States parties to the Convention, thus establishing an objective legal regime.[190]

As in the case of the continental shelf regime, the legal status of the superjacent waters and that of the airspace above those waters remains unaffected.[191] The freedoms of the high seas are, however, to be exercised with due regard for the rights under the Convention with respect to activities in the international seabed "Area". This requirement does not qualify the exercise of these freedoms as such, but rather recognizes that this exercise might interfere with the exploration and exploitation of the resources of the "Area".[192] All rights in these resources are vested in mankind as a whole on whose behalf the ISA is to

[187] R. Wolfrum, *Common Heritage of Mankind*, in: Encyclopedia of Public International Law, Vol. I, R. Bernhardt (ed.), at 693 (1992).
[188] Art. 311 (6) UNCLOS. See also Wolfrum, *The Principle of the Common Heritage of Mankind* (note 167), at 313–314.
[189] Id., at 316.
[190] Wolfrum, *Common Heritage of Mankind* (note 187), at 693.
[191] See Arts 78 (1) and 135 UNCLOS.
[192] See also B.H. Oxman, The *High Seas and The International Seabed Area*, 10 Michigan Journal of International Law, at 537–538 (1989).

act. A further revolutionary new element has thus been introduced into the law of the sea as the States parties which are ipso facto members of the Authority have to act through it as a kind of trustee on behalf of mankind.[193]

The principal organs of the ISA – which is based at Kingston, Jamaica – are the Assembly, consisting of all its members, the Council and the Secretariat. The thirty-six-member Council elected by the Assembly is the executive organ of the Authority, the Enterprise its operating arm with the task of directly carrying out activities in the "Area".[194] Article 140 sets forth the obligation of the ISA to carry out its activities for the benefit of mankind as a whole, irrespective of the geographical location of States, whether coastal or landlocked, and taking into particular consideration the interests and needs of the developing States and of peoples who have not attained full independence or self-governing status recognized by the United Nations. It must ensure the equitable sharing of the financial and other economic benefits derived from activities in the "Area", taking into particular consideration the interests and needs of the aforementioned States and peoples. The tasks of the ISA include the promotion of marine scientific research in the "Area", the transfer of technology to developing States and the protection of the environment[195] – which may be considered one of its main functions.

Controversy at the Conference over the utilization system concerning the deep seabed centred upon the question of how to ensure that deep seabed mining would benefit mankind as a whole.[196] The developing countries favored a broad application of the principle of the common heritage of mankind which in their view implicitly rejected freedom of access to areas beyond national jurisdiction and their resources, and invested mankind with property rights analogous to ownership. Common property required common management and exploitation through a global, institutionalized mechanism endowed with exclusive exploitation rights, with the task of equitably distributing the benefits derived therefrom.[197] The industrialized countries believed that the common heritage of mankind concept should be limited to a certain improvement in the distribution of the benefits derived from the exploitation of the resources of the "Area" on the basis of equity, with the States exploiting the resources to make the determination. The notion of the common heritage as being common property – which also clearly went beyond the original Maltese proposal –

---

[193] Id.; Wolfrum, *The Principle of the Common Heritage of Mankind* (note 167), at 317.

[194] See Arts. 158, 166, 170 UNCLOS.

[195] See Arts. 143–145 UNCLOS.

[196] Wolfrum, *The Principle of the Common Heritage of Mankind* (note 167), at 320.

[197] G.M. Danilenko, *The Concept of the 'Common Heritage of Mankind' in International Law*, XIII Annals of Air and Space Law, at 249 (1988).

was rejected, in particular as contradicting the principle of non-appropriation.[198] While the developed countries had advocated a licensing system for resource exploitation, the developing countries held the view that only the Enterprise should carry out mining operations in the "Area".[199] The compromise achieved, on the basis of a proposal by the United States, was the so-called "parallel system":[200] that is, that both these options would be enshrined in the Convention. The mechanism by which this was to be achieved was the so-called "site banking" system, whereby an applicant for a mine site has to divide the respective area into two parts of equal estimated commercial value, and the ISA will designate which part is to be reserved solely for the conduct of activities through the Enterprise or in association with developing States.

According to Article 141 UNCLOS the use of the "Area" is foreseen exclusively for peaceful purposes by all States, whether coastal or landlocked, without discrimination. The controversial question of whether to interpret the notion of peaceful uses as precluding any military activities or only those of an aggressive nature has, in principle, been resolved by Article 301 according to which States parties shall refrain from any threat or use of force against the territorial integrity or political independence of any State, or in any other manner inconsistent with the principles of international law embodied in the Charter of the United Nations.[201] A complete prohibition of military uses would moreover have been inconsistent with the regime of the high seas which undoubtedly permits military manoeuvres. The adoption in 1971 of the Treaty on the Prohibition of the Emplacement of Nuclear Weapons and Other Weapons of Mass Destruction on the Seabed and the Ocean Floor and the Subsoil thereof, had, to a large extent, been also a consequence of this discussion. This Treaty, which only prohibits specific uses of certain weapons in a specified environment, falling short of complete demilitarization, can be regarded as an important result of the Maltese initiative of 1967.[202]

As already indicated, the results of the Third United Nations Conference on the Law of the Sea with respect to the continental shelf constituted a further milestone with major potential effects, not only with respect to the freedom of the seas, but also the principle of the common heritage of mankind. Today, about one third of the world's oil production is from offshore, and that

---

[198] Id., at 251.

[199] See also Wolfrum, *The Principle of the Common Heritage of Mankind* (note 167), at 324.

[200] See J.M. Van Dyke, *Sharing Ocean Resources – in a Time of Scarcity and Selfishness*, in: Law of the Sea, the Common Heritage and Emerging Challenges, H.N. Scheiber (ed.), at 5 (2000). Wolfrum, *The Principle of the Common Heritage of Mankind* (note 167), at 328.

[201] See also id., Wolfrum, at 320.

[202] Id.; see also Guntrip, *The Common Heritage of Mankind: An Adequate Regime?* (note 182), at 390.

percentage is still growing as production is moving into ever deeper waters.[203] As all the natural resources of the continental margin have been placed under coastal State jurisdiction and hydrocarbons were almost totally excluded from the international seabed "Area", the result is a prolongation for an unforeseeable timeframe until a commercially viable exploitation of the deep seabed can occur. With respect to the Arctic Ocean – according to estimates, the entire Arctic region might hold as much as 25% of the world's undiscovered energy resources – it appears that it may be possible for the five surrounding coastal States to advance legitimate claims to most of its seabed. There is thus a very real possibility that the common heritage of mankind will be reduced to just a few so-called "donut" holes in the central Arctic Ocean.[204] In this context it should be recalled that the Maltese proposal of a "Draft Ocean Space Treaty" had provided that States parties would "agree to surrender against equitable and appropriate compensation their claims to jurisdiction over the seabed of submarine areas more than 200 nautical miles from their coast which are subjacent to waters less than 200 meters deep".[205]

Although directly affected by the delineation of the continental shelf beyond 200 nautical miles by coastal States – on the basis of recommendations by the Commission on the Limits of the Continental Shelf – no role in the proceedings was given to the ISA, entrusted with administering the international seabed "Area".[206] It has rightly been pointed out that it might have been sensible to provide for such a possibility in a contentious case, since an extensive continental shelf reduces the geographical extent of the "Area", and correspondingly the scope of the activities of the Authority.[207] The question may be asked, if any State party to UNCLOS could challenge outer continental shelf limits, giving rise to doubts with the argument of being affected by the consequential diminution of the area of the common heritage of mankind.[208]

---

[203] See S. Scott, *'Minerals on Land, Minerals in the Sea'* in: Geotimes – December 2002, at 4, available at: www.geotimes.org/dec02/feature_minerals.html (last visited: 1 July 2011).

[204] See T. Potts & C. Schofield, *Current Legal Developments: The Arctic*, 23/1 The International Journal of Marine and Coastal Law, at 163–164 (2008).

[205] Art. 38 (1) Draft Ocean Space Treaty (note 184).

[206] See International Seabed Authority, www.isa.org.jm/en/about. See Suarez, *The Outer Limits of the Continental Shelf* (note 121), at 234.

[207] J.E. Noyes, *Judicial and Arbitral Proceedings and the Outer Limit of the Continental Shelf*, 42 Vanderbilt Journal of Transnational Law, at 10 (2009).

[208] See also L.D.M. Nelson, *The Settlement of Disputes Arising From Conflicting Outer Continental Shelf Claims*, 24 International Journal of Marine and Coastal Law, at 409–422 (2009); see further Judge R. Wolfrum, President of ITLOS, *The Outer Continental Shelf: Some Considerations Concerning Applications and the Potential Role of the International Tribunal for the Law of the Sea*, Statement at the 73rd Biennial Conference of the International Law Association, Rio De Janeiro, Brazil, 21 August 2008 (on file with author).

The previously mentioned revenue-sharing provision of Article 82 UNCLOS sets the final rate of the payments or contributions to be made by coastal States with a continental shelf extending beyond 200 nautical miles – on the basis of an informal Austrian compromise proposal[209] – at 7 per cent of the value or the volume of production at the site as of the twelfth year after the commencement of exploitation. The duty to make payments or contributions from the exploitation of the continental margin beyond 200 nautical miles has thus been fixed at quite a low level that also includes a five-year grace period after the beginning of production. The rationale for this relatively low figure was not to cause a disincentive for the exploitation of the seabed beyond 200 nautical miles.[210] A developing State which is a net importer of a mineral resource produced from its continental shelf is furthermore exempt from making such payments or contributions in respect of that resource.

That provision raises a number of questions which will have to be dealt with once commercial exploitation of the outer continental shelf is to become a reality.[211] First of all, it seems clear that the obligation to make such payments or contributions is one of the coastal State and not of the producer. In this context, producers might well argue that they already provide benefits to the economy in form of taxes, employment and existing royalties so that it should not be incumbent upon them to bear the additional cost of meeting the State's treaty obligation. It is left to the coastal State to determine whether there shall be a payment of value or a contribution in kind or volume. If a State should choose to make contributions in kind, practical difficulties are bound to emerge, for instance whether the ISA should distribute the contributions in the form of resources or convert them into money.[212] The question also arises of how to calculate the "value of production at the site". The negotiating history of Article 82 suggests that reference to the "well-head value" is intended.[213]

The payments or contributions are to be made through the ISA which shall distribute them to States parties to the Convention on the basis of equitable sharing criteria, taking into account the interests and need of developing States,

---

[209] Put forth by the author.

[210] See also G. Mingay, *Article 82 of the LOS Convention: Revenue Sharing – The Mining Industry's Perspective*, 21/3 The International Journal of Marine and Coastal Law, at 346 (2006); see further Tuerk, *The Idea of the Common Heritage of Mankind* (note 166), at 162.

[211] See M.W. Lodge, *The International Seabed Authority and Article 82 of the UN Convention on the Law of the Sea*, 21/3 The International Journal of Marine and Coastal Law, at 325 (2006). See also ISA Technical Study No.5, *"Non-living Resources of the Continental Shelf beyond 200 Nautical Miles: Speculations on the Implementation of Article 82 of the United Nations Convention on the Law of the Sea"* (2010), available at: www.isa.org.jm/files/documents/EN/Pubs/TechStudy5.pdf (last visited 1 July 2011).

[212] Id., Lodge at 325–326.

[213] Id., at 328.

particularly the least developed and the landlocked among them.[214] A fundamental issue is whether the Authority has any role to play in the process of determining the value or volume of the resources and the amount of the payments or contributions. The prevailing view seems to be that, at the very least, there needs to be consultation and agreement between the coastal States and the ISA in order that the latter can discharge its fiduciary duty to mankind as a whole.[215] The same is true with respect to the determination of whether a particular developing country qualifies for the resource specific exemption. If such decisions were left to the sole discretion of the coastal State concerned, the value of the entire revenue-sharing provision would be greatly diminished. At present, there are, however, no indications as to when the system of distribution of benefits to States parties, particularly to the developing ones, will become operational; it therefore lacks any true compensatory effect,[216] at least for the foreseeable future.

The importance of Article 82 as part of the overall legal regime for the continental shelf, nevertheless, should not be overlooked: it is part and parcel of the common heritage concept.[217] In 2000, the ISA commissioned a preliminary study of the potential mineral resources of the outer continental shelf, which concluded that the major resource potential in these areas is held in ferromanganese nodules and crusts, hydrocarbons, and gas hydrates. The most important driving factor behind the exploitation of the outer continental shelf is, however, likely to be increasing demand for oil and gas in the face of dwindling supply.[218] Therefore, current indications reveal the first source of revenue for the international community will be the payments and contributions made on the basis of Article 82 rather than any revenues derived from the exploitation of the deep seabed.[219] When that time comes the ISA will have to determine how to proceed with respect to the payments and contributions made pursuant to that Article and how to define "equitable sharing criteria". In that context the Secretary-General of the Authority has already proposed the establishment of a special fund for the promotion of marine scientific research in developing countries.[220]

As the broad-margin States through UNCLOS were able to gain recognition for their claims to the resources of vast areas of the seabed beyond the EEZ, dramatically diminishing the economic viability of the international seabed "Area", it has even been said that this extension of maritime zones with national jurisdiction has deprived the common heritage principle of its primary content and

---

[214] See also Tuerk, *Landlocked States* (note 11), at 106–107.

[215] See Lodge, *The International Seabed Authority and UNCLOS* (note 211), at 328.

[216] Tuerk, *Landlocked States* (note 11), at 106–107.

[217] Lodge, *The International Seabed Authority and UNCLOS* (note 211), at 332–333.

[218] Id., at 331.

[219] Id., at 333.

[220] Id., at 330.

rendered it a mere political slogan.[221] At one of the sessions of the Conference on the Law of the Sea a delegate of Austria[222] pointed out that the idea of the common heritage of mankind had been given "a first class burial", whereupon another delegate[223] commented that this assessment was too pessimistic – was it really?

C. *The 1994 "Implementation Agreement" to Part XI of UNCLOS*

The 1982 UNCLOS attempted to reach the objective of equal participation in the deep seabed mining regime through a system of distributive justice. This meant restrictions imposed upon potential deep seabed miners, affirmative action benefitting non-mining States, especially developing countries, and conferring jurisdiction over deep seabed mining on the ISA, so that all States parties can equally, though indirectly participate therein.[224] These provisions of the Convention were clearly influenced by the efforts of developing States to establish a "New International Economic Order" which sought to close the gap between industrialized and developing countries through interdependence and cooperation as well as an increased role of developing countries in international decision-making and better access to modern technology.[225] Major industrialized countries, in particular the United States, considered the approach to the deep seabed mining regime laid down in Part XI as too heavily weighted in favor of the developing countries and therefore decided to stay out of UNCLOS. Besides having substantial financial implications, this put in question the success of the entire endeavor of creating a new and universal law of the sea.

In order to avoid the entry into force the Convention without the adherence of important industrialized countries and to promote universal membership, the UN Secretary-General called informal consultations between 1990 and 1994 to identify the controversial issues and search for solutions which resulted in the Implementation Agreement of 28 July 1994.[226] This Agreement,

---

[221] See W. Graf Vitzthum, *Die Bemühungen um ein Regime des Tiefseebodens*, 38 Zeitschrift für ausländisches öffentliches Recht und Völkerrecht, at 769–770 (1978).
[222] The author; see Tuerk, *Landlocked States* (note 11), at 106.
[223] Professor Djamchid Momtaz, Iran.
[224] Wolfrum, *The Principle of the Common Heritage of Mankind* (note 167), at 332; Wolfrum, *Common Heritage of Mankind* (note 187), at 694.
[225] M.V. White, *The Common Heritage of Mankind: An Assessment*, 14 Case Western Reserve Journal of International Law, at 524 (1982); see also Danilenko, *The Concept of the 'Common Heritage of Mankind'* (note 197), at 250.
[226] Agreement Relating to the Implementation of Part XI of the United Nations Convention on the Law of the Sea of 10 December 1982 (hereinafter referred to as the Implementation Agreement), 1836 UNTS 3. See also L.D.M. Nelson, *The New Deep Seabed Mining Regime*, 10 International Journal of Marine and Coastal Law, at 190–192 (1995); see further

adopted without a negative vote, provisionally entered into force together with UNCLOS on 16 November 1994 and definitely on 28 July 1996. To date 140 States and the European Union are party to it.[227] The procedure adopted in that case was highly innovative as the Agreement and Part XI of the Convention are to be "interpreted and applied together as a single instrument". In the event of any inconsistency between the two documents the Agreement "shall prevail". If a State becomes a party to the Convention after the adoption of the Agreement, that act shall also represent consent to be bound by it.[228]

Concern over the financial implications of establishing the deep seabed mining regime played a cardinal role in the consultations.[229] The Agreement therefore reiterates the principle of cost-effectiveness with respect to all organs and subsidiary bodies of the ISA. A particular cause of concern for many States parties was the cost of running the Enterprise which was thus effectively shelved by designating the Secretariat of the Authority to perform its functions for the foreseeable future.[230] Seabed mining operations are to be conducted through joint-ventures in accordance with sound commercial principles. The financial terms of contracts contained in UNCLOS were viewed by some States as imposing unduly burdensome obligations on commercial operators. The Agreement therefore sets aside that whole complex body of rules and instead spells out a series of general principles which would in the future provide the basis for detailed rules on the matter. The fees payable to the Authority by contractors were also considerably reduced.[231]

The decision-making processes of the Assembly and the Council of the ISA – which were at the heart of the consultations – were changed in order to give technologically advanced States a stronger voice that fairly protects their interests.[232] Failing a consensus, a system of chambered voting is to be applied, requiring a two-thirds majority on questions of substance, provided that such decisions are not opposed by a majority in any one of the five chambers constituted on the basis of different interest groups as well as geographical criteria, except where the Convention provides for decisions by consensus in the Council. This mechanism on the one hand ensures a right of veto for certain

---

B.H. Oxman, *The 1994 Agreement and the Convention*, 88 American Journal of International Law, at 687–696 (1994).

[227] See status of the Implementation Agreement, available at: treaties.un.org/Pages/ViewDetails .aspx?src=TREATY&mtdsg_no=XXI-6-a&chapter=21&lang=en (last visited: 1 July 2011).

[228] See D. Freestone, *A Decade of the Law of the Sea Convention: Is It a Success?*, 39/3 George Washington International Review, at 514 (2007).

[229] Nelson, *The New Deep Seabed Mining Regime* (note 226), at 196.

[230] Id., at 196–197, see also Freestone, *A Decade of UNCLOS – a Success?* (note 228), at 512.

[231] Nelson, *The New Deep Seabed Mining Regime* (note 226), at 198–200.

[232] Id., at 197.

categories of States and on the other that at least some international community interests will play a part in the decision-making process.[233]

The Agreement further dropped the controversial Review Conference which was supposed to take place fifteen years after the first commercial seabed exploitation. That Conference could have adopted amendments to Part XI of the Convention by a three-fourths majority which would also have entered into force for those countries that had not approved them. The Assembly of the Authority on the recommendation of the Council may now make such a review any time. Amendments relating to the Agreement and Part XI are subject to the regular amendment procedure set out in the respective articles of the Convention.[234] Any amendment shall, however, in particular ensure the maintenance of the principle of the common heritage of mankind, the international regime designed to ensure equitable exploitation of the resources of the "Area" for the benefit of all States, especially the developing ones, and an Authority to organize, conduct and control activities therein.

Part of the original "package deal" had been the mandatory transfer of technology to developing countries which from the very beginning had met with objections from industrialized countries. The Agreement therefore provides that this requirement shall not apply, putting the emphasis instead on the promotion of international cooperation with respect to the transfer of technology.[235] In the same manner, the idea of limiting production from deep seabed minerals so as not to adversely impact land-based producers was eliminated as major industrialized countries had viewed such limitation as being based on outmoded concepts of central economic planning. The Agreement sets forth new general principles on which the production policy of the Authority shall be based, including no subsidization of activities in the "Area" and no discrimination between minerals derived therefrom and from other sources. In addition, the GATT rules and its relevant codes and successor, or superseding agreement, that is the WTO, apply.[236]

The Agreement also established a new organ of the ISA, a Finance Committee on the recommendation of which decisions by the Assembly and the Council having financial or budgetary implications have to be based. Before the Authority has sufficient funds to meet its administrative expenses that Committee is to include the five largest contributors to its budget. Decisions in the Finance Committee on questions of substance are to be taken by consensus.[237]

---

[233] Id., at 198.

[234] Id.

[235] Id. See also Freestone, *A Decade of UNCLOS – a Success?* (note 228), at 513–514.

[236] Nelson, *The New Deep Seabed Mining Regime* (note 226), at 199; see also id. Freestone, at 514.

[237] Id., Nelson, at 200. See Implementation Agreement, Section 9.

The 1994 Implementation Agreement substantively changed the 1982 UNCLOS without using its amendment provisions. It can certainly be regarded as a protocol of amendment which appears to "unpack" an important part of the "package deal",[238] bringing the deep seabed mining regime closer in line with political and economic realities. Commercial concerns had eroded the original redistributionist ideals, shifting the balance between use and distribution in favor of the former. The General Assembly resolution to which the Agreement was annexed expressly recognized that "political and economic changes, including in particular a growing reliance on market principles have necessitated the re-evaluation of some aspects of the regime for the "Area" and its resources".[239] The negotiators of the Agreement also refrained from laying down detailed rules on important economic and financial issues which had extensively been dealt with in UNCLOS, but merely set forth general principles instead which would be applied when commercial deep seabed mining would be imminent. At the same time, the Agreement preserved and reaffirmed the fundamental principle on which the deep seabed mining regime is based – that of the common heritage of mankind.[240]

It is also important to note that mining of the deep seabed will not only disrupt the ocean floor environment but also affect the surface waters and the remainder of the ocean's ecosystem.[241] Any future exploitation of seabed minerals will thus have to face increased environmental concerns, including the protection of marine biodiversity and of life forms around volcanic vents.[242] The need to set aside areas in order to preserve their unique flora and fauna was already recognized by the drafters of the Convention. The ISA has endeavored to base its regulations not only on sound economic principles, but also on rigorous environmental standards, including the application of the precautionary approach.[243]

D. *The Current State of the Principle of the Common Heritage of Mankind*

The principle of the common heritage of mankind is today enshrined in two international agreements – UNCLOS and the Moon Treaty, with only the

---

[238] Freestone, *A Decade of UNCLOS – a Success?* (note 228), at 515.

[239] UN General Assembly Res. 48/263 of 28 July 1994. See also L.B. Sohn, *International Law Implications of the 1994 Agreement*, 88 American Journal of International Law, at 697 (1994).

[240] See Nelson, *The New Deep Seabed Mining Regime* (note 226), at 198; see also Nicholson, *The Common Heritage of Mankind and Mining* (note 170), at 186.

[241] Heim, *Exploring the Last Frontiers for Mineral Resources* (note 172), at 824.

[242] Freestone, *A Decade of UNCLOS – a Success?* (note 228), at 541–546.

[243] See Statement by Satya Nandan, Secretary-General of the ISA, before the UN General Assembly, UN doc. A/62/PV.65), at 31(2007).

former containing a detailed elaboration of the concept to date.[244] Important aspects of that principle – non-appropriation, peaceful use of the international commons and protection of the environment – which are also to be found in other international instruments, have won general acceptance from the outset. The appropriate regime of utilization of areas beyond national jurisdiction for the benefit of mankind as a whole has, however, given rise to divergent views in the past, and may do so in the future. The regime originally foreseen by UNCLOS with respect to the exploitation of the international seabed "Area" was eventually brought in line with political and economic realities, removing the stumbling blocks to universal adherence to the Convention.[245] Any attempt to frame an international regime of utilization of the resources with respect to the Moon Treaty was purposely avoided, as being premature and also in view of the problems that had arisen in the field of the law of the sea.[246]

Working on the basis of the Implementation Agreement, the ISA in 2000 approved the Regulations on Prospecting and Exploration for Polymetallic Nodules in the "Area" – a part of the so-called mining code – which has enabled it to sign contracts for exploration with eight investors.[247] The excitement at the Conference on the Law of the Sea about the exploitation of manganese nodules has since been overtaken by the possibility of commercial development of other seabed minerals, such as polymetallic sulphide and cobalt-rich crust deposits. Mining activities for resources different from polymetallic nodules have therefore also been envisaged by the Authority. In 2010 a second part of the "mining code", the "Regulations on prospecting and exploration for polymetallic

---

[244] Kiss, *Conserving the Common Heritage of Mankind* (note 169), at 775; see also A.C. Kiss, *The common heritage of mankind: utopia or reality?*, 40 International Journal, at 432 (1984–1985).

[245] See also Oxman, *The 1994 Agreement and the Convention* (note 226), at 695.

[246] See also White, *The Common Heritage of Mankind: An Assessment* (note 225), at 529. Adherence to the Moon Treaty has nevertheless remained quite limited, as it only counts 13 States parties and four more signatories; see www.oosa.unvienna.org/oosatdb/showTreatySignatures.do (last visited 1 July 2011).

[247] Scovazzi, *The Seabed beyond the Limits of National Jurisdiction* (note 173), at 5. These investors are: Yuzhmorgeologiya (Russian Federation), Interoceanmetal Joint Organization (IOM) (Bulgaria, Cuba, Czech Republic, Poland, Russian Federation, and Slovakia), the Government of the Republic of Korea, China Ocean Mineral Resources Research and Development Association (COMRA) (China), Deep Ocean Resources Development Company (DORD) (Japan), L'IFREMER (France), the Government of India, and the Federal Institute for Geosciences and Natural Resources (Germany). See Report of the Secretary-General of the ISA under Article 166, paragraph 4 of UNCLOS, ISA Assembly doc. ISBA/15/A/2 (23 March 2009), para. 54, available at: www.isa.org.jm/files/documents/EN/15Sess/Ass/ISBA-15A-2.pdf (last visited 1 July 2011). Furthermore, two applications by private companies to conduct activities in reserved areas have been submitted, sponsored by Nauru, respectively Tonga; see website of the ISA: www.isa.org.jm/en/sessions/2011/documents (last visited 1 July 2011).

sulfides in the "Area" was approved,[248] and work is going on regarding another
similar instrument relating to cobalt-rich ferromanganese crusts.[249] Pursuant to
Article 145 UNCLOS the Authority is also elaborating rules, regulations and
procedures to ensure the effective protection of the marine environment, for,
inter alia, the protection and conservation of the natural resources of the "Area"
and for the prevention of damage to the flora and fauna of the marine environment from harmful effects that may arise from the activities therein.[250]

The regime for the deep seabed contained in Part XI of UNCLOS was negotiated on the assumption and the expectation that deep seabed mining would
become an economic reality well before the end of the twentieth century.[251]
These assumptions or predictions have proven to be mistaken in important
respects. Thus, it was predicted that demand for minerals derived from polymetallic nodules would continue to increase steadily at previous rates. It was even
believed that, at an early date, the production of manganese nodules from the
deep seabed would be competitive with the increasingly expensive extraction
of the same minerals from depleted and/or less accessible land-based resources.
Altered market conditions, discoveries of additional land-based sources and the
improved efficiency of land-based mining have, however, resulted in at least a
long postponement of commercial deep seabed mining operations which we
have been witnessing over the past decades.[252]

The Third United Nations Conference on the Law of the Sea certainly devoted
too much time and effort to the deep seabed mining regime laying down too
many details with a view to regulating commercial activities to take place at an
unknown time in the future.[253] International legal rules were elaborated which
were too far ahead of economic developments. Theory thus overtook facts on the
basis of overoptimistic assumptions and predictions, while voices sounding a note

---

[248] See ISA Assembly doc. ISBA/16/A/12 (7 May 2010), available at: www.isa.org.jm/files/documents/EN/16Sess/Assembly/ISBA-16A-12.pdf (last visited 1 July 2011).

[249] See Statement by the Secretary-General of the ISA before the UNGA (note 243). The China Ocean Mineral Resources Research and Development Association (COMRA) has submitted an application to the ISA for approval of a plan of work for exploration for polymetallic sulfides; the general location of the application area is on the Southwest Indian Ocean Ridge; see www.isa.org.jm/en/node/518 (last visited 1 July 2011); The Ministry of Natural Resources and the Environment of the Russian Federation also submitted an application to the ISA for approval of a plan of work for exploration for polymetallic sulfides in the "Area". The general location of the application is on the Mid-Atlantic Ridge; see www.isa.org.jm/en/node/627 (last visited 1 July 2011).

[250] See UN General Assembly Res. 65/37 of 7 December 2010, Oceans and the law of the sea, at op. para. 42.

[251] See Statement by Expert Panel: *Deep Seabed Mining and the 1982 Convention on the Law of the Sea*, 82 American Journal of International Law, at 363 (1988).

[252] See id., at 364.

[253] See also Freestone, *A Decade of UNCLOS – a Success?* (note 228), at 539.

of caution were ignored. Although the major flaws of the mining regime from the point of view of the industrialized countries have been remedied by the 1994 Implementation Agreement it still remains to be seen whether its provisions and the regulations based upon them will really be adequate and appropriate at the time when commercial deep seabed mining may become a reality. Rising metal prices in the last years driven by surging economic growth in developing new economies had been seen as a ray of hope that economic conditions for seabed mining might become increasingly favorable. A target date of 2010 for commercial production of marine mineral resources in the Western Pacific had even been announced by the private sector.[254] The depth of the global recession has, however, had an unexpectedly profound and severe impact upon metal markets and thus also adversely affected the prospects for seabed mining.[255]

The two applications for exploration of reserved areas by private sector entities sponsored by developing States – Nauru and Tonga – submitted to the ISA are considered a new milestone in the life of the Authority and for the regime for deep seabed mining under UNCLOS and the 1994 Implementation Agreement. The applications submitted by China and the Russian Federation for contracts for exploration for polymetallic sulfides are also seen as groundbreaking in nature as they represent the first applications under the aforementioned regulations.[256]

At the United Nations intense discussions have been going on for quite some time whether besides minerals also genetic resources of the seabed in the "Area", which are considered to be of substantial economic importance in the future, form part of the common heritage of mankind – as advocated by the developing countries. Industrialized countries, biotechnology-interested entities and marine scientists argue that access to these resources falls within the high seas freedoms under Part III of UNCLOS. The view has also been expressed that all access and conservation issues are not covered by the existing legal framework and that there is thus a legal gap to close[257] which might be filled by a multilateral agreement under UNCLOS creating a new regime for marine biodiversity and

---

[254] Statement by the Secretary-General of the ISA before the UNGA (note 243), at 30. See also Report of the Secretary-General on oceans and the law of the sea, Addendum 1, UN doc. A/63/63/Add.1 (2008), at 15–16.

[255] Id., Secretary-General of the ISA (note 243), para. 64.

[256] See the information reported by the Secretary-General of the ISA at the Twenty-first Meeting of States Parties to UNCLOS; see www.isa.org.jm/files/documents/EN/SG-Stats/SPLOS-21 .pdf (last visited 1 July 2011). The reported discovery of large deposits of "rare earth" minerals on the floor of the Pacific Ocean may also be of importance for the future work of the ISA; see S. Buck, *Scientists Discover Large Deposit of rare Minerals Used in iPads*, available at: mashable.com/2011/07/04/rare-earth-minerals-ipads (last visited 4 July 2011).

[257] F. Lehmann, *The Legal Status of Genetic Resources of the Deep Seabed*, 11 New Zealand Journal of Environmental Law, at 43–44 (2007).

genetic resources beyond national jurisdiction.[258] The controversial question of the legal status of genetic resources in the "Area" is thus still awaiting a resolution.[259] While it is generally agreed that UNCLOS provides the overarching legal framework for marine activities and resources, including biodiversity and marine genetic resources, views are deeply divided on the adequacy of that framework.[260]

In the negotiations regarding these resources, the question of benefit-sharing in favor of developing countries to be derived from their exploitation also plays an important role. In view of the unsatisfactory experience with mineral resource exploitation from the deep seabed expectations in this respect should probably not be too high, in particular because it is not the resources as such that are highly valuable, but rather the end-product resulting from long and expensive processing. Any promising regulatory regime would have to ensure that economic operators have high incentives to invest in the growth of the activities in question in order that benefits for humankind may truly be realized.[261] Initially, benefit-sharing could perhaps also consist in the sharing of scientific knowledge.[262]

A commencement of commercial production of minerals from the deep seabed is at present still not in sight.[263] Consolation could be drawn from considering the idea of the common heritage of mankind which has become an important principle of international law primarily as a concept of conservation and of transmission of a heritage to future generations.[264] The question may rightly be asked if and when we will ever see it translated into a tangible economic reality.

---

[258] See also L.A. de La Fayette, *A New Regime for the Conservation and Sustainable Use of Marine Biodiversity and Genetic Resources Beyond the Limits of National Jurisdiction*, 24/2 The International Journal of the Marine and Coastal Law, at 226 (2009).

[259] Id., at 8–9. See also A.G. Oude Elferink, *The Regime of the Area: Delineating the Scope of Application of the Common Heritage Principle and Freedom of High Seas*, 22/1 The International Journal of Marine and Coastal Law, at 43 (2007); see further A. Proelss, *Marine Genetic Resources under UNCLOS and the CBD*, 51 German Yearbook of International Law, at 417–466 (2008); see also N. Matz-Lück, *The Concept of the Common Heritage of Mankind: Its Viability as a Management Tool for Deep-Sea Genetic Resources*, in: The International Legal Regime of Areas beyond National Jurisdiction: Current and Future Developments, A.G. Oude Elferink & E.J. Molenaar (eds.), at 61–75 (2010).

[260] L. Ridgeway, *Marine Genetic Resources: Outcomes of the United Nations Informal Consultative Process (ICP)*, 24 The International Journal of Marine and Coastal Law, at 321 (2009).

[261] S. Beslier, *The Protection and Sustainable Exploitation of Genetic Resources of the High Seas from the European Union's Perspective*, 24/2 The International Journal of Marine and Coastal Law, at 338 (2009).

[262] See id., at 340.

[263] See Statement by the Secretary-General of the ISA before the UNGA (note 243), para. 64.

[264] Kiss, *Conserving the Common Heritage of Mankind* (note 169), at 776; see also Kiss, *The Common Heritage of Mankind: Utopia or Reality?* (note 244), at 435.

Chapter Four

The Landlocked States and the Law of the Sea[265]

A. *Landlocked States and Maritimes Uses*

UNCLOS defines landlocked States in a very clear and forthright manner, based on an earlier pertinent legal instrument: "landlocked State" means a State which has no sea-coast.[266] It is by no means general knowledge that the law of the sea is also of interest to landlocked countries. The fact is even much less known that quite a number of these countries,[267] among them Austria, Switzerland, Luxembourg, Slovakia, Paraguay, Bolivia, Ethiopia and Mongolia, have a merchant marine under their own flag, Bolivia even a small high seas fishing fleet. Apart from having ships sailing under their flag, landlocked States have developed other maritime interests as well. Austria and Switzerland have, for instance, for a long time been members of the Intergovernmental Oceanographic Commission (IOC).[268] Both countries have been involved in marine scientific research for quite a number of years, and Austria's petroleum company has engaged in offshore drilling and oil exploration activities.[269] The geographical location of a State – at least in Europe – can therefore no longer be considered a real impediment to maritime uses.[270]

Regarding the manifold uses of the sea, landlocked States differ from other States in one decisive respect: as they do not border the sea, they need transit across the territory of other countries in order to be able to benefit from maritime uses. The lack of a coast of their own deprives them of exclusive

---

[265] For this chapter see in particular Tuerk, *Landlocked States* (note 11).

[266] Art 124 (1) (a) UNCLOS, based on Art. 1 (a) Convention on Transit Trade of Landlocked States, 8 July 1965, 597 UNTS 3.

[267] World Fleet Statistics 2005 (compiled by Lloyd's Register – Fairplay Ltd.), table 1 A, available at: www.emsa.europa.eu (last visited 1 July 2011).

[268] G. Hafner, *The Regulation of Marine Scientific Research Activities of Landlocked and Geographically Disadvantaged States in the Draft Convention on the Law of the Sea*, in: The Law of the Sea in the 1980s: Proceedings/Law of the Sea Institute Fourteenth Annual Conference, C. Park (ed.), 20–23 October 1980, at 345 (1983).

[269] G. Hafner, *Austria and the Law of the Sea*, in: The Law of the Sea: the European Union and its Member States, T. Treves and L. Pineschi (eds.), at 30, 35 (1997).

[270] Tuerk, *Landlocked States* (note 11), at 92.

rights with respect to maritime areas, rights which coastal States derive from the sovereignty they enjoy over the coast.[271] Their geographical location thus places landlocked States at a severe disadvantage relative to their coastal counterparts.[272] The availability of suitable transit facilities is normally subject to little or no control by the landlocked State, and countries of transit have sometimes also used their strategic position as an economic or political lever against their landlocked neighbors. Occasionally, transit has been denied altogether, thereby forcing the landlocked countries to seek alternative routes or means of transport of their goods to and from the sea. It is therefore not at all surprising that many landlocked States in the developing world belong to the Group of Least Developed Countries.[273]

B. *The Historic Evolution of the Maritime Rights of Landlocked States*

The thorny question of access to and from the sea for landlocked territories has a long history. As early as the in the 11th century, coastal territories in Europe began granting treaty rights to landlocked entities to allow them access to the sea, and certain rivers were internationalized.[274] Landlocked States at times even strove to gain direct territorial access to the sea, some, such as Paraguay in the nineteenth century, even employed military force in order to obtain that goal. Switzerland first raised the question of the right of landlocked States to fly their own maritime flag. In 1864, the Swiss Government requested and obtained from the Swiss Parliament permission to form a merchant marine under Swiss flag. However, the attitude of the main Powers – France, Prussia, Britain – was guarded if not negative, owing to Switzerland's lack of a home port and its resulting inability to provide guarantees with regard to the nationality of the ships and marine policing.[275] The Swiss Government abandoned its plan, and ships belonging to Swiss nationals were thus obliged to sail under foreign flags, which gave rise to problems in times of war.[276] In the course of World War I, landlocked States like neutral Switzerland clearly felt the great disadvantage of

---

[271] Id.

[272] M. Sinjela, *Freedom of Transit and the Right of Access for Landlocked States: The Evolution of Principle and Law*, 12 Georgia Journal of International Comparative Law, at 31 (1982).

[273] Virginia Commentary, Vol. III, S.N. Nandan and S. Rosenne (Volume Editors), N.R. Grandy (Assistant Editor), at 375 (1995).

[274] L.M. Alexander, *The 'Disadvantaged' States and the Law of the Sea*, 5 Marine Policy, at 185 (1981); M. Glassner, *The Status of Developing Landlocked States since 1965*, 5/3 Lawyer of the Americas, at 480 (1973).

[275] J. Monnier, *Right of Access to the Sea and Freedom of Transit*, in: A Handbook on the New Law of the Sea, R.-J. Dupuy & D. Vignes (eds.), at 502 (1981).

[276] Id., at 503.

not having ships under their own flag in order to safeguard the supply of their population.

It was not until new States lacking a sea-coast – Austria, Hungary, Czecho-slovakia – appeared on the map of Europe, with the disintegration of the Austro-Hungarian Empire at the end of World War I, that the right of land-locked States to fly a national flag was formally recognized.[277] At first, this right was granted, by the Treaties of Versailles and Neuilly, only to vessels of an Allied or Associated Power having no sea-coast; the Treaties of Saint Germain and Trianon – which were concluded respectively with Austria and Hungary – extended that right to all Contracting parties.[278] This was later confirmed by the Declaration of Barcelona of 1921, adopted by a Conference on Communica-tion and Transit, convened by the League of Nations, recognizing the right to a flag of States having no sea-coast.[279] By choosing the form of a declaration rather than that of a convention, the Barcelona Conference emphasized that it was restating an existing principle of international law.[280]

However, the right of landlocked States to fly their own flag on the seas could only be effective if at the same time they also enjoyed the right of access thereto.[281] Their claims regarding access to the sea were originally founded on principles of natural law. It was argued that the right of free transit was con-ferred on every landlocked country by its very sovereignty, a necessary corollary to accepted notions of freedom of the high seas. As the oceans are open to all States, coastal and landlocked alike, the latter should be entitled to free transit in exercise of their equal rights within the *res communis*. Another theory sup-porting a right of transit by landlocked States was derived from the civil law concept of "servitude".[282] The view was also expressed that the right of land-locked States to free transit over land was the same as the right of innocent passage through the territorial waters of a coastal State. The transit countries, however, considered access to the sea merely a privilege, contingent upon terms and conditions unilaterally imposed by them.[283]

The only generally acceptable way to resolve this problem appeared to be by way of bilateral or multilateral treaty arrangements on transit rights. The liberal-istic trend in the economic field prevailing after World War I fostered solutions providing for transit rights in general. The Barcelona Convention and Statute

---

[277] Id.

[278] Id.; see also P. Tavernier, *Les nouveaux États sans littoral d'Europe et d'Asie et l'accès à la mer*, 97/3 Revue générale de droit international public, at 733 (1993).

[279] Glassner, *The Status of Developing Landlocked States since 1965* (note 274), at 481.

[280] Monnier, *Right of Access to the Sea and Freedom of Transit* (note 275), at 504.

[281] Tuerk & Hafner, *The Landlocked Countries and UNCLOS* (note 3), at 59.

[282] Sinjela, *Freedom of Transit and the Right of Access for Landlocked States* (note 272), at 32.

[283] Tuerk, *Landlocked States* (note 11), at 95.

on Freedom of Transit of 1921 provided for an internationally recognized right of transit, although with several important restrictions.[284] It did not specifically cater to the particular needs of the landlocked countries, and applied only to railway and waterway transport, thus excluding land transport. That Convention, furthermore, received only a limited number of ratifications. The failure of the Barcelona Convention, which focused primarily on Europe, to address road transport, excluded extensive portions of Africa and Asia, continents that are largely dependent on overland routes to and from the sea.[285] The principle of a general right of transit – applicable to all States – was confirmed after World War II, in Article V of the 1947 General Agreement on Tariffs and Trade (GATT), once again without express reference to landlocked countries.[286]

The right of the ships of landlocked States to have access to sea ports was enshrined in the Convention and Statute on the International Regime of Maritime Ports, concluded by the Second General Conference on Communications and Transit, convened in Geneva in 1923. This Statute does not lay down the principle of freedom of access to ports, but only one of equality of treatment with regard to such access, equality being achieved by granting national and most-favored nation treatment.[287]

C. *The 1958 Geneva Conventions on the Law of the Sea*

A further important step regarding the relationship between landlocked countries and the sea was the adoption, by the First United Nations Conference on the Law of the Sea, of the four Geneva Conventions on the Law of the Sea of 1958 already referred to. A total of ninety States participated in that Conference, of which only ten were landlocked. These 1958 Conventions were based on draft articles elaborated by the ILC which were characterized by a certain lack of understanding of the specific position of landlocked States in maritime matters, since these countries were not even mentioned in these articles. This might have been a reflection of the outdated view that landlocked States and their nationals were not able to make a reasonable use of the sea. However, Switzerland had taken the initiative to convene a preliminary conference of landlocked States preceding the United Nations Conference, which contributed to a heightening of the awareness of landlocked States with respect to their

---

[284] Tuerk & Hafner, *The Landlocked Countries and UNCLOS* (note 3), at 59.
[285] Id.
[286] Hafner, *Austria and the Law of the Sea* (note 269), at 28; see also Virginia Commentary Vol. III (note 273), at 374.
[287] Monnier, *Right of Access to the Sea and Freedom of Transit* (note 275), at 505–506.

particular situation and led to a common position of these countries at the Conference itself.[288]

This First United Nations Conference on the Law of the Sea, apart from the now undisputed recognition of the right of landlocked States to their own flag on the seas, however, produced only a rather meagre result, namely Article 3 of the Convention on the High Seas. This Article states that, "in order to enjoy the freedom of the seas on equal terms with coastal States, States having no sea-coast *should* have free access to the sea". This access was, however, made contingent on agreement among the States concerned based on the principle of reciprocity. Thus, the transit rights were in fact made dependent on the good will of the coastal States concerned.[289] The question regarding access and use of sea ports was settled jointly with that of freedom of transit in Article 3: operations take place entirely in territory under the sovereignty of the transit States which were prepared to tolerate them only within the framework of special agreements.[290]

As already pointed out, one of the most important decisions taken at the 1958 Conference related to the Convention on the Continental Shelf, nationalizing the most valuable areas of the seabed in favor of coastal States. At that time the tendency had already emerged to also apply a similar system to the living resources of the seas. It has, however, to be admitted that the landlocked countries themselves were not yet quite aware of the importance of the oceans as a repository of resources. Thus, they did not defend their position with the necessary resolve, thereby prejudging themselves to their own detriment for the future.[291] The view that the continental shelf would not be of any interest to landlocked States not only prevailed at the 1958 Conference on the Law of the Sea, but was also expressed as late as 1969 by the ICJ in its North Sea Continental Shelf judgement.[292] An opinion that has been shown not to correspond to reality.

---

[288] G. Hafner, *Die Gruppe der Binnen- und geographisch benachteiligten Staaten auf der Dritten Seerechtskonferenz der Vereinten Nationen*, 38 Zeitschrift für ausländisches öffentliches Recht und Völkerrecht, at 570 (1978); Tuerk & Hafner, *The Landlocked Countries and UNCLOS* (note 3), at 59; Virginia Commentary, Vol. III (note 273), at 376.

[289] Tuerk & Hafner, *The Landlocked Countries and UNCLOS* (note 3), at 60.

[290] Monnier, *Right of Access to the Sea and Freedom of Transit* (note 275), at 506.

[291] Tuerk & Hafner, *The Landlocked Countries and UNCLOS* (note 3), at 60.

[292] See G. Hafner, *The Rights of Landlocked States in the Baltic Area*, in: The Baltic Sea: New Developments in National Policies and International Cooperation, R. Platzöder & P. Verlaan (eds.), at 371 (1996), quoting ICJ Reports 1969, at 43; see also G. Hafner, *Bemerkungen zur Funktion und Bestimmung der Betroffenheit im Völkerrecht anhand des Binnenstaates*, 31 German Yearbook of International Law, at 187 (1988).

D. *The 1965 Convention on Transit Trade of Landlocked States*[293]

The accelerated process of decolonization in the early 1960s led to an increase in the number of landlocked States, particularly in Africa. In 1965, the pressing demands of newly-independent landlocked States led to the elaboration within the framework of UNCTAD of the New York Convention on Transit Trade of Landlocked States. This Convention in its Preamble sets forth several principles reflecting the main aspirations of the landlocked countries, including, *inter alia,* free access to the sea, identical treatment for vessels flying the flag of landlocked States to those of coastal States, free and unrestricted transit – however, once again on the basis of reciprocity. These principles are to a certain extent further spelled out in the substantive articles of that Convention.

The 1965 Transit Convention was the first multilateral treaty devoted exclusively to the special transit problems of landlocked States. It has nevertheless drawn criticism from many landlocked countries, mainly because it is based on reciprocity and requires additional agreements with transit States to make transit rights self-executing.[294] The Convention entered into force in 1967 following its ratification by the required minimum of two landlocked and two transit States having a sea-coast. It has thus far been adhered to by 40 States, among them only 22 coastal States, some of which do not even border a landlocked country.[295] Although the Convention has remained largely a dead letter, it nevertheless provided a good basis for negotiations on the question of the transit of landlocked countries,[296] first in the Seabed Committee – which laid some of the groundwork for the new law of the sea – and later at the Conference on the Law of the Sea itself.

E. *The Third United Nations Conference on the Law of the Sea*

The extension of national jurisdiction over vast, valuable maritime areas in the decades following World War II, which led to what has been called a "New International Maritime Order" embracing all human activities at sea, even

---

[293] The Convention on Transit Trade of Landlocked States was adopted on 8 July 1965 by the United Nations Conference on Transit Trade of Landlocked Countries, which had been convened pursuant to a decision of the General Assembly (note 266); see also Glassner, *The Status of Developing Landlocked States since 1965* (note 274), at 484–485.

[294] See also Tavernier, *Les nouveaux États sans littoral* (note 278), at 734; see further Virginia Commentary, Vol. III (note 273), at 377.

[295] See status of the Convention, available at: treaties.un.org/doc/publication/mtdsg/volume%20i/chapter%20x/x-3.en.pdf (last visited 1 July 2011).

[296] Tuerk & Hafner, *The Landlocked Countries and UNCLOS* (note 3), at 61.

further increased the disadvantages of landlocked States in comparison with coastal States.[297] That development, however, made landlocked countries realize their "handicapped situation" even more. Unlike coastal States, they could not enlarge the amount of resources reserved only for a certain State and its population, simply by claiming a 200 nautical mile EEZ.[298] The landlocked countries became increasingly aware of the danger to their interests of this transition of the law of the sea.[299] Thus, they wholeheartedly welcomed the initiative of Malta in 1967 to declare the seabed beyond the limits of national jurisdiction the "common heritage of mankind".[300] Already in the Seabed Committee, established following that initiative, they forged an alliance with the so-called "geographically disadvantaged States", i.e. those coastal countries which would derive little or no benefit from the massive extensions of coastal State jurisdiction.[301] That interest group of "Landlocked and Geographically Disadvantaged States" chaired by Austria, was marked by a true spirit of solidarity between its developing and developed members.[302]

When the Third United Nations Conference on the Law of the Sea began its substantive work in 1974 there were already 29 landlocked States participating. Together with the "geographically disadvantaged States" they endeavored to forestall a partition of oceanic resources, which under traditional international law were common to all nations, among the primarily coastal States alone. The "Group of Landlocked and Geographically Disadvantaged States", which in the end comprised 55 countries, vigorously sought to defend the interests of its members at the Conference,[303] which caused quite a surprise among some of the other Conference participants.

The demands of that Group at the Conference can be categorized as follows:[304]

---

[297] Id.; M. Glassner, *Developing Land-locked States and the Resources of the Seabed*, 11/3 San Diego Law Review, at 636 (1973–1974).

[298] Tuerk & Hafner, *The Landlocked Countries and UNCLOS* (note 3), at 61.

[299] R.-J. Dupuy, *The Law of the Sea: Current Problems* (1974), as quoted by G. Hafner, *The 'landlocked' viewpoint* (note 45), at 281.

[300] Tuerk, *Landlocked States* (note 11), at 99.

[301] L.C. Caflisch, *Land-locked States and their Access to and from the Sea*, 49 British Yearbook of International Law, at 71 (1978).

[302] For a list of the members of the Group of Landlocked and Geographically Disadvantaged States see Alexander, *The 'Disadvantaged' States and the Law of the Sea* (note 274), at 187. Romania is missing on that list as it joined that Group only at a very late stage of the Conference. See also Hafner, *Die Gruppe der Binnen- und geographisch benachteiligten Staaten* (note 288), at 568–615.

[303] See also S. Vasciannie, *Land-Locked and Geographically Disadvantaged States in the International Law of the Sea*, at 218 (1990).

[304] Tuerk & Hafner, *The Landlocked Countries and UNCLOS* (note 3), at 61.

a) participation in the exploration and exploitation of the marine resources by virtue of a right of their own, marine scientific research being included;
b) effective enjoyment of the benefits to be derived from the application of the principle that the seabed and the ocean-floor beyond the limits of national jurisdiction are the common heritage of mankind;
c) participation in the institutions to be created by the new Convention on the Law of the Sea;
d) transit rights to and from the sea.

It was emphasized by this Group that the breadth of the territorial sea should not exceed 12 nautical miles; the establishment of a contiguous zone outside that limit should not be permitted. The new concept of a coastal State EEZ was at first rejected altogether. Once it became clear that the recognition of such a zone could not be avoided, as it had already been accepted by the major maritime powers, the landlocked and geographically disadvantaged States conceded, on condition that the coastal States would recognize their rights in such a zone. They demanded the right to participate in the exploration and exploitation of the living resources and the non-living resources of the economic zones of "neighbouring" coastal States, respectively of the same region or sub-region, on an equal and non-discriminatory basis.[305]

The provisions on the economic zone in a new Convention on the Law of the Sea should replace the 1958 Convention on the Continental Shelf;[306] therefore, the continental shelf beyond 200 nautical miles should be part of the international seabed "Area". All States deriving revenues from the exploitation of the non-living resources of the economic zone should make contributions to the International Seabed Authority to be created.[307] Regarding marine scientific research, the landlocked countries stated that the respective regulations should permit them to participate in research projects carried out in the economic zones of "neighbouring" coastal States.[308]

With respect to the regime concerning the international seabed "Area", it was requested that contracts should be awarded by the ISA with special regard to the need for the widest possible participation of developing countries, particularly the landlocked among them. As for the organs of the Authority, it was pointed out that an adequate representation of landlocked and geographically disadvantaged States in the Council should be ensured; at least two-fifths of its members should be representatives of that group of States. Furthermore, the system applied by the ISA for the distribution of revenues should take special account of the need to compensate landlocked and geographically disadvantaged

---

[305] Id., at 62.
[306] See also Virginia Commentary, Vol. II (note 82), at 848.
[307] Tuerk & Hafner, *The Landlocked Countries and UNCLOS* (note 3), at 62.
[308] Id.

States for the extension of coastal States' jurisdiction by allotting to these States a larger share of such revenues. The organs of the Authority should also deal specifically with questions relating to the particular geographical position of landlocked States.[309]

The landlocked States stressed that their right of free access to and from the sea was one of the basic principles of the law of the sea and formed an integral part of the principles of international law. Such rights were considered the only effective instrument for reducing the additional costs incurred by the landlocked countries due to their unfavorable geographical location in relation to the sea.[310]

F. UNCLOS and the Landlocked States

The overall result of the intense negotiating effort at the Third United Nations Conference on the Law of the Sea is certainly far from wholly satisfying the interests and needs of landlocked States, as their views are only to some degree reflected in UNCLOS. The Convention, however, constitutes the only solution on which agreement with the coastal States was possible and which nevertheless to a certain – albeit rather narrow – extent reflects the legitimate demands of landlocked States.[311]

The Preamble of the Convention recognizes the necessity to take into account the interests and needs of mankind as a whole and, in particular, the special interests and needs of developing countries, whether coastal or landlocked. As mentioned before, UNCLOS in Article 17 affirms that ships under the flag of landlocked States enjoy the right of innocent passage through the territorial sea of other States and Article 87 that the high seas are open to all States, whether coastal or landlocked – both kinds of States enjoying exactly the same rights as regards the freedom of the high seas. Similar provisions were already contained in the 1958 Geneva Conventions on the Territorial Sea and Contiguous Zone and on the High Seas respectively, and are undoubtedly also part of international customary law.[312]

---

[309] Id., at 62–63.

[310] Id., at 63.

[311] Id., at 67; S. Vasciannie, *Landlocked and Geographically Disadvantaged States*, 31 Commonwealth Law Bulletin, at 60 (2005).

[312] See also id., Vasciannie. See further Virginia Commentary, Vol. II (note 82), at 155, respectively, Vol. III (note 273), at 80.

An entire Chapter of UNCLOS – Part X[313] – is devoted to the overriding problem of the landlocked States' transit to and from the sea.[314] The respective articles found their final formulation only after extremely difficult negotiations in a small consultative group, in which the main spokesperson for the land-locked countries was Austria[315] and for the transit States, Peru. Although the outcome of these negotiations came under sharp criticism at the Conference, both from some landlocked and some transit countries, in the end it proved to be the generally acceptable compromise.[316]

The provisions of Part X share to some extent the narrow scope of the rel-evant articles of the 1958 Geneva Convention on the High Seas and the 1965 New York Convention on Transit Trade, but at the same time improve the legal situation of the landlocked States.[317] The core provision of this Part is Article 125,[318] which enshrines the right of access by landlocked countries to and from the sea, and freedom of transit through the territory of transit States by all means of transport. These means are defined in the same manner as in the 1965 Convention as comprising railway rolling-stock, sea, lake and river craft and road vehicles and, where local conditions so require, also porters and pack animals, omitting such important means as aircraft and pipelines. The right of access is, however, contrary to the 1965 Convention, made contingent upon bilateral, sub-regional or regional agreements between the landlocked States and transit States, laying down the terms and modalities for exercising freedom of transit.

The right of access is, furthermore, closely linked with and therefore restricted to the purpose of exercising the "maritime rights" enshrined in UNCLOS, including those relating to the freedom of the high seas and the common heri-tage of mankind. A relatively broad escape clause allows the transit States to take all necessary measures to protect their sovereignty if such transit threatens to infringe their legitimate interests. Some sort of counterbalance is only estab-lished by the non-applicability of the most-favored nation clause in Article 126 regarding the exercise of the right of access to and from the sea.[319] The require-ment of reciprocity has been dropped, which certainly represents an improve-ment over the Conventions of 1958 and 1965.[320] Further provisions of Part X[321] relate to the prohibition of the imposition of financial burdens on transit and

---

[313] Arts 124–132 UNCLOS.
[314] Tuerk & Hafner, *The Landlocked Countries and UNCLOS* (note 3), at 64.
[315] Represented by the author.
[316] See also Virginia Commentary, Vol. III (note 273), at 372.
[317] Tuerk & Hafner, *The Landlocked Countries and UNCLOS* (note 3), at 64.
[318] Virginia Commentary, Vol. III (note 273), at 409.
[319] Tuerk & Hafner, *The Landlocked Countries and UNCLOS* (note 3), at 64.
[320] See also Monnier, *Right of Access to the Sea and Freedom of Transit* (note 275), at 519.
[321] See Arts. 127–132 UNCLOS.

to free zones, oblige the transit State to avoid or reduce delays or other technical difficulties to transit, and provide for some sort of cooperation among the States concerned to improve the technical conditions for transit in cases of their inadequacy. Finally, UNCLOS as a whole does not derogate from any greater rights in respect of transit that landlocked States may have, by agreement, with particular transit States.[322]

Part X of UNCLOS, compared to the 1958 Geneva Convention on the High Seas, undoubtedly marks some progress by putting the rights of the landlocked States to access to and from the sea within a multilateral and more general context, integrating it into the broader framework of the law of the sea.[323] The right of the transit State to suspend transit nevertheless leaves certain loopholes in favor of that State. UNCLOS has reduced the degree of dependence of the landlocked on the transit States in comparison to 1958, but has increased it in relation to the 1965 Convention on Transit Trade of Landlocked States which, however, – as has been pointed out – never really had much practical impact. Complete and unrestricted freedom of access to the sea was not within the grasp of general agreement at the Third United Nations Conference on the Law of the Sea.[324]

It must, however, also be noted that many landlocked States are at the same time transit countries. Thus at the Conference, they only offered qualified support for complete freedom of access to and from the sea for landlocked countries. In spite of the undeniable shortcomings – from the point of view of landlocked States – of the transit provisions of the UNCLOS, it can, however, be said that, on the whole, Part X by striking a certain balance between the interests of landlocked on the one and transit States on the other hand,[325] nevertheless constitutes a significant achievement by the landlocked countries.

A major deficiency of UNCLOS undoubtedly concerns the treatment of ships flying the flag of landlocked States in the ports of a transit State. Pursuant to Article 131 these ships are only accorded treatment equal to that of other foreign ships, whereas Article 3 of the 1958 Convention on the High Seas provided for combined most-favored nation or national treatment, whichever was more favorable to the vessel. That rule of UNCLOS only means that vessels may not be discriminated against in maritime ports for the sole reason that they fly the flag of a landlocked State. Accordingly, this provision amounts to no more than a corollary of the right of landlocked countries to sail ships under

---

[322] Tuerk, *Landlocked States* (note 11), at 103.
[323] Id., at 67; Virginia Commentary, Vol. III (note 273), at 382.
[324] Tuerk & Hafner, *The Landlocked Countries and UNCLOS* (note 3), at 68.
[325] Id., at 64.

their own maritime flag.[326] Furthermore, provisions on legally guaranteed access to those ports from the sea are lacking.

UNCLOS certainly grants the landlocked States a right to participate in the exploration and exploitation of the living resources of EEZs. The relevant provisions of Article 69, however, are not only restricted to living resources, but also limited by additional requirements and conditions as to the object and the substantial and geographical scope of that participation right. Thus, this right exists only in relation to a surplus as defined by the coastal State, with a very narrow exception clause for developing landlocked States. Furthermore, it only becomes effective within a sub-region or a region, but even in this restricted area, does not take precedence over other participation rights. Rather, it must compete with them, with the final decision being left to the coastal State.[327]

Following the same system as for the right of transit, the exercise of the right of landlocked States relating to fisheries is made contingent upon additional agreements with the coastal States concerned. It also cannot be enjoyed in the EEZ of coastal States which are overwhelmingly dependent on fisheries, nor by developed landlocked States in the EEZs of developing States. The prohibition of the transfer of these participation rights to other States is accompanied by their subordination under Article 62 UNCLOS, which permits the coastal State to require the landlocked States to share with itself the benefit from those exploitation activities.[328] In this context, the constantly diminishing yields already causing economic difficulties for many coastal States as well as the rising demand for fish caused by population increase must also be borne in mind. Hence, the fishing rights granted to landlocked States constitute in practice a *nudum ius*, certainly for developed landlocked States.

The determined resistance by the coastal States did not allow for a right to some participation by the landlocked States in the exploration and exploitation of the non-living resources of the continental shelf to be enshrined in UNCLOS,[329] nor did an informal Austrian draft resolution,[330] containing a mere recommendation regarding such participation, find favor among coastal States.[331] The continental shelf doctrine granting sovereign rights to these States over the continental shelf for the purpose of exploring it and exploiting its natural resources was already too firmly anchored in international law.[332]

---

[326] Art. 90 UNCLOS; Caflisch, *Land-locked States and their Access to and from the Sea* (note 301), at 97–98.

[327] Tuerk & Hafner, *The Landlocked Countries and UNCLOS* (note 3), at 65.

[328] Id., at 65.

[329] See also Virginia Commentary, Vol. III (note 273), at 371.

[330] Proposed by the author.

[331] See also Hafner, *Austria and the Law of the Sea* (note 269), at 32.

[332] See also Vasciannie, *Landlocked and Geographically Disadvantaged States and the Outer Limit of the Continental Shelf* (note 158), at 272.

As pointed out before, in the international seabed "Area" activities are to be carried out for the benefit of mankind as a whole, irrespective of the geographical location of States, whether coastal or landlocked. The same holds true of the use of the "Area" exclusively for peaceful purposes by all States, whether coastal or landlocked.[333] Article 148 UNCLOS deals with the promotion of the effective participation of developing States in activities in the "Area", with due regard, in particular, to the special need of the landlocked and geographically disadvantaged among them to overcome obstacles arising from their disadvantaged location, including remoteness from the "Area" and difficulty of access to and from it. In addition, Article 152 excludes particular consideration for the developing landlocked and geographically disadvantaged States from the non-discrimination rule to be applied by the ISA in the exercise of its powers and functions.

Within the ISA, the landlocked States are also accorded some, albeit very few, special rights. The 1994 Implementation Agreement provides that developing landlocked and geographically disadvantaged States are to have representation on the Council of the Authority[334] – in the same manner, however, as several other groups of States. In electing the members of the Council, the Assembly of the Authority shall ensure that landlocked and geographically disadvantaged States are represented to a degree which is reasonably proportionate to their representation in the Assembly.[335] The Assembly is also endowed with the competence to consider problems for States in connection with activities in the "Area" that are due to their geographical location, particularly for landlocked and geographically disadvantaged States.[336]

On the whole, the effect of the provisions of Part XI of UNCLOS relating to landlocked States does not consist so much in granting them preferential treatment over the coastal States as a kind of compensation for their other maritime disadvantages, as in ensuring their participation in the benefits to be derived from the "Area" and in defeating any attempt to exclude them therefrom.[337] It seems likely that for any foreseeable future the landlocked States will be obliged to continue to bear costs with respect to the deep seabed rather than

---

[333] See Art. 140, respectively Art. 141 UNCLOS.

[334] Annex, Section 3 Implementation Agreement to UNCLOS. See also Virginia Commentary, Vol. III (note 273), at 383.

[335] Art. 161 UNCLOS. The issue of representation of the Group of Landlocked and Geographically Disadvantaged States in the organs of the ISA was also raised by the Chairman of that Group – at that time the author – in a letter addressed to the Chairman of the Preparatory Commission for the International Seabed Authority and for the International Tribunal for the Law of the Sea; see Document LOS/PCN/114 of 28 August 1990.

[336] Art. 160 (2) (k) UNCLOS.

[337] Tuerk & Hafner, *The Landlocked Countries and UNCLOS* (note 3), at 64.

enjoy benefits, which, however, also holds true for the other members of the international community.[338]

The rights of the landlocked as well as the geographically disadvantaged States regarding marine scientific research activities are enshrined in Article 254 UNCLOS. Although these States are entitled to be informed of planned marine scientific research projects and to participate in such projects, this right depends on additional conditions and requirements. It permits them to participate only in projects carried out by third States and competent international organizations in the EEZ of neighboring coastal States; detailed information must be given to the landlocked and geographically disadvantaged States only if "appropriate", and they must be given the "opportunity" to participate in such research activities only "whenever feasible";[339] experts nominated by them may be objected to by the coastal State.[340] It is doubtful whether these provisions constitute an appropriate substitute for the freedom of scientific research in the oceans, which in the past has created the most favorable conditions for increasing the knowledge of humankind regarding the marine world.[341]

The provisions of UNCLOS on the settlement of disputes – despite their progressive and promising effect from a general point of view – do not endow landlocked States, despite their efforts at the Conference, with all the judicial or other means necessary to guarantee the full use of their limited rights.[342]

G. *Developments since the Adoption of UNCLOS*

Since the adoption of UNCLOS in 1982, the number of landlocked States has further increased, mainly due to the disintegration of the Soviet Union and Yugoslavia. At present, the number of these countries with United Nations membership stands at 42[343] – 15 in Africa, 13 in Europe, 12 in Asia and two in South America; 25 of them are parties to the Convention.[344] It is to be noted that none of the Central Asian landlocked States has adhered to UNCLOS and

---

[338] Id., at 67.

[339] Legislative history indicates that "feasibility" must be determined according to the practicability of participation in light of available research facilities, and may be affected by the degree of anticipated participation by the coastal State – see Virginia Commentary, Vol. IV, M.H. Nordquist (Editor-in-Chief), S. Rosenne and A. Yankov (Volume Editors), N.R. Grandy (Assistant Editor), at 596.

[340] Tuerk & Hafner, *The Landlocked Countries and UNCLOS* (note 3), at 66.

[341] Id., at 68.

[342] Id., at 70.

[343] See landlocked States with UN membership: www.un.org/en/members/ (last visited 1 July 2011).

[344] See status of the Convention (note 6).

that several landlocked States, particularly in Africa, have signed the Convention without so far ratifying it.

All the landlocked countries in Africa, Asia and South America as well as two of them in Central and Eastern Europe are developing countries, facing severe challenges to growth and development, *inter alia*, due to a poor physical infrastructure and remoteness from world markets.[345] The UN General Assembly resolution on "Oceans and the law of the sea", adopted annually, continues to call upon donor agencies and international financial institutions to bear in mind the interests and needs of landlocked developing States in ensuring the availability in all States of the economic, legal, navigational, scientific and technical skills necessary for the full implementation of UNCLOS as well as the sustainable development of the oceans and seas nationally, regionally, and globally.[346]

The transit provisions of UNCLOS seem to have had a positive effect on some of the bilateral agreements since concluded between landlocked and transit States. The probably most far-reaching agreement was signed between Peru and Bolivia in 1992 by which Bolivia was granted an industrial and commercial free zone on the Peruvian coast, including port installations as well as the right of free transit to and from that zone.[347] Paraguay has been granted road access to the sea by Brazil, and Argentina has accorded that country such free access via the Paraná river.[348] In 1991, Mongolia and China concluded an agreement on the access to and from the sea, and transit transport by Mongolia through China's territory.[349] The Preamble to this Agreement specifically refers to the special needs of Mongolia as a landlocked State for transit through the territory of China and access to and from the sea. In 1994, Ethiopia and Djibouti signed an agreement by which Djibouti guaranteed to Ethiopia the permanent right of access to the sea and to transit goods from and to Ethiopia through its territory.[350] Furthermore, Ethiopia was guaranteed the right to use the installations

---

[345] See UNCTAD, UN Recognition of the Problems of Landlocked Developing Countries, available at: www.unctad.org/Templates/Page.asp?intItemID=3619&lang=1 (last visited 1 July 2011).

[346] See UN General Assembly Res. 65/37 (note 250), op. para. 9.

[347] See www.eluniverso.com/2010/10/20/1/1361/bolivia-alcanza-un-acceso-oceano-pacifico.html (last visited 1 July 2011).

[348] See www.observatoriomercosul.ufsc.br/Arquivos/para-merco.pdf (last visited 1 July 2011).

[349] Agreement between the Government of the Mongolian People's Republic and the Government of the People's Republic of China on the Access to and from the Sea and Transit Transport by Mongolia through China's territory of 26 August 1991 (on file with author).

[350] Djibouti Port Utilization Agreement between the Transitional Government of Ethiopia and the Government of the Republic of Djibouti of 12 December 1993 (on file with author). See also the Transit and Port Services Agreement between the Transitional Government of Ethiopia and the Government of the State of Eritrea of 27 September 1993 (on file with author).

and equipment of the Port of Djibouti and if necessary to invest in order to promote Ethiopia's foreign trade.

Besides such bilateral agreements, treaties providing for regional economic integration are playing an increasingly important role in overcoming the plight of developing landlocked countries, by also facilitating access to and from the sea. Bolivia has joined the Andean Community, also comprising Colombia, Ecuador and Peru; Paraguay, together with Brazil, Argentina and Uruguay, is a member of "Mercosur" (Southern Common Market). Both these treaties have established customs unions that are components of the continuing process of South American integration.[351] Africa, the continent with the largest number of land-locked countries, counts several organizations promoting economic integration. The largest such grouping is the Common Market for Eastern and Southern Africa (COMESA), formed in 1994, which comprises 19 States, including eight landlocked countries.[352] The Economic Community of West African States (ECOWAS) was already founded in 1975 and consists of 15 States, including three landlocked ones.[353] The Southern African Development Community (SADC), set up in 1992, has a membership of 15 States, including six landlocked countries.[354] When founded in 1999 the East African Community (EAC) only comprised Kenya, Uganda and Tanzania; Rwanda and Burundi acceded to the Community in 2007.[355]

With respect to developing landlocked countries, reference should also be made to the so-called São Paolo Consensus adopted by the United Nations Conference on Trade and Development (UNCTAD) in June 2004,[356] which *inter alia*, deals with the special problems of landlocked developing countries as well as the related challenges faced by transit developing countries. The

---

[351] See www.comunidadandina.org/ingles/who.htm (last visited 1 July 2011); see also: www.mercosur.int/t_generic.jsp?contentid=655&site=1&channel=secretaria&seccion=2 (last visited 1 July 2011).

[352] The members are: Angola, Burundi, Comoros, D. R. Congo, Eritrea, Ethiopia, Kenya, Madagascar, Malawi, Mauritius, Namibia, Rwanda, Seychelles, Sudan, Swaziland, Tanzania, Uganda, Zambia, Zimbabwe; available at: actrav.itcilo.org/actrav-english/telearn/global/ilo/blokit/comesa.htm (last visited 1 July 2011).

[353] The members are: Benin, Burkina Faso, Cape Verde, Cote d'Ivoire, Gambia, Ghana, Guinea, Guinea Bissau, Liberia, Mali, Niger, Nigeria, Senegal, Sierra Leone, Togo; see ECOWAS in Brief; available at: www.comm.ecowas.int/sec/index.php?id=about_a&lang=en (last visited 1 July 2011).

[354] The members are: Angola, Botswana, D.R. Congo, Lesotho, Madagascar, Malawi, Mauritius, Mozambique, Namibia, Seychelles, South Africa, Swaziland, United Republic of Tanzania, Zambia and Zimbabwe; available at: www.sadc.int/index/print/page/715 (last visited 1 July 2011).

[355] See East African Community; available at: http://www.eac.int/about-eac.hmtl.

[356] See Report of the Secretary-General on Oceans and the law of the sea, UN doc. A/59/62/Add.1 (2004), at 17–18.

document outlines the goals of UNCTAD in addressing these problems within a new global framework for transit transport cooperation between landlocked and transit developing countries. These goals, which include technical assistance, should make it easier for both landlocked and transit States to build the legal framework containing the agreed terms and modalities for exercising freedom of transit, at the bilateral, sub-regional or regional level.

The 2005 World Summit recognized the special needs of, and challenges faced by landlocked developing countries, and reaffirmed the commitment by the international community to urgently address these needs and challenges through the full, timely and effective implementation of relevant internationally agreed programmes.[357] Particular reference was made to the Declaration and Programme of Action which had been adopted in 2003 by an international ministerial conference convened by the United Nations in Almaty, Kazakhstan, to enhance transit transport cooperation between landlocked and transit developing countries.[358] Already in 1998, the UN Special Programme for the Economies of Central Asia (SPECA) was launched to strengthen sub-regional cooperation in that area and its integration into the economies of Europe and Asia, also dealing with questions of transport and border crossing.[359]

As regards the EEZ, coastal States in their national legislation generally appear to have ignored the provisions of UNCLOS in respect of the sharing of surplus living resources with landlocked and geographically disadvantaged States. There are, however, some exceptions. In 1992, Bolivia and Peru concluded an agreement which also contemplates the possibility that Bolivia may enter into joint ventures with Peruvian companies to engage in fishing activities in the Peruvian EEZ.[360] Morocco and Togo, for instance, in their relevant legislation, referring to African solidarity, have indicated their readiness to allow neighboring landlocked countries access to the living resources of their EEZs.[361] Regarding

---

[357] The 2005 World Summit was held at United Nations Headquarters in New York from 14–16 September 2005; see UN General Assembly Res. 60/1, para. 65.

[358] See UNCTAD, UN Recognition of the Problems of Landlocked Developing Countries (note 344).

[359] See SPECA Background Information, available at: www.unescap.org/oes/SPECA/about/index .asp (last visited 1 July 2011)

[360] Vasciannie, *Landlocked and Geographically Disadvantaged States* (note 311), at 65.

[361] Id., at 65, footnote 6; see also *Paper by the Commonwealth Secretariat, Landlocked and Geographically Disadvantaged States under UNCLOS*, 30 Commonwealth Law Bulletin, at 792 (2004). It should further be noted that, in its declaration upon accession to UNCLOS in 2007, Moldova affirmed, as a country without a seashore, the necessity of developing international cooperation for the exploitation of the living resources of the economic zones on the basis of just and equitable agreements that should ensure the access of the countries of this category to the fishing resources in the economic zones of other regions or sub-regions. Declaration upon accession, 6 February 2007 of Moldova, available at: www.un.org/Depts/los/convention_agreements/convention_declarations.htm (last visited 1 July 2011).

marine scientific research, coastal States in their domestic legislations do not seem to have taken any account of the rights of landlocked countries.[362]

In assessing the present situation of the landlocked countries with respect to the law of the sea, it must also not be overlooked that a fundamental change has occurred with respect to those landlocked States that have become members of the European Union.[363] When signing UNCLOS in 1984, the European Community[364] indicated that its Member States have transferred competence to it with regard to the conservation and management of sea fishing resources, competences concerning rules and regulations for the protection and preservation of the marine environment as well as certain powers with regard to the provisions of Part X.[365]

European Union Law applies to the entire area under the sovereignty of the Member States and thus the four basic freedoms – freedom of movement of persons, goods, services and capital – are applicable,[366] and any discrimination against nationals of Member States is prohibited. If a Member State extends its area of jurisdiction, the area of applicability of European Union Law is automatically extended. This also holds true for instance for the continental shelf.[367] The Common European Fisheries Policy provides for the allotment of quotas of the total allowable catch to individual Member States.[368] Although the criteria underlying

---

[362] Tuerk, *Landlocked States* (note 11), at 110.

[363] See also Hafner, *Austria and the Law of the Sea* (note 269), at 34.

[364] On 1 December 2009, the Treaty of Lisbon amending the Treaty on the European Union and the Treaty Establishing the European Community entered into force. As a consequence, as of that date, the European Union has replaced and succeeded the European Community – see Art. 1 (3) of the Treaty on the European Union as it results from the amendments introduced by the Treaty of Lisbon. Therefore, as from that date the European Union is exercising all rights and assuming all obligations of the European Community.

[365] Declaration by the European Economic Community upon signature on 7 December 1994, www.un.org/Depts/los/convention_agreements/convention_declarations.htm (last visited 1 July 2011). See also W. Graf Vitzthum, *Die Europäische Gemeinschaft und das Internationale Seerecht*, 111 Archiv des Öffentlichen Rechts, at 36–37, footnote 15 (1986); Hafner, *The Rights of Landlocked States in the Baltic Area* (note 292), at 384.

[366] See Art. 299(1) consolidated version of 29 December 2006 of the Treaty Establishing the European Community (hereinafter the Rome Treaty establishing the EC), 25 March 1957, OJ C 321 E.

[367] J. Schwarze (ed.), EU-Kommentar 2000, at Art. 299, Rz 5 (2000), and C. Thun-Hohenstein et al. (eds.), Europarecht, at 49 (2005).

[368] The allocation is decided annually; see Regulation No. 53/2010, 2010 OJ (L21) 1, last amended by Regulation No. 1004/2010 OJ (L291) 31. The Member States divide their quota among the ships of their fishing fleet; the ships must be under the flag of the Member State or registered in that Member State. The freedom of establishment enables any citizen of the Union to register a ship in any Member State. There must not be any limitations in this respect as underlined by the European Court of Justice (ECJ); see Case C-221/89, R vs. Secretary of State for Transport, *ex parte* Factortame (No. 3), 1991 ECR I-3905.

the quota allocation, namely the traditional fishing patterns, do not favor fishing activities by nationals of landlocked countries,[369] there do not seem to be fundamental obstacles regarding such activities. On the contrary, the European Court of Justice has ruled explicitly that coastal Member States are prohibited from restricting the fishing activities of nationals of other Member States – thus including landlocked States – undertaken from the territory of the coastal States. In view of this situation, the landlocked Member States of the European Union are landlocked in theory rather than in practice.[370]

It has taken quite some time for certain legitimate interests of the landlocked States with regard to the sea to be recognized in international law. UNCLOS undoubtedly represents a major step forward in this respect by reaffirming and in some ways also extending the nevertheless still rather limited rights of these States regarding maritime uses. Moreover, one of the major and lasting results of the Third United Nations Conference on the Law of the Sea was to heighten the awareness of the international community that the law of the sea is also of considerable importance and interest to the landlocked States. At the same time, these States themselves have become more conscious of that fact than ever before and endeavor to continue contributing to the further development of that important field of international law.

---

[369] Hafner, *The Rights of Landlocked States in the Baltic Area* (note 292), at 385.

[370] Graf Vitzthum, *Die Europäische Gemeinschaft und das Internationale Seerecht* (note 365), at 62.

Chapter Five

The Resurgence of Piracy[371]

A. *The Present Situation*

Most of the oceans are under no State's jurisdiction, acting as both a barrier and a conduit for threats to the security of people everywhere,[372] with piracy and armed robbery at sea having once again become the most prominent maritime threat. There are critical chokepoints for maritime traffic, in particular, the Strait of Malacca, transited by around 50.000 vessels annually transporting about 50% of the total volume of oil transported by sea and the Gulf of Aden, with about 22.000 vessels annually coming from or sailing to the Suez Canal, carrying more than 12% of that volume.[373] Pirate attacks basically occur in four major geographical areas: the Gulf of Aden and off the coast of Somalia; the Gulf of Guinea, near Nigeria and the Niger River delta; the Malacca Strait between Indonesia and Malaysia, and the Indian subcontinent.[374]

According to the IMO the total number of acts of piracy and armed robbery against ships so far reported to the Organization since it began compiling relevant statistics in 1984 was 6023 by 1 July 2011;[375] it is, however, also believed that, in general, incidents of piracy and armed robbery at sea are considerably

---

[371] For this chapter see in particular H. Tuerk, *The Resurgence of Piracy: A Phenomenon of Modern Times*, 17/1 University of Miami International and Comparative Law Review, at 1–42 (2009).

[372] See National Strategy for Maritime Security (note 1), at 333.

[373] See IMO, Reports on Acts of Piracy and Armed Robbery Against Ships, MSC.4/Circ.169 of 1 April 2011, available at: www.imo.org/OurWork/Security/PiracyArmedRobbery/Monthly%20 and%20annual%20piarcy%20and%20armed%20robbery%20report/169_Annual2010.pdf (last visited 1 July 2011).

[374] S. Hanson, *Combating Maritime Piracy, Council on Foreign Relations*, 7 January 2010 (updated), available at: http://www.cfr.org/publication/18376/combating_maritime_piracy.html (last visited 1 July 2011); see also Lloyds list Regulation article, *"South China Sea is new piracy hot spot"*, available at: www.lloydslist.com/ll/sector/regulation/article345194.ece (last visited 11 July 2011).

[375] IMO, doc. MSC.4/Circ.173, para. 3, 11 July 2011; see Global Integrated Shipping Information System website: gisis.imo.org/Public.

underreported.[376] Thus the actual number of such incidents might be much higher. In recent years, the region off the coast of Somalia has become the leading area plagued by pirate attacks. The IMO has expressly recognized the strategic importance of the navigational routes in that area for regional and global seaborne trade and the need to ensure that they remain safe at all times. It has furthermore pointed out that the particular character of the present situation in Somalia requires an exceptional response in order to safeguard the interests of the maritime community making use of the waters off the coast of that country.[377]

In 2010, maritime piracy reached its then highest annual level since the Piracy Reporting Centre (PRC) of the International Maritime Bureau (IMB), a specialized division of the International Chamber of Commerce (ICC), started monitoring piracy incidents worldwide in 1991. In that year a total of 445 incidents of piracy and armed robbery – as compared to 406 in 2009 – were reported, with 219 incidents attributed to Somali pirates. Altogether 1016 seafarers were captured and 8 killed. At the end of 2010, Somali pirates held 28 vessels for ransom and 638 seafarers as hostages.[378] It is also worth noting that the periods of detention of hostages by Somali pirates became lengthier, the modus operandi of the pirates became more sophisticated and the area of attacks extended further to the south – as far as Mozambique – and east to less than 200 nautical miles from India.[379] The Security Council has also expressed concern about the reported involvement of children in piracy off the coast of Somalia.[380]

In the first half of 2011, piracy at sea hit a new all-time high with 266 attacks worldwide, a sharp rise driven by a further surge in piracy off the coast of Somalia, where 163 incidents were recorded during that period.[381] This dramatic increase in sea robbery is unprecedented and perhaps the most significant

---

[376] See IMO, Piracy and Armed Robbery at Sea, Focus on IMO, January 2000, available at: www.imo.org/KnowledgeCentre/ReferencesAndArchives/FocusOnIMO(Archives)/Documents/Focus%20on%20IMO%20-%20Piracy%20and%20armed%20robbery%20at%20sea .pdf (last visited 1 July 2011), at 2.

[377] See IMO, Piracy and Armed Robbery Against Ships in Waters Off the Coast of Somalia, IMO Assembly Resolution A.1026 (26) of 3 December 2009, available at: www.classnk.or.jp/ hp/SMD/isps/pdf/IMO/A1026(26).pdf (last visited 1 July 2011).

[378] ICC IMB Annual Report 1 January–31 December 2010, Piracy and Armed Robbery Against Ships (January 2011); at 23. A short summary is available at: www.simsl.com/Downloads/ Piracy/IMBPiracyReport2010.pdf (last visited 1 July 2011).

[379] Report of the Special Adviser to the Secretary-General on Legal Issues related to Piracy off the Coast of Somalia, UN doc. 11-20621, 19 January 2011, at para. 2.

[380] See UN Security Council Res. 1950 of 23 November 2010, preambular para. 3.

[381] See ICC IMB, Piracy and Armed Robbery against Ships, available at: www.icc-ccs.org/piracy-reporting-centre/piracynewsafigures (last visited 1 July 2011).

eruption of such criminal activity in 200 years,[382] with the pirates making no discrimination among vessels.[383] There is concern that the number of reported piracy incidents could increase to more than 600 per year by 2015 and that piracy risks could become a significant problem across all major African, Middle Eastern and Pacific Rim maritime systems.[384]

It has been pointed out that pirate groups may often be linked to other forms of organized crime, since they maintain relatively sophisticated intelligence collection networks and are engaged in the systematic corruption of local officials. Funds from ransoms are widely distributed within local communities, and in some areas of Somalia, piracy is becoming a major source of income. A parallel illicit economy has been created, leading to a growing dependency of coastal communities on funds obtained from piracy. There is also evidence that the rise of maritime piracy feeds the conflicts in Somalia and contributes to destabilizing the country further by strengthening the resources available to certain groups. Finally, there is an emerging concern that maritime piracy could become linked with extremist movements.[385]

Today's pirates constitute a serious threat not only for those at the front line – seafarers, fishermen and shipping companies – but also for the international community at large, due to the repercussions they have on world trade and international security. Current day piracy has been estimated to cost between $13 and $16 billion every year, a figure that could even be substantially higher in the future.[386] This resurgence of piracy and armed robbery against ships is attributable to many factors, from the poverty of coastal populations and desire for financial gain, to the weakness of some States' policing functions, or even, as in the case of Somalia, the absence of an effective government and economic collapse, to the deficiencies of the legal environment characterized by both an insufficient legal framework and the lack of a response mechanism to counter piratical activities.[387]

---

[382] See also M. Silva, *Somalia: State Failure, Piracy, and the Challenge to International Law*, 50/3 Virginia Journal of International Law, at 560 (2010).

[383] E. Kontorovich, *International Legal Responses to Piracy off the Coast of Somalia*, 13/2 ASIL Insights, No. 2, at 1 (2009).

[384] See *The Economics of Piracy, Pirate Ransoms and Livelihoods off the Coast of Somalia*, Geopolicity Inc., Executive Summary iii (2011); available at: www.geopolicity.com/upload/content/pub_1305229189_regular.pdf (last visited 1 July 2011).

[385] Joint European Commission/UNODC Programme "EU support to the trial and the related treatment of piracy suspects", May 2009 (on file with author).

[386] J. Kraska & B. Wilson, *Piracy Repression, Partnering and the Law*, 40/1 Journal of Maritime Law and Commerce, No. 1, at 45 (2009).

[387] J.L. Jesus, *Protection of Foreign Ships against Piracy and Terrorism at Sea: Legal Aspects* (note 71); see also N. Stracke & M. Bos, *Piracy – Motivation and Tactics*, at 16 (2009).

Somali pirates, whose total number is estimated to be between 1500 and 3000,[388] have often sought to justify their actions as a response to illegal foreign fishing and the dumping of toxic waste in Somali waters,[389] respectively the country's 200-nautical mile EEZ. Although the nexus between piracy, on the one hand, and illegal fishing and the dumping of toxic waste, on the other, continues to be invoked, today piracy off the coast of Somalia has in essence became an organized, lucrative and attractive criminal activity. The shift of acts of piracy further afield from the Somali coast shows that those acts have nothing to do with a desire to protect national interests.[390]

B. *The History of Piracy*

What is commonly thought of as piracy has existed for thousands of years.[391] Early historians have suggested that acts of piracy can be traced back to the beginnings of navigation, having been regarded only as one of the means of livelihood that the sea offered.[392] Homer's epic poems, the *Iliad* and the *Odyssey* addressed the issue of piracy as early as the 7th or 8th century B.C.[393] The most famous victims of this practice were the Greek philosopher Plato and the young Julius Caesar, both eventually freed against a ransom.[394] The concept of piracy has, however, undergone an important evolution from that time until its codification in the 20th century. In antiquity almost anyone who attacked another on the open sea was referred to as a "pirate".[395] The fundamental Greek and Roman conception of piracy distinguished between robbers, who were criminals under

[388] See *The Economics of Piracy* (note 384), at 12.
[389] See Piracy off the Somali Coast, Final report (Assessment and recommendations) of the International Expert Group on Piracy off the Somali Coast, Workshop commissioned by the Special Representative of the Secretary-General of the UN to Somalia (Nairobi, 21 November 2008), at 27, available at: www.imcsnet.org/imcs/docs/somalia_piracy_intl_experts_report_consolidated.pdf (last visited 1 July 2011); see also Stracke & Bos, *Piracy – Motivation and Tactics: The Case of Somali Piracy*, (note 387), at 45.
[390] Report of the Special Adviser to the Secretary-General on Legal Issues related to Piracy off the Coast of Somalia (note 379), at para. 13
[391] J.M. Goodwin, *Universal Jurisdiction and the Pirate: Time for an Old Couple to Part*, 39 Vanderbilt Journal of Transnational Law, at 976 (2006).
[392] See id., at 977.
[393] J. Power, Maritime *Terrorism: A New Challenge for National and International Security*, 10 Barry Law Review, at 112 (2008); see also J.D. Peppetti, *Building the Global Maritime Security Network: A Multinational Legal Structure to Combat Transnational Threats*, 55 Naval Law Review, at 87 (2008).
[394] See Kraska & Wilson, *Piracy Repression, Partnering and the Law* (note 386), at 44; see also Goodwin, *Universal Jurisdiction and the Pirate* (note 391), at 978.
[395] See id., Goodwin.

domestic law and communities referred to as "piratical". These were political societies pursuing an economic and political course which accepted the legitimacy of seizing the goods and persons of strangers without the religious and formal ceremonies considered a prerequisite for beginning a war. It was believed that "pirate communities" were in a "permanent state of war" with everyone around them[396] except with whom they had concluded an alliance.

It was only in the late Middle Ages that the word "*piratae*" began to be understood as "sea thieves" while the old Greek and Roman usage of this term also seems to have survived in the Mediterranean Sea.[397] At about the same time, the legal status of war no longer applied to many lawful private takings. It was, in fact, in an effort to avoid bringing about a state of war between princes that "letters of marque and reprisal" were issued to private persons authorizing them to recapture goods from foreigners that had been wrongfully taken by those foreigners, not necessarily the original goods, nor from the original taker, but from his fellow-citizens.[398]

In the early 17th century the Italian jurist Alberico Gentili, who taught at the University of Oxford, argued that only princes had the power to resort to war and that the label "pirate" carried with it unmistakeably the connotation of outlawry, stating that "pirates are enemies of all men [*Piratae sunt hostes omnium*]".[399] The laws of war could not apply to them and their actions were forbidden by international law. In his view, any taking of foreign life or property at sea not authorized by a sovereign was synonymous with robbery on land.[400] The concept employed by him was based on the writings of Cicero, who had declared that "pirates were the common enemies of all communities".[401] Cicero had, however, used this phrase in a context different from that of Gentili and others who emulated him, namely with respect to politically significant communities in the Eastern Mediterranean who pursued a course of behaviour similar to that of the Vikings many centuries later.[402]

---

[396] See id., at 979.

[397] A.P. Rubin, *The Law of Piracy*, 2nd ed., at 13 (2006).

[398] See id., at 21, 22.

[399] See id., at 23, 24.

[400] See id., at 20.

[401] See Goodwin, *Universal Jurisdiction and the Pirate* (note 391), at 989, 990. The source of the paraphrase "*hostis humani generis*" has not been found. It has been attributed to Sir Edward Coke who used it in a book published in 1644; see Rubin, The Law of Piracy (note 397), at 55, footnote 61. Already in 1615, British courts had determined "*pirata est hostis humani generic*"; see M. Bahar, *Attaining Optimal Deterrence at Sea: A Legal and Strategic Theory for Naval Anti-Piracy Operations*, 40/1 Vanderbilt Journal of Transnational Law, at 11 (2007).

[402] See Rubin, *The Law of Piracy* (note 397), at 83; see also Goodwin, *Universal Jurisdiction and the Pirate* (note 391), at 978.

The Dutch lawyer Hugo Grotius, in his seminal work *De Jure Belli ac Pacis*, published in its final version in 1646, defined the term "pirate" quite differently from Gentili and asserted that the term "piratical" should be applied to those who are banded together for wrongdoing but did not include societies formed for other reasons even if also committing illegal acts. A gathering of pirates and brigands was not a State, while the members of a State, even if at times not free from crime, nevertheless had been united for the enjoyment of rights, and they did render justice to foreigners.[403] Thus, Grotius' conception of the term "pirate" would rather fit robber bands on sea or land, not, however, the Barbary States or other communities engaged in piratical activities whose primary purpose of association was nevertheless considered lawful.[404]

The growth of modern international law in the post-Westphalian order had to take account of the rapid increase of piracy, which was most prevalent in the Mediterranean Sea and on the trade routes between Europe and the Americas, reaching its heyday during the 17th and 18th centuries.[405] While piracy was cracked down on as disturbing "the commerce and friendship betwixt different nations",[406] privateering authorized by a sovereign was often openly encouraged and became the preferred method of plunder on the high seas.[407] With trade flourishing in the relative calm after Napoleon's demise, nations, however, began to increasingly view not only piracy but also the activities of privateers or corsairs as detrimental to their commercial and national interests.[408] Therefore, to counter a menace that affected all nations indiscriminately and that could not be controlled by the normal means of diplomacy or warfare, the "Declaration Respecting Maritime Law"[409] was signed in Paris in 1856, outlawing such state-sponsored piracy,[410] by stating that "privateering is, and remains, abolished".[411]

Piracy dwindled to a controllable and almost unnoticeable activity at the end of the 19th century, only to make a strong comeback, though in a different cast, in recent years. Indeed, at the turn of the 19th century and for the greater part of the 20th century, piracy seemed to have faded away into the mists of history. Though a phenomenon as old as shipping and maritime trade, it was

---

[403] See Rubin, *The Law of Piracy* (note 397), at 26, 27.

[404] See id., at 28.

[405] I. Shearer, *Piracy*, Max Planck Encyclopaedia of Public International Law (R. Wolfrum ed., online ed. June 2008), at 2.

[406] Goodwin, *Universal Jurisdiction and the Pirate* (note 391), at 978.

[407] See id., at 981.

[408] Bahar, *Attaining Optimal Deterrence at Sea* (note 401), at 12.

[409] See Peppetti, *Building the Global Maritime Security Network* (note 393), at 88.

[410] See Bahar, *Attaining Optimal Deterrence at Sea* (note 401), at 12, 13.

[411] See Declaration Respecting Maritime Law, Paris, 16 April 1856, available at: www.icrc.org/IHL.nsf/INTRO/105?OpenDocument (last visited 1 July 2011).

thought to have "forever" been eradicated[412] from most of the seven seas. The crime of piracy thus also began to disappear from some criminal codes or was not included therein in the first place.[413] In the 1960s, piracy, however, slowly started its surge towards emerging once more as a regional, if not a global, menace by the 1980s. South-East Asia first took centre stage in this unfolding drama, only recently to be replaced by the region off the coast of Somalia as the piracy hotspot of the world.[414]

The notion of piracy was first codified by the 1958 Geneva Convention on the High Seas[415] and later by UNCLOS in Articles 100 to 107 and 110 which almost literally repeat Articles 14 to 22 of the 1958 Convention. These provisions are based on the preparatory work of the ILC, which in turn was greatly assisted by the research carried out at the Harvard Law School, having culminated in a draft Convention already in 1932.[416] Some countries which are not yet parties to UNCLOS are nevertheless bound by the 1958 Convention so that the respective articles state the international law on piracy currently in force.[417]

C. *The Definition of Piracy*

Under customary international law there is no authoritative definition of piracy and the municipal law of a number of countries is based on an extensive interpretation of that term which has been defined as broadly as "any armed violence at sea which is not a lawful act of war".[418] Thus many countries criminalize "piracy" that takes place in their own territorial waters which is, however,

---

[412] See Jesus, *Protection of Foreign Ships against Piracy and Terrorism at Sea* (note 71), at 364.

[413] Spain, for instance, deleted the offence of piracy from its Criminal Code in 1995, France, as late as 2007 and only restored it at the beginning of 2011; see F. LeSieur, *Commentaire sur la nouvelle loi française relative à la lutte contre la piraterie et à l'exercice des pouvoirs de police de d'état en mer*, 4/1 Journal of East Asia and International Law, at 115–129 (2011); see also P. Obelleiro, *Juristas internaciones debaten en La Coruña sobre la piratería*, El Pais, May 16, 2009. The offence of piracy has hitherto not existed in Somali law; see Nairobi Workshop Final Report on Piracy off the Somali Coast (note 389); it is now to be included in the new Somali Criminal Code.

[414] S. Eklöf, *Pirates in Paradise: A Modern History of Southeast Asia's Maritime Marauders*, 7/2 WMU Journal of Maritime Affairs, Book Review, at 509 (2008).

[415] See 1958 Geneva Convention on the High Seas (note 52).

[416] See Articles concerning the Law of the Sea with Commentaries, Yearbook of the International Law Commission (ILC), Vol. II (1956), at 282, available at: untreaty.un.org/ilc/texts/ instruments/english/commentaries/8_1_8_2_1956.pdf (last see 1 July 2011).

[417] T. Treves, *Piracy, Law of the Sea, and Use of Force: Developments off the Coast of Somalia*, 20/2 European Journal of International Law, at 401 (2009).

[418] M. Halberstam, *Terrorism on the High Seas: The Achille Lauro, Piracy and the IMO Convention on Maritime Safety*, 82/2 American Journal of International Law, at 273 (1988).

not piracy under international law.[419] Piracy was first authoritatively defined in the afore-mentioned Convention on the High Seas and later in UNCLOS, although being circumscribed by these legal instruments in a rather narrow manner. Article 15 of the 1958 Convention and Article 101 UNCLOS define piracy as:

> (a) Any illegal acts of violence or detention, or any act of depredation, committed for private ends by the crew or the passengers of a private ship or a private aircraft, and directed:
>   (i) On the high seas, against another ship or aircraft, or against persons or property on board of such ship or aircraft;
>   (ii) Against a ship, aircraft, persons or property in a place outside the jurisdiction of any State;
> (b) any act of voluntary participation in the operation of a ship or of an aircraft with the knowledge of facts making it a pirate ship or aircraft;
> (c) any act of inciting or intentionally facilitating an act described in subparagraph (a) or (b).

When drafting this definition, the ILC considered certain controversial points as to the essential features of piracy reaching the conclusion that the intention to rob (*animus furandi*) is not required, that acts of piracy may also be prompted by feelings of hatred or revenge and not merely by the desire for gain, and that the acts must be committed for private ends.[420] The Commission further concluded that piracy can only be committed by private ships and not by warships or other government ships – except when the crew has mutinied and taken control of the ship and that piracy can only be committed on the high seas or in a place outside the territorial jurisdiction of any State – such as an island constituting *terra nullius*, which today is a rather remote possibility.[421]

The ILC also pointed out in the Commentary that acts committed on board a ship by the crew or passengers and directed against the ship itself or against persons or property on the ship cannot be regarded as acts of piracy.[422] The inclusion of aircraft within the definition went beyond earlier customary law.[423] The scope of this provision was further extended by the cited Conventions to include acts of violence from one aircraft to another on the high seas and

---

[419] M.H. Passman, *Protections Afforded to Captured Pirates Under the Law of War and International Law*, 33/1 Tulane Maritime Law Journal, at 5 (2008).
[420] An attempt at the Third United Nations Conference on the Law of the Sea to have the words "for private ends" omitted "in order to include, within the definition [...] acts of violence or depredation committed for professed political ends" failed; see Virginia Commentary, Vol. III (note 273), at 199; see also J. Hjalmarsson, *Piracy and International Law*, 8/10 Shipping & Trade Law, at 1 (2008).
[421] ILC Articles concerning the Law of the Sea (note 414), at 282.
[422] Id.
[423] See Shearer, *Piracy* (note 405), at 3.

not only against ships, which had originally been proposed. The Commission, however, dismissed the idea that the sinking of merchant ships by submarines can be considered piratical acts – as had been expressed in the 1937 Nyon Agreement[424] – as "to assimilate unlawful acts committed by warships to acts of piracy would be prejudicial to the interests of the international community".[425] It should also be pointed out that the meaning of the word "illegal" in the definition of piracy is unclear and the legislative history is not enlightening. It is thus for the courts of the prosecuting State to decide whether the act of violence under consideration was illegal under international law or the national law of that State.[426]

The definition of piracy as codified on the basis of the draft submitted by the ILC is thus quite limited, as it includes only acts committed for "private ends" on the high seas and only undertaken by one ship or aircraft against another ship or aircraft. This excluded some earlier conceptions of piracy that allowed for the crime to be constituted by acts committed on board a vessel by passengers or crew, so-called "internal seizures".[427] Such acts, even when consisting of holding the ship, its crew and the passengers for ransom as a follow-up to the seizure, are thus not covered.[428] The same holds true for violence in internal waters, the territorial sea or archipelagic waters. Furthermore, "the private-ends" criterion removes attacks on shipping "for the sole purpose of achieving some political end" from the concept of piracy under current international law. Acts of violence and depredation exerted by environmentally-friendly groups or persons, in connexion with their quest for enhanced protection of the marine environment, seem likewise to be excluded.[429] It should, however, also be mentioned that in 1986 the Belgian Court of Cassation held that a Greenpeace vessel had committed piracy against an allegedly polluting Dutch vessel when attacking it, because the act of violence was "in support of a personal point of view and not political".[430]

It has also been stated that the definition of piracy under UNCLOS might lead to a misunderstanding as it refers to the high seas without mentioning the

---

[424] See id., at 2.

[425] See ILC Articles concerning the Law of the Sea (note 416), at 282.

[426] R. Wolfrum, *Fighting Terrorism at Sea: Options and Limitations Under International Law*, in: Legal Challenges in Maritime Security, M.H. Nordquist et al. (eds.), at 8 (2008); see also Virginia Commentary, Vol. III (note 273), at 201; see further A. Morita, *Piracy Jure Gentium Revisited: For Japan's Future Contribution*, 51 Japanese Yearbook of International Law, at 79 (2008).

[427] See Shearer, *Piracy* (note 405), at 3.

[428] See Treves, *Piracy*, Law of the Sea, and Use of Force – Somalia (note 417), at 402.

[429] See Jesus, *Protection of Foreign Ships against Piracy and Terrorism at Sea* (note 71), at 379.

[430] See Shearer, *Piracy* (note 405), at 2.

EEZ.[431] A proposal to expressly mention that zone in defining piracy was not accepted at the Third United Nations Conference on the Law of the Sea.[432] This omission, however, does not mean that piracy under international law cannot be committed within that area. As mentioned earlier, Article 58 (2) UNCLOS states that "Articles 88 to 115 and other pertinent rules of international law apply to the EEZ in so far as they are not incompatible with this Part" of the Convention, which includes the articles relating to piracy. The EEZ also encompasses the contiguous zone, by reason of the definition of the spatial extent of that zone as defined in Article 55 UNCLOS.[433] Piratical acts beyond the limits of the territorial sea are thus treated as though they had been committed on the high seas.

The effectiveness of the rules on piracy enshrined in UNCLOS has certainly suffered from the fact that these are limited to the high seas and the EEZ. Pirates are thus able to evade pursuit by crossing into the territorial sea which constitutes a genuine problem.[434] The geographical limitation regarding the applicability of the rules on piracy has to a certain extent been aggravated by the fact that UNCLOS has granted the right to establish a territorial sea of twelve nautical miles instead of the previously most widely accepted limit of three nautical miles.[435] Although, due to the effects of increased Somali piracy, in recent years most of the pirate attacks worldwide have occurred in international waters, in other regions the majority of such incidents continues to take place when ships are transiting the territorial sea or when in port or at anchor.[436] The IMB has therefore, for statistical purposes, adopted a broader definition than the one retained by UNCLOS. Under that definition, piracy and armed robbery at sea is "an act of boarding or attempting to board any ship with apparent intent to commit theft or any other crime with the apparent intent or capability to use force in the furtherance of that act".[437] This definition covers all actual or attempted acts of armed robbery against ships, perpetrated in the

---

[431] See id., at 3, 4.

[432] See Virginia Commentary, Vol. III (note 273), at 199.

[433] See Shearer, *Piracy* (note 405), at 4.

[434] C.D. Guilfoyle, *Piracy off Somalia: UN Security Council Resolution 1816 and IMO Regional Counter Piracy Efforts*, 57 International & Comparative Law Quarterly, at 694 (2008).

[435] R. Collins & B. Hassan, *Applications and Shortcomings of the Law of the Sea in Combating Piracy: A South East Asian Perspective*, 40/1 Journal of Maritime Law & Commerce, at 97 (2009).

[436] See IMO, Reports on Acts of Piracy and Armed Robbery against Ships (note 373), at para. 6; see also R.C. Beckman, *The 1988 SUA Convention and 2005 SUA Protocol: Tools to Combat Piracy, Armed Robbery and Maritime Terrorism*, in: Lloyd's MIU Handbook of Maritime Security, R.H. Burns et al. (eds.), at 188 (2009).

[437] See D. Johnson & E. Pladdet, *Maritime Piracy in Asia*, 32 IIAS Newsl. 45 (2003), available at: www.iias.nl/iiasn/32/IIASNEWS_maritime_piracy_in_Asia.pdf (last visited 1 July 2011).

territorial sea and archipelagic waters, as well as attacks against ships at anchor or berthed. Petty thefts are excluded unless the thieves are armed.[438]

The IMO, in 2001, adopted the "Code of Practice for the Investigation of the Crimes of Piracy and Armed Robbery against Ships",[439] which defines "piracy" as "unlawful acts as set forth in Article 101 UNCLOS". "Armed robbery" is defined as "any unlawful act of violence or detention or any act of depredation, or threat thereof, other than an act of 'piracy', directed against a ship or against persons or property on board such a ship within a State's jurisdiction over such offences". This clear distinction between piracy and "armed robbery against ships" also makes it evident that the special jurisdictional rules on piracy – universal jurisdiction – are not applicable to the latter.[440]

D. *Universal Jurisdiction*

Piracy is the oldest and one of the few crimes where universal jurisdiction has been generally recognized under customary international law,[441] whereas universal jurisdiction for other offenses depends upon specific requirements. The right to take enforcement measures against pirates is vested in all States. Anyone of them has therefore the right to capture and punish pirates under

---

[438] See ICC IMB Annual Report 2009, Piracy and Armed Robbery Against Ships (January 2010), at 4. A short summary is available at: www.iccs.org/index.php?option=com_contentandview=articlesandid=385:2009-worldwide-piracy-figues-surpass-400andcatid=60:newsandItemid=51 (last visited 1 July 2011). See also J.I. Winn & K.H. Govern, *Maritime Pirates, Sea Robbers, and Terrorists: New Approaches to Emerging Threats*, 2 Homeland Security Review, at 137 (2008).

[439] See IMO, Code of Practice for the Investigation of the Crimes of Piracy and Armed Robbery Against Ships, IMO Assembly Resolution A.922 (22) of 29 November 2001, available at: www.imo.org/includes/blastDataOnly.asp/data_id%3D23528/A922(22).pdf (last visited 1 July 2011). In June 2009, the Maritime Safety Committee (MSC) agreed on amendments to the Code; see IMO, Report of the MSC on its 86th Session, MSC 86/26/Add. 1 of 25 June 2009, available at: www.uscg.mil/imo/msc/docs/msc86-report-add-1.pdf (last visited 1 July 2011).

[440] It has been noted that the IMO's definition of "armed robbery against ships" is not without ambiguity. It is called "armed robbery" even though it includes offences committed without weapons. Also, the phrase "within a state's jurisdiction over such offences" does not seem entirely clear. It may be intended to be confined to ocean areas within a state's territorial jurisdiction, such as ports, territorial sea, and archipelagic waters. However, as worded, it could include attacks on ships in internal waters, such as lakes or rivers, as well as attacks on ships on the high seas that do not fall within the narrow definition of piracy. It furthermore does not appear to include acts of robbery aboard ships that do not involve violence or detention. See R.C. Beckman, *Combatting Piracy and Armed Robbery Against Ships in Southeast Asia: The Way Forward, 33 Ocean Development & International Law*, at 319, 320 (2002).

[441] Halberstam, *Terrorism on the High Seas* (note 418), at 272.

its own municipal law even when the accused pirate is not a national of the State and the crime was neither committed against its nationals nor within its territorial waters. States accepted universal jurisdiction over piracy because pirates indiscriminately attacked all States' ships and were a threat to everyone.[442] Universal jurisdiction with respect to pirates was theoretically justified by applying to them the concept of *hostes humani generis*, enemies of all mankind.[443] Furthermore, pirates were not subject to the authority of any State; no State could therefore be held responsible under international law for their acts.[444] The principle of universal jurisdiction is reflected in Article 105 UNCLOS[445] which provides that on the high seas, or in any place outside the jurisdiction of any State,[446] every State may seize a pirate ship or aircraft, arrest the persons responsible and seize the property on board. This is an exception to the general principle that ships on the high seas are subject to the exclusive jurisdiction of the flag State.[447]

According to Article 107 UNCLOS a seizure on account of piracy may, however, only be carried out by warships or military aircraft, or other ships or aircraft clearly marked and identifiable as being on government service and authorized to that effect. The ILC has pointed out with respect to this provision that it does not apply in the case of a merchant ship which has repulsed an attack by a pirate ship and, in exercising its right of self-defence, overpowers the pirate ship and subsequently hands it over to a warship or to the authorities of a coastal State. This would not be considered a "seizure" within the meaning of that provision.[448]

The respective article does not authorize the seizure of a pirate ship or aircraft in territorial waters, archipelagic waters or internal waters, even for acts falling within the definition of piracy that have been committed on the high seas.[449] A provision that would have required a State encountering a pirate ship or aircraft

---

[442] See id., at 288.

[443] See id.; see also Jesus, *Protection of Foreign Ships against Piracy and Terrorism at Sea* (note 71), at 384; see further T. Garmon, *International Law of the Sea: Reconciling the Law of Piracy and Terrorism in the Wake of September 11th*, 27 Tulane Maritime Law Journal, at 259 (2002–2003).

[444] See Halberstam (note 418) at 288.

[445] Passman, *Protections Afforded to Captured Pirates* (note 419), at 5.

[446] In its Commentary on Article 39 of its 1956 draft articles, the ILC stated that piracy "cannot be committed within the territory of a State or in its territorial sea" as it considered it to be a matter for the State affected to take the necessary measures for the repression of the acts committed within its territory. See Virginia Commentary, Vol. II (note 82), at 201.

[447] See id., at 213; see also Beckman, *The 1988 SUA Convention and 2005 SUA Protocol* (note 436), at 188.

[448] See ILC Articles concerning the Law of the Sea (note 416), at 283.

[449] See Virginia Commentary Vol. II (note 82), at 215.

in the EEZ of another State to notify the coastal State and cooperate with it in taking appropriate measures was not accepted at the Conference on the Law of the Sea.[450] If the seizure of a ship or aircraft on suspicion of piracy has been affected without adequate grounds, the State making the seizure is liable to the State of nationality of the ship or aircraft for any loss or damage caused by the seizure.[451]

The courts of the seizing State may decide on the penalties to be imposed and determine the action to be taken with regard to the seized vessel and property, subject to the rights of third parties acting in good faith.[452] The language of Article 105 – "may" – seems to indicate that the exercise of jurisdiction by the seizing State's court is a possibility, not an obligation, notwithstanding the "duty" to cooperate in the repression of piracy laid down in Article 100. As the rule in Article 105 does not establish the exclusive jurisdiction of the seizing State's courts, courts of other States are not prevented from exercising jurisdiction under conditions they determine.[453] It has, however, also been asserted that the drafting history of this provision indicates that it was intended to preclude transfers of captured pirates to third States.[454] In any case, the rules of international law on action to be taken against pirates permit action, but are far from ensuring that such action is effectively taken.[455]

The principle of universal criminal jurisdiction with respect to piracy is also reflected in Article 110 (1) UNCLOS relating to the right of visit of vessels on the high seas. This provision generally prohibits all acts of interference by warships regarding foreign ships on the high seas save for certain exceptions, one of which is that "the ship is engaged in piracy".[456] The warship or military aircraft or other duly authorized ships or aircraft may proceed to verify the ship's right to fly its flag and if suspicion remains further examination on board of the ship may take place. If the suspicion proves to be unfounded the ship is to be compensated for any loss or damage that it may have sustained. Furthermore, the right of "hot pursuit" may be exercised against a pirate ship or aircraft. An unjustified stop or arrest outside the territorial sea is likewise subject to compensation for loss or damage.[457]

---

[450] See id., at 214.

[451] See Art. 106 UNCLOS.

[452] See Shearer, *Piracy* (note 405), at 3.

[453] See Treves, *Piracy, Law of the Sea, and Use of Force – Somalia* (note 417), at 402.

[454] See Kontorovich, *International Legal Responses to Piracy off the Coast of Somalia* (note 383), at 3; see also A. Fischer-Lescano & L. Kreck, *Piraterie und Menschenrechte: Rechtsfragen der Bekämpfung der Piraterie im Rahmen der europäischen Operation Atalanta*, 47/4 Archiv des Völkerrechts, at 514 (2009).

[455] See Treves, *Piracy, Law of the Sea, and Use of Force – Somalia* (note 417), at 402.

[456] See Shearer, *Piracy* (note 405), at 3.

[457] See Art. 101 (1) and (8) UNCLOS.

It has been stated that the labelling of pirates as "*hostes humani generis*" is neither accurate nor can it provide a good reason to apply universal jurisdiction to piracy. A pirate did not need to be truly the "enemy of all mankind" to be found guilty of piracy and have universal jurisdiction applied, nor was piracy more heinous than a number of other serious crimes.[458] Applying universal jurisdiction to piracy had the potential to cause international tension as it might be used merely to harass political opponents or for aims extraneous to criminal justice. Furthermore, the right of a pirate to due process was violated,[459] in particular, as he could not know in advance to whose law he would be subject when a country exercised universal jurisdiction; the punishments for piracy greatly vary, ranging from three years in prison, to life imprisonment, or even capital punishment, which had been the universal penalty in previous centuries.[460]

In spite of these arguments, which do not seem without some merit as regards the right to due process, the principle of universal jurisdiction continues to be upheld by the international community with good cause. A U.S. Federal Appeals Court, for instance, held that a non-U.S. national who forcibly seized control of a non-U.S. vessel in international waters, and who was later found in the United States, could be prosecuted in that country. The Court noted that "universal jurisdiction" is based on the premise that offences against all States may be punished by any State where the offender is found, and accordingly, it allows a State to claim jurisdiction over such an offender even if the offender's acts occurred outside its boundaries and even if the offender has no connexion to that State. The Court further pointed out that due process did not require a nexus between the U.S. and a foreign defendant accused of piracy because the universal condemnation of the defender's conduct put him on notice that his acts would be prosecuted by any State where he is found.[461]

E. *The Repression of Piracy*

The basic provision dealing with the repression of piracy is Article 100 UNCLOS, literally corresponding to article 14 of the Geneva Convention on

---

[458] See Goodwin, *Universal Jurisdiction and the Pirate* (note 391), at 994, 995.

[459] See id., at 1003–1007.

[460] See id., at 997, 998; see also Collins & Hassan, *Combating Piracy: A South East Asian Perspective* (note 435), at 102; see further N. Dahlvang, *Thieves, Robbers & Terrorists: Piracy in the 21st Century*, 4 Regent Journal of International Law, at 39, 40 (2006).

[461] United States v. Lei Shi, 525 F.3d 709, 723, 724 (9th Circuit 2008), cert. denied, 129 South Circuit 324 (US, 6 October 2008) (No. 08-5942), at para. 3; see also J. Romero et al., *The Pirates of Puntland: Practical, Legal and Policy Issues in the Fight Against Somali Piracy*, at 1, 5 (2009), available at: www.klgates.com/files/Publication/ac22f46f-de64-41d5-a99c-8566b961c41e/Presentation/PublicationAttachment/fbdacf5a-55e1-408d-833b-a4b-c8a15dc70/3_09_The_Pirates_of_Puntland.pdf (last visited 1 July 2011).

the High Seas as suggested by the ILC, according to which "all States shall cooperate to the fullest possible extent in the repression of piracy on the high seas or in any other place outside the jurisdiction of any State". The question has arisen whether UNCLOS regulates the seizure of pirates as a right or a duty, whether the parties to UNCLOS are obliged to adopt and implement anti-piracy legislation. The view seems justified that the suppression of piracy besides being a right is also an international duty.[462] As the ILC pointed out in its Commentary, "Any State having an opportunity of taking measures against piracy, and neglecting to do so, would be failing in a duty laid upon it by international law. Obviously, the State must be allowed a certain latitude as to the measures it should take to this end in any individual case".[463]

According to Article 102 UNCLOS piracy may not only be committed by a private vessel or aircraft, but also by a government ship or government aircraft whose crew has mutinied or taken control of the ship or aircraft. The significance of this provision is that in cases of mutiny, the ship or aircraft can no longer be regarded as engaging the responsibility of the flag State and therefore may be apprehended at will.[464] It would, however, be going too far to assimilate to a pirate ship a government vessel the crew of which has disobeyed orders or even resorted to criminality as this would ordinarily fall short of mutiny. A ship or aircraft is defined as being a pirate ship or aircraft if it is intended by the persons in dominant control to be used for the purpose of piracy,[465] or has been used to commit such act, so long as it remains under the control of the persons guilty of that act.

The problem of preventing and repressing piracy and armed robbery against ships has been drawing increasing attention from the international community, particularly since the early 1990s, with the IMO playing a leading role in providing guidance to States and the shipping community with respect to this phenomenon.[466] In view of the rising number of pirate attacks, the IMO,

---

[462] A. Blanco-Bazán, *War Against Piracy? Some Misconceptions and Oversights in the Repression of Crimes at Sea*, Il diritto marittimo, Anno CXI, Terza Serie, Fascicolo I, at 266 (2009); see also Wolfrum, *Fighting Terrorism at Sea* (note 426), at 9; see further R. Wolfrum, *The Obligation to Cooperate in the Fight Against Piracy – Legal Considerations*, 116 3/4 Chuo Law Review at 89 (2009). According to Wolfrum, one may argue that Article 100 UNCLOS addresses three levels of cooperation: cooperation in general, cooperation in a particular region, and cooperation to act against a particular incident of piracy.

[463] ILC Articles concerning the Law of the Sea (note 416), at 282.

[464] Shearer, *Piracy* (note 405), at 3.

[465] Id.

[466] M. Hayashi, *Introductory Note to the Regional Cooperation Agreement on Combating Piracy and Armed Robbery Against Ships in Asia*, 44 ILM, at 826 (2005); see also Dahlvang, *Piracy in the 21st Century* (note 460), at 35.

as early as in 1983, adopted Resolution A.545 (13),[467] which noted with great concern the increasing number of incidents involving piracy and armed robbery against ships and recognized the grave danger to life and the grave navigational and environmental risks to which such incidents can give rise. Governments concerned were urged to take as a matter of highest priority, "all measures necessary to prevent and suppress acts of piracy and armed robbery from ships in or adjacent to their waters, including the strengthening of security measures".[468]

In the following years the IMO adopted further recommendations addressed to governments regarding the prevention and suppression of piracy and armed robbery against ships; it also dealt with measures to prevent unlawful acts against passengers and crews on board ships and further gave guidance to shipowners and ship operators, shipmasters and crews.[469] The purpose of the aforementioned "Code of Practice for Investigation of the Crimes of Piracy and Armed Robbery Against Ships" was to provide IMO Member States with an "aide-memoire" to facilitate the investigation of these crimes. The Code, which is recommendatory in nature, was adopted with full awareness of the fact that the fight against piracy and armed robbery against ships is often impeded, in some countries, by the absence of an effective legislative framework to facilitate not only the investigation of such crimes, but also the arrest and punishment of those accused of such acts. Consequently, one of the measures it recommends is for States to fill this legislative gap.[470]

In 2005, the IMO adopted Resolution A.979(24),[471] which strongly urged nations to take legislative, judicial and law enforcement action to receive and prosecute or extradite pirates arrested by warships or other government vessels and to continue consultations by which technical assistance can be brought to regional States to enhance their capacity for repressing piracy.[472] Addressing the problem of piracy off the coast of Somalia in 2007 it adopted

---

[467] See IMO, Measures to Prevent Acts of Piracy and Armed Robbery Against Ships, IMO Assembly Resolution A.545 (13) of 17 November 1983, available at: www.imo.org/includes/ blastDataOnly.asp/data_id%3D22356/A545%2813%29.pdf (last visited 1 July 2010), reaffirmed by IMO Assembly Resolutions A.783 (18) of 4 November 1993, A.979 (24) of 23 November 2005 and A.1002 (25) of 29 November 2007.

[468] See id.

[469] See IMO, Maritime Safety Committee, Piracy and Armed Robbery Against Ships: Guidance to shipowners and ship operators, shipmasters and crews on preventing and suppressing acts of piracy and armed robbery against ships, IMO doc. MSC/Circ.623/Rev. 3 of 29 May 2002, available at: www.skuld.com/upload/News%20and%20Publications/Publications/ Piracy/IMO%20MSC%20Circ%20623.pdf (last visited 1 July 2011).

[470] R. Balkin, *The International Maritime Organization and Maritime Security*, 30/1 *Tulane Maritime Law Journal*, at para. 11 (2006).

[471] See IMO Assembly Resolution A.979(24), available at: www.imo.org/includes/blastDataOnly .asp/data_id%3D25750/A979%2824%29.pdf (last visited 1 July 2011).

[472] See Kraska & Wilson, *Piracy Repression, Partnering and the Law* (note 386), at 50.

Resolution A.1002(25)[473] in which it asked the Transitional Federal Government (TFG) of that country to advise the Security Council that it consents to warships or military aircraft, or other government ships or aircraft, entering its territorial sea when engaging in operations against pirates or suspected pirates and armed robbers and of its readiness to conclude any necessary agreements to enable warships or military aircraft to escort ships employed by the World Food Programme for the delivery of humanitarian aid. In 2009, Resolution A.1026(26) was adopted, strongly urging Governments to increase their efforts to prevent and suppress, within the provisions of international law, acts of piracy and armed robbery against ships irrespective of where such acts occur and, in particular, to co-operate with other Governments and international organizations in the interests of the rule of law, safety of life at sea and environmental protection, in relation to acts occurring or likely to occur in the waters off the coast of Somalia.[474]

It seems obvious that the eradication of piracy and armed robbery at sea not only calls for coordination among the international community but also for the close involvement of regional actors.[475] An excellent example is to be found in the Strait of Malacca, one of the "world's vital maritime passages",[476] an area which until 2005 was the main hotspot for piracy and was in that year even classified as a "war zone" for purposes of indemnity coverage.[477] In 2004 the "Regional Cooperation Agreement on Combating Piracy and Armed Robbery against Ships in Asia (ReCAAP)"[478] was adopted with the purpose of strengthening regional cooperation and coordination of all States affected to effectively prevent and suppress piracy and armed robbery against ships, expressly reaffirming the respective duty of States under UNCLOS.[479]

The central feature of that Agreement, which entered into force in 2006 and to which 18 States are party,[480] is the establishment of an Information Sharing

---

[473] See IMO Assembly Resolution A.1002 (25), available at: www.imo.org/includes/blastDataOnly .asp/data_id%3D27087/1026.pdf (last visited 1 July 2011).

[474] See IMO Resolution A.1026 (26) of 2 December 2009, available at: www.classnk.or.jp/hp/ SMD/isps/pdf/IMO/A1026(26).pdf (last visited 1 July 2011).

[475] Commissioner J. Borg, Address at the Seminar on Piracy and Armed Robbery Against Shipping: "Combating Piracy: Strength in Unity": *To Prevent, Deter, Protect and Fight Against an ACTUAL Threat*, at 3 (2009), transcript available at: ec.europa.eu/transport/maritime/events/ doc/2009_01_21_piracy/dr_borg_closing.pdf (last visited 1 July 2011).

[476] See id.

[477] See Winn & Govern, *Maritime Pirates, Sea Robbers, and Terrorists* (note 438), at 133.

[478] Regional Cooperation Agreement on Combating Piracy and Armed Robbery against Ships in Asia, 11 November 2004, 44 ILM 829 (2005).

[479] See Hayashi, *Introductory Note to the Regional Cooperation Agreement* (note 466), at 827.

[480] These States are: Bangladesh, Brunei Darussalam, Cambodia, China, India, Indonesia, Japan, Korea, Laos, Myanmar, Philippines, Singapore, Sri Lanka, Thailand, Viet Nam as well as

Centre in Singapore, which also deals with information relating to individuals and transnationally organized criminal groups. The Agreement further envisages a system of cooperation among States parties in detecting, arresting or seizing pirates and persons who have committed armed robbery, as well as in detecting the victim ships and rescuing victimized persons. The narrow scope of customary and codified law of the sea with respect to piracy is being expanded by including armed robbery in the territorial sea, archipelagic waters and internal waters as well as attacks directed "against a ship" and not only those "against another ship" as defined in Article 101 UNCLOS.[481] This Agreement is certainly a model worth considering for other regions blighted by piracy[482] – the Malacca Strait has seen a notable decline in attacks against shipping in recent years.[483] By working together, Indonesia, Malaysia, Singapore and Thailand have cut the number of pirate attacks by more than half since 2004.[484]

Another interesting regional model has been created in the Gulf of Guinea. The Maritime Organization of West and Central Africa (MOWCA), in July 2008 through a Memorandum of Understanding established an institutional framework for close cooperation on suppression of piracy and armed robbery, countering terrorism at sea, illegal, unreported, and unregulated (IUU) fishing, drug trafficking, etc. That Agreement also provides guidelines for coastal surveillance, maintaining presence in the EEZs and enforcement of international treaties, especially the Law of the Sea and related IMO instruments. It is remarkable that of the twenty-five MOWCA States, five are land-locked, demonstrating that all States concerned with facilitating international trade and enhancing regional stability have a stake in maritime security.[485]

In the aforementioned Resolution A.1002(25) the IMO also called upon regional States in East Africa to conclude an international agreement to prevent, deter and suppress piracy. The Organization further developed such a

---

Norway, Denmark and the Netherlands, available at: www.recaap.org/AboutReCAAPISC .aspx (last visited 1 July 2011).

[481] See Hayashi (note 466), at 828.

[482] See Borg, *Combating Piracy: Strength in Unity*, Address (note 475), at 3.

[483] See Guilfoyle, Piracy off Somalia: UNSC and IMO Efforts (note 434), at 691.

[484] A. Costa, Testimony to the U.S. House of Representatives, Foreign Affairs Subcommittee on International Organizations, Human Rights and Oversight, *"Fighting Piracy on Land and at Sea"* (2009), available at: www.unodc.org/unodc/en/about-unodc/speeches/2009-14-05. html (last visited 1 July 2011). In this context, also the Jakarta Initiative and the Singapore Cooperative Mechanism to enhance the Safety, Security and the Environmental Protection in the Straits of Malacca and Singapore should be mentioned; see Wolfrum, *The Obligation to Cooperate in the Fight Against Piracy* (note 462), at 94. Singapore Statement of 6 September 2007, IMO doc. IMO/SGP 1/4, available at: www.mpa.gov.sg/sites/pdf/spore_statement.pdf (last visited 1 July 2011).

[485] J. Kraska, *Coalition Strategy and the Pirates of the Gulf of Aden and the Red Sea*, 28/3 Comparative Strategy, at 204–205 (2009).

draft regional agreement[486] which may be applied to any region and presents an ideal model for States seeking to work more closely together. Provisions of the draft include procedures for States to conduct boarding and search of suspected vessels as well as provisions for criminal enforcement and determining choice of jurisdiction among coastal and flag States.[487] As a result of these endeavors, a "Code of Conduct concerning the Repression of Acts of Piracy and Armed Robbery against Ships in the Western Indian Ocean and the Gulf of Aden" was adopted in Djibouti on 29 January 2009[488] which is open for signature by the 21 countries in the region and has so far been signed by 17 States.[489] The Code provides for information sharing, interdicting ships suspected in engaging in acts of piracy or armed robbery at sea, reviewing relevant national legislation and the apprehension and prosecution of suspects. It also covers the possibilities of shared operations, such as nominating law enforcement or other authorized officials to embark in the patrol ships or aircraft of another signatory.[490] The IMO has undertaken a broad capacity-building initiative to assist the signatories in the implementation of the Code.[491]

Although much less plagued by piracy than other geographical regions, the Member States of the Caribbean Community in the CARICOM Maritime and Airspace Security Co-operation Agreement[492] of 2008 expressly referred to piracy as well as hijacking, terrorism, illicit trafficking in narcotic drugs, etc.

---

[486] See IMO, Piracy and Armed Robbery Against Ships: Recommendations to Governments for Preventing and Suppressing Piracy and Armed Robbery Against Ships, IMO doc. MSC/ Circ. 622/Rev.1 of 16 June 1999, Appendix 5, Annex, at 12, available at: www5.imo.org/ SharePoint/blastDataHelper.asp/data_id%3D1951/622REV1.PDF (last visited 1 July 2011).

[487] See Kraska & Wilson, *Piracy Repression, Partnering and the Law* (note 386), at 54.

[488] IMO, Press Briefing, High-level meeting in Djibouti adopts a Code of Conduct to repress acts of piracy and armed robbery against ships (30 January 2009), (hereinafter referred to as the Code of Conduct) available at: www.imo.org/MediaCentre/PressBriefings/Archives/ Pages/2009.aspx (last visited 1 July 2011).

[489] These States are: Comoros, Djibouti, Egypt, Eritrea, Ethiopia, Jordan, Kenya, Madagascar, Maldives, Mauritius, Oman, Saudi-Arabia, Seychelles, Somalia, Sudan, Tanzania and Yemen, available at: www.imo.org/OurWork/Security/PIU/Pages/DCoC.aspx (last visited 1 July 2011).

[490] See Id.

[491] See Report of the Secretary-General on possible options to further the aim of prosecuting and imprisoning persons responsible for acts of piracy and armed robbery at sea off the coast of Somalia, including, in particular, options for creating special domestic chambers possibly with international components, a regional tribunal or an international tribunal and corresponding imprisonment arrangements, taking into account the work of the Contact Group on Piracy off the Coast of Somalia, the existing practice in establishing international and mixed tribunals, and the time and resources necessary to achieve and sustain substantive results, UN doc. S/2010/394, 26 July 2010, at 12.

[492] The States parties are: Antigua and Barbuda, Bahamas, Barbados, Belize, Dominica, Grenada, Guyana, Haiti, Jamaica, Montserrat, St. Kitts and Nevis, St. Lucia, St. Vincent and the Grenadines, Surinam, and Trinidad and Tobago; see text of the Agreement at: www.caricomlaw

as an activity likely to compromise the security of a State party. A major objective of this Agreement is to promote co-operation among the parties to enable them to conduct such law enforcement operations as may be necessary to address more effectively their own security as well as the security of the Region. This instrument is supplemented by the CARICOM Arrest Warrant Treaty[493] concluded at the same time. In the Treaty Establishing the Regional Security System of 1996[494] the Member States had already granted each other the right of "hot-pursuit" within each other's territorial sea and EEZ.

In 2009, the IMO Maritime Safety Committee (MSC) agreed on updated Recommendations to Governments for preventing and suppressing piracy and armed robbery against ships; and Guidance to shipowners, ship operators, shipmasters and crew, which includes a new annex aimed at seafarers, fishermen and other mariners who may be kidnapped or held hostage for ransom, based on the current United Nations guidance on "surviving as a hostage".[495] Furthermore, an MSC Circular on Piracy and Armed Robbery against Ships was agreed which includes Best Management Practices to Deter Piracy in the Gulf of Aden and off the Coast of Somalia as well as additional guidance to vessels engaged in fishing, identified as being particularly vulnerable to attack.[496] In 2010, the MSC adopted Guidelines on Operational Procedures for the Promulgation of Maritime Safety Information concerning Acts of Piracy and Piracy Counter-measure Operations.[497] The IMO Secretariat is also reviewing existing

---

.org/docs/CARICOM%20Maritime%20and%20Airspace%20Security%20Co-operation%20 Agreement.pdf (last visited on 1 July 2011).

[493] See www.caricomlaw.org/Details.aspx?EntryId=90 (last visited on 1 July 2011).

[494] The membership of the System is open to the following States: Antigua and Barbuda, Barbados, the Commonwealth of Dominica, Grenada, St. Christopher and Nevis, St. Lucia, St. Vincent and the Grenadines; see www.state.gov/p/wha/rls/70686.htm (last visited on 1 July 2011).

[495] See IMO, MSC, Revised guidance on combating piracy agreed by IMO Maritime Safety Committee, MSC 86th Session, available at: reliefweb.int/node/314971 (last visited 1 July 2011).

[496] IMO, MSC 86th Session, The Secretariat, Piracy and Armed Robbery Against Ships: Outcome of the Contact Group on Piracy off the Coast of Somalia, Note to the Maritime Safety Committee, IMO doc. MSC 86/INF. 13 of 19 May 2009, available at: merchantmarine. financelaw.fju.edu.tw/data/IMO/MSC/86/MSC%2086-INF.13 (last visited 1 July 2011); see also Best Management Practices to Deter Piracy in the Gulf of Aden and off the Coast of Somalia (February 2009), available at: www.marisec.org/piracy-gulf-of-aden-indian-ocean-industry-best-management-practice (last visited 1 July 2011). These Best Management Practices were supported by a large number of industry representatives.

[497] IMO MSC 87th Session, Resolution MSC 305(87), IMO doc. MSC 87/26/Add.2 of 17 May 2010, available at: www.uscg.mil/imo/msc/docs/msc87-report-add-2.pdf (last visited 1 July 2011). These Operational Procedures provide specific additional guidance for naval and military authorities involved in the gathering and interpretation of information on acts of piracy and piracy counter-measure operations.

national legislation to prevent and punish the crimes of piracy and armed robbery at sea as part of the Organization's anti-piracy strategy, in response to UN Security Council Resolution 1851 (2008) which noted with concern the lack of capacity, domestic legislation, and clarity about how to deal with pirates following their capture. This problem has hindered more robust international action being taken against pirates off the coast of Somalia and has led to pirates frequently being released without facing justice.[498]

The work of the IMO has the full support of the UN General Assembly as well as the Security Council when repeatedly expressing concern at the increasing threat to shipping from piracy and armed robbery at sea. The General Assembly in Resolution 65/37 on "Oceans and the law of the sea",[499] adopted in 2010, once again recognized the crucial role of international cooperation in combating threats to maritime security, including piracy, armed robbery at sea, terrorist acts against shipping etc. through bilateral and multilateral instruments and mechanisms. States are also being called upon to take appropriate steps under national law to facilitate the apprehension and prosecution of suspected pirates. The Resolution furthermore encourages national, bilateral and trilateral initiatives as well as regional cooperative mechanisms to address piracy and armed robbery at sea in the Asian region.[500]

F. *Measures against Somali Piracy*

The steadily increasing danger for navigation in the Gulf of Aden and off the coast of Somalia as well as the outrage caused by pirate attacks on ships carrying humanitarian supplies to the Somali population have been decisive in prompting the international community into action in that region. In 2008, the UN Security Council passed several resolutions dealing with Somali piracy,[501] each of these pursuant to Chapter VII of the United Nations Charter, under which the Council may authorize the use of military force against threats to international security. These resolutions aim at remedying the limitations of the rules of current international law with respect to piracy – as far as their application to the situation in Somalia is concerned[502] – and also provide a legal basis for interception operations by the warships of a large number of countries,

---

[498] See IMO, Legal Committee, Report of the Legal Committee on the Work of its Ninety-Fifth Session, at para. 9(c)(1) (30 March–3 April 2009), available at: www.imo.org/Newsroom/mainframe.asp?topic_id=280&doc_id=11167 (last visited 1 July 2011).

[499] UN General Assembly Res. 65/37 (note 250), op. paras. 82, 85, 89.

[500] See id., at op. paras. 82, 86 and 89.

[501] Kontorovich, *International Legal Responses to Piracy off the Coast of Somalia* (note 383), at 2.

[502] See Treves, Piracy, *Law of the Sea, and Use of Force – Somalia* (note 417), at 402.

including the United States, several European Union Member States, China, India, Japan and Russia, patrolling the waters of the Gulf of Aden and off the coast of Somalia.

The Security Council in Resolution 1816,[503] (2008), expressed its grave concern at "the threat that acts of piracy and armed robbery against vessels pose to the prompt, safe and effective delivery of humanitarian aid to Somalia, the safety of commercial maritime routes and to international navigation". It also determined that "the incidents of piracy and armed robbery against vessels in the territorial waters of Somalia and the high seas off the coast of Somalia exacerbate the situation in Somalia, which continues to constitute a threat to international peace and security in the region".

Attention has been drawn to the fact that it is the situation in Somalia which constitutes the threat to international peace and security, not the piracy and armed robbery as such.[504] As in the Gulf of Aden, where international shipping must pass through a narrow corridor, pirates are able to launch attacks in international waters and then quickly return to Somali territorial waters, the Security Council with the express consent of the TFG of Somalia authorized States cooperating with that Government "in the fight against piracy and armed robbery at sea off the coast of Somalia" to enter the territorial waters of Somalia for that purpose "in a manner consistent with such action permitted on the high seas with respect to piracy under relevant international law" and to use under the same conditions "all necessary means to repress acts of piracy and armed robbery". The original limitation to a period of six months of the authorization given by that Resolution has been renewed by the Security Council on the basis of consent by the TFG.[505]

The basic effect of these provisions of Resolution 1816 is to make the rules of international law concerning piracy on the high seas applicable also to territorial waters permitting *inter alia* pursuit from the high seas into these waters,[506] or to counter violence against or aboard vessels occurring exclusively within Somalia's territorial sea.[507] These provisions also clarify that States acting under these rules within the territorial waters of Somalia may use "all necessary means" – commonly associated with a general authorization to use military force.[508] It has correctly been stated that international law has little to say about the manner in

---

[503] See UN Security Council Res. 1816 of 2 June 2008, The Situation in Somalia, preamb. paras. 1, 12, op. para. 7.

[504] See Guilfoyle, *Piracy off Somalia: UNSC and IMO Efforts* (note 434), at 695.

[505] See UN Security Council Res. 1846 of 2 December 2008, op. para. 10 and 1897 (2009) of 30 November 2009, The situation in Somalia, op. para. 7.

[506] See Treves, *Piracy, Law of the Sea, and Use of Force – Somalia* (note 417), at 404.

[507] See Guilfoyle, *Piracy off Somalia: UNSC and IMO Efforts* (note 434), at 695.

[508] See id.

which piracy may be suppressed.[509] Self-defence against armed attack or threat thereof seems to be a guiding principle of States the navies of which are engaged in these anti-piracy efforts. Action against pirates can be assimilated to the exercise of the power to engage in police action on the high seas with respect to foreign vessels in accordance with international legal rules.[510] It would, however, seem that in any case the use of force must be necessary, proportionate and should be preceded by warning shots where practicable. As ITLOS has emphasized in a case before it "considerations of humanity must apply in the law of the sea, as they do in other areas of international law".[511]

Furthermore, the Security Council passed Resolution 1851 (2008)[512] extending the authorization of military force to land-based operations on the mainland of Somalia as that Resolution authorizes nations for a one-year period to "undertake all necessary measures that are appropriate in Somalia, for the purpose of suppressing acts of piracy and armed robbery at sea".[513] This authorization has likewise since been renewed.[514] The resolution also invites all States and regional organizations fighting piracy off the coast of Somalia to conclude special agreements or arrangements with countries willing to take custody of pirates in order to embark law enforcement officials, so called "shipriders" from the latter countries, in particular countries from the region, to facilitate the investigation and prosecution of piracy suspects. The exercise of third State jurisdiction by shipriders in Somali territorial waters is, however, subject to the advance consent of the TFG and such agreements or arrangements must not prejudice the effective implementation of the SUA Convention. Where a shiprider arrangement is in place, transfer of suspects from sea to shore is straightforward: they remain subject to the jurisdiction of the shiprider's government throughout.[515] Shipriders have already been used to great effect against drug smugglers in the Caribbean.[516]

---

[509] See id.

[510] See Treves, *Piracy, Law of the Sea, and Use of Force – Somalia* (note 417), at 413; see also Blanco-Bazán, *War Against Piracy? Some Misconceptions* (note 462), at 266; see further A. von Arnauld, *Die moderne Piraterie und das Völkerrecht*, 47/4 Archiv des Völkerrechts, at 464 (2009).

[511] *M/V Saiga II* (Saint Vincent and the Grenadines v. Guinea), Merits, Judgment of 1 July 1999, 3 ITLOS Reports (1999), at para 155; ITLOS Press Release No. 23 and Supplement No. 1, 1 July 1999, available at: www.itlos.org.

[512] See UN Security Council Res. 1851 of 16 December 2008, The situation in Somalia, op. para. 6.

[513] See Kontorovich, *International Legal Responses to Piracy off the Coast of Somalia* (note 383), at 2.

[514] See UN Security Council Res. 1897 (2009) (note 505).

[515] See Nairobi Workshop, Final Report on Piracy off the Somali Coast (note 389), at 9.

[516] See Costa, *Testimony, Fighting Piracy on Land and at Sea* (note 484), at 2. The Maritime Safety Committee agreed that the use of unarmed security personnel is a matter for individual

Authorizing armed action against pirates in sovereign territory is certainly an unprecedented measure by the Security Council. Because the resolutions allow for responses beyond those permitted under current international law they have caused some apprehension on the part of States with a history of piracy problems, fearing a precedent potentially eroding national territorial sovereignty.[517] It has, however, rightly been pointed out that there are important limitations to the authorization accorded by the Security Council which make the relevant provisions less "revolutionary" than they might appear.[518] First, as already mentioned, the authorization is limited *ratione temporis*. Second, its scope is clearly limited *ratione loci* as the authorization provided "applies only with respect to the situation in Somalia". Third, cooperating States are requested to ensure that anti-piracy activities they undertake "do not have the practical effect of denying or impairing the right of innocent passage to the ships of any third State". Fourth, it has repeatedly been affirmed by the Security Council that the authorization provided "shall not affect the rights or obligations or responsibilities of member states under international law, including any rights or obligations" under UNCLOS, with respect to any other situation. It is also underscored in particular that the authorization by the Security Council "shall not be considered as establishing customary international law".[519] The point that the integrity of UNCLOS must be maintained was made by several members of the Council when Resolution 1816 was adopted and was probably a precondition for its unanimous acceptance.[520]

It must be emphasized that these resolutions of the Security Council were adopted on the basis of consent given by the TFG of Somalia – pursuant to the aforementioned request by the IMO – which sought and welcomed these measures as it lacks the capacity to interdict pirates or patrol and secure its territorial waters. The reference to the consent by the coastal State concerned

---

shipowners, companies, and ship operators to decide. The carriage of armed security personnel or the use of military or law-enforcement officials (duly authorized by the Government of the flag State to carry firearms for the security of the ship) should be subject to flag State legislation and policies and is a matter for the flag State to authorize, in consultation with shipowners, companies and ship operators. The Maritime Safety Committee further expressed the view that flag States should strongly discourage the carrying and use of firearms by seafarers for personal protection or for the protection of a ship. Carriage of firearms may pose an even greater danger if the ship is carrying flammable cargo or similar types of dangerous goods; see IMO, Report of the MSC 86th Session (note 439), at 2. On 11 March 2010 the European Commission published a Recommendation addressed to all Member States re-asserting the IMO's disinclination for armed security on vessels; see Jason Chuah, EU Maritime security – protecting maritime transport from piracy, 16/1 The Journal of International Maritime Law: EDITORIAL, at 6 (2010).

[517] See Kontorovich, *International Legal Responses to Piracy off the Coast of Somalia* (note 383), at 2.

[518] See Treves, *Piracy, Law of the Sea, and Use of Force – Somalia* (note 417), at 404.

[519] See id., at 404–405. See also UN Security Council Res. 1897 (note 505).

[520] Id., Treves.

greatly limits the "revolutionary content" of the resolutions as the activities authorized could also be conducted in the absence of any Security Council resolution on the basis of an agreement given by the coastal State.[521] It is further to be noted that Resolution 1851 requires that any measure undertaken in Somali territory must be consistent with applicable international humanitarian and human rights law. It has been stated that the latter condition may greatly limit the scope of possible anti-piracy operations under the Resolution as under international humanitarian law civilians may not be specifically targeted except in immediate self-defence.[522] Pirates are, however, not combatants but rather civilians.[523] United States military officials have warned that any action against pirates on land would likely result in civilian deaths. Still, Resolution 1851 clearly broadens the scope of permissible "hot pursuit", allowing pirates to be chased from the high seas into Somali waters and farther onto dry land.[524]

The European Union, since December 2008, has been conducting a military operation – EUNAVFOR Somalia – Operation ATALANTA – in support of the relevant Security Council Resolutions, the first EU maritime operation conducted in accordance with the European Security and Defence Policy.[525] The duration of this mission has been extended until the end of 2012.[526] Its object is to protect deliveries by the World Food Programme as well as merchant ships and also to avert pirate attacks.[527] NATO, after having instigated two

---

[521] See id.

[522] Id., at 412.

[523] See Bahar, *Attaining Optimal Deterrence at Sea* (note 401), at 6; see also C. Laly-Chevalier, *Lutte contre la piraterie maritime et droits de l'homme*, 42/1 Revue belge de droit international, at 23 (2009).

[524] See Kontorovich, *International Legal Responses to Piracy off the Coast of Somalia* (note 383), at 2; see Kraska & Wilson, *Piracy Repression, Partnering and the Law* (note 386), at 56.

[525] See Council Joint Action 2208/749/CFSP, 2008 OJ (L 252) 39, on the European Union military coordination action in support of UN Security Council Res. 1816 (note 501) [EU NAVCO9]; see also Council Joint Action 2008/851/CFSP, 2008 OJ (L 301) 34, on a European Union military operation to contribute to the deterrence, prevention and repression of acts of piracy and armed robbery off the Somali coast; see further Romero et al., *The Pirates of Puntland* (note 461), at 4. Until December 2010, 26 countries had made some kind of contribution to Operation ATALANTA; this includes 13 EU Member States – France, Spain, Germany, Greece, Sweden, Netherlands, Italy, Belgium, United Kingdom, Portugal, Luxembourg, Malta and Estonia; the first non-EU country to participate in this operation was Norway; see: www.eunavfor.eu/about-us/mission/ (last visited 1 July 2011).

[526] European Union, EU Council Extends ATALANTA Operation (15 June 2010), available at: www.upi.com/Top_News/Special/2010/06/15/EU-extends-piracy-operations-near-Somalia/UPI-20451276615949/ (last visited 1 July 2011).

[527] The EUNAVFOR operation is in permanent liaison with several other naval forces operating in the area – US-led coalition Combined Task Forces (CTF) 151, NATO, Russian, Indian, Japanese, Malaysian and Chinese vessels. CTF-151 is responsible for the Gulf of Aden and the Somali Basin and is the primary counter-piracy operation of the allied effort. See R.I. Rotberg, Combating Maritime Piracy: A Policy Brief with Recommendations for Action, World Peace

short-term missions against piracy off the Somali coast, in June 2009 decided to launch "Operation Ocean Shield" which is anticipated to run for an analogous period of time.[528] The international navies play a critical role in the prevention of piracy in Somalia and it is considered vital that they remain. Their increased presence has certainly contributed to the fact that although the total number of incidents attributed to Somali pirates continues to rise, the number of successful hijackings is proportionately less.[529]

These international efforts have, however, also partly been hampered by the fact that the naval forces have to answer to individual national authorities with varied rules of engagement as well as by incompatible communications.[530] It has, furthermore, been pointed out that there is an obvious disparity between the high-technology force operating in the area from distant water States and the nearly complete lack of maritime security capacity among the States of East Africa. Large warships are extremely capable but too few in number and are inefficient for conducting maritime security operations. Smaller warships should therefore be deployed that could serve as the training force while at the same time hunting for pirates. Attention has also been drawn to the need of East African States for assistance in developing and operating a vast network of small littoral and coastal forces. Providing military training to Somali government forces so that they can prevent maritime piracy is considered an important step in the right direction.[531]

G. *Current Legal Problems*

As previously pointed out, international law recognizes universal jurisdiction in the case of piracy which, under the aforementioned Security Council resolutions,

---

Foundation, Policy Brief #11 (26 January 2010), available at: www.worldpeacefoundation .org/WPF_Piracy_PolicyBrief_11.pdf (last visited 1 July 2011).

[528] NATO expands anti-piracy operation off the coast of Somalia until 2012, available at: en.rian .ru/world/20100311/158156287.html (last visited 1 July 2011).

[529] See ICC IMB Annual Report 2010 (note 378), at 23. While attacks off the coast of Somalia remain high, the number of incidents in the Gulf of Aden more than halved in 2010, with 53 attacks as compared to 117 in 2009. This reduction is attributed to the deterrent work of naval forces that have been controlling the area since 2008, and to ships' application of self-protection measures recommended in Best Management Practices. See also Council of Europe, Parliamentary Assembly, Resolution 1722 (2010), Piracy – a crime and a challenge for democracies, 28 April 2010, para. 5, available at: assembly.coe.int/Documents/Adopted-Text/ta10/ERES1722.htm (last visited 1 July 2011).

[530] C. Turner, *Recent Development in Military Operations, Seoul High Level Meeting on Piracy off the Coast of Somalia*, 10 June 2009, at 6 (on file with author).

[531] J. Kraska & B. Wilson, *Combating pirates of the Gulf of Aden: The Djibouti Code and the Somali Coast Guard*, 52 Ocean and Coastal Management, at 5 (2009).

also applies to seizures and arrests in the territorial sea of Somalia. The seizing States are, however, reluctant to exercise such broad powers by prosecuting and submitting to criminal proceedings in their courts the pirates and armed robbers arrested in view of legal complexities and in particular human rights implications.[532] Thus, in quite a number of instances pirates have been let free or not been detained in the first place.[533] The Security Council in Resolution 1918 (2010) therefore stated that "the failure to prosecute persons responsible for acts of piracy and armed robbery at sea off the coast of Somalia undermines anti-piracy efforts of the international community."[534]

Member States of the European Convention on Human Rights[535] are obviously concerned that pirates might request asylum in the respective countries as they certainly would claim to risk torture or the death penalty if returned to Somalia.[536] Furthermore, after pirates had served a sentence and been granted asylum they may also ask for family reunion; no country would, however, be eager having to import pirate clans. The question may further arise whether the requirement under the European Convention on Human Rights of bringing an arrested or detained person promptly before a judge can be met in the case of a prolonged detention of a pirate suspect on a naval vessel.[537] The jurisprudence

---

[532] See Treves, *Piracy, Law of the Sea, and Use of Force – Somalia* (note 417), at 408; see also C. Laly-Chevalier (note 523) at 9–11.

[533] Over 60% of the pirates apprehended under Operation ATALANTA are released, which illustrates the impunity of the pirates; see Non-Paper for the Creation of a Special Somali Court, Relocated to a State in the Region, with International Support (on file with author); see also E. Kontorovich, *"A Guantanamo on the Sea": The Difficulty of Prosecuting Pirates and Terrorists*, 98 California Law Review, at 1–29 (2010).

[534] See UN Security Council Res. 1918 of 27 April 2010, preambular para. 17. A similar concern has been expressed by the Parliamentary Assembly of the Council of Europe with respect to the practice of some Member States, see Resolution 1722 (2010), (note 529), para. 7. Prosecutions of acts of piracy are ongoing in 10 States: Kenya, Seychelles, Somalia (in the Somaliland and Puntland regions), Maldives, Yemen, the Netherlands, United States of America, France, Spain, and Germany; only around 40 prosecutions are taking place outside of the region; see Report of the Secretary-General (note 491), paras. 19 and 20.

[535] See Convention for the Protection of Human Rights and Fundamental Freedoms, 4 November 1950, *inter alia* amended by Protocol No. 11, available at: http://conventions.coe.int/Treaty/en/Treaties/Html/005.htm (last visited 1 July 2011). See also C. Laly-Chevalier (note 523) at 49.

[536] See id., European Convention on Human Rights, Art. 3: "No one shall be subjected to torture or to inhuman or degrading treatment or punishment." See also the United Nations Convention Against Torture and Other Cruel, Inhuman or Degrading Treatment or Punishment, 10 December 1984, 1465 UNTS 85, Art. 3(1): "No State party shall expel, return ('refouler') or extradite a person to another State where there are actual or substantial grounds for believing that he would be in danger of being subjected to torture."

[537] See id., European Convention on Human Rights, Art. 5(3): "Everyone arrested or detained in accordance with the provisions [...] of this article shall be brought promptly before a judge or other officer authorized by law to exercise judicial power and shall be entitled to trial within a reasonable time or to release pending trial [...]."; see also Art. 6(1): "In the determination

under the international and regional human rights instruments suggests that the period of delay before a detainee is brought before a judicial officer must not exceed a few days. This requirement, of course, raises practical difficulties in the context of detention on a naval vessel patrolling off the coast of Somalia.[538]

Ideally, pirate suspects should be tried in the country where they originated, but in the case of Somalia – with the exception of the Somaliland and Puntland regions – this does not seem to be a realistic option under present circumstances. Flag States could, of course, prosecute the pirates, but in many cases ships in the region fly flags of convenience of far away countries. An option which has been made use of is to conclude bilateral agreements with a country in the region, defining procedures for the detention, transfer and prosecution of persons suspected of having committed acts of piracy, as Canada, China, Denmark, the United Kingdom, the United States and the European Union have done with Kenya.[539] The latter agreement expressly provides that such transfer may only take place on condition of humane treatment and that no one will be subjected to the death penalty, to torture or to any cruel, inhuman or degrading treatment or punishment. There is further a guarantee that any transferred person will be brought promptly before a judge and is entitled to trial within a reasonable time or to release.[540] In view of the fact that pirates are already operating far from the coast of Somalia, agreements were also concluded by the United Kingdom and the European Union with the Seychelles, with the latter agreement based on the same conditions and framework as the agreement with Kenya.[541]

---

of his civil rights and obligations or of any criminal charge against him, everyone is entitled to a fair and public hearing within a reasonable time and by an independent and impartial tribunal established by law."

[538] See Contact Group on Piracy off the Coast of Somalia, Working Group 2, 21 May 2010, para. 27 (on file with author).

[539] See Costa, *Testimony, Fighting Piracy on Land and at Sea* (note 484), at 2. See also Report of the Secretary-General (note 491), para. 23.

[540] See Exchange of Letters between the European Union and the Government of Kenya on the Conditions and Modalities for the Transfer of Persons Suspected of Having Committed Acts of Piracy and Detained by the European Union-led Naval Force (EUNAVFOR), and Seized Property in the Possession of EUNAVFOR, from EUNAVFOR to Kenya and for their Treatment after such Transfer, 6 March 2009, Annex, provisions, paras 3(a), 3(b), 3(c), 2009 OJ (L 79) 51. See further: www.fco.gov.uk/en/global-issues/conflict-prevention/piracy/prisoners/ (last visited 1 July 2011).

[541] Exchange of Letters between the European Union and the Republic of Seychelles on the Conditions and Modalities for the Transfer of Suspected Pirates and Armed Robbers from EUNAVFOR to the Republic of Seychelles and for their Treatment after such Transfer, 30 October 2009, 2009 OJ (L 315) 37. See also: Report of the Secretary-General (note 491), para. 23.

With respect to the question whether part of the legal response of the international community to piracy should be the establishment of an international mechanism a number of suggestions have been made. These include the creation of an entirely new international tribunal on the basis of a Security Council Resolution following the pattern of the international criminal tribunals for the former Yugoslavia and Rwanda, of a hybrid tribunal following the model of the Special Court for Sierra Leone and the Special Tribunal for Lebanon, the establishment of an African regional anti-piracy court based upon a multilateral agreement among regional States, or by amending the statutes of ITLOS, the African Court on Human and People's Rights or the International Criminal Court by an international treaty.[542] Further proposals refer to the creation of special domestic chambers with international components in one or more countries in the region or the establishment of a special Somali court in another East African country.

As regards ITLOS, it has to be borne in mind that it could deal with piracy issues only insofar far as they relate to disputes between States or if a legal question would be submitted to it on which it might render an advisory opinion.[543] Under its Statute, ITLOS has no criminal jurisdiction, which also holds true of the African Court on Human and People's Rights. With respect to the International Criminal Court, it has been pointed out that it has been established to prosecute individuals for crimes of a much more serious nature than piracy, i.e. genocide, crimes against humanity, war crimes and the crime of aggression. That Court would, therefore, not be suitable for dealing with common criminals like pirates in cases where national tribunals are unwilling or unable to prosecute them.[544] Amending the statutes of existing tribunals on a treaty basis would undoubtedly require a number of years and thus would not constitute a short or medium term remedy for the present situation in Somalia. The States

---

[542] See United Nations Contact Group on Piracy Off the Coast of Somalia: Working Group on Legal Issues, Discussion Paper on Prosecution of Pirates: An International Mechanism?, Copenhagen, 3 March 2009, at 2–3 (on file with author).

[543] UNCLOS does not contain any provision conferring advisory jurisdiction on the Tribunal as such, which may, however, on the basis of Article 21 of its Statute give an advisory opinion on a legal question if that is provided for by an international agreement related to the purposes of the Convention conferring jurisdiction on it. Thus far, no use has been made of that interesting option in any international instrument. See H. Tuerk, *The Contribution of the International Tribunal for the Law of the Sea to International Law*, 26/2 Penn State International Law Review, at 292 (2007); see also Press Release, Clarification, 24 April 2009, available at: www.itlos.org/news/press_release/2009/press_release_135_en.pdf (last visited 1 July 2011) setting forth that the Tribunal deals mainly with disputes between States parties to the Convention, is not a criminal court, and has no competence to try pirates; see further C. Thedwall, *Choosing the Right Yardarm: Establishing an International Court for Piracy*, 41/2 Georgetown Journal of International Law, at 1–17 (2010), advocating the establishment of an ITLOS Piracy Chamber.

[544] See Contact Group on Somali Piracy (note 538), at 3.

parties to the respective multilateral conventions have, furthermore, given no indication whatsoever that they would be willing to consider such a course of action. The question may certainly be asked whether such an enlargement of competence could also be effected by way of a Security Council resolution.

In connection with the suggestion to establish an international tribunal, it must not be overlooked that such tribunals depend on State cooperation for the enforcement of sentences since they do not have long-term prison facilities, and the States in whose territory they are based do not necessarily want the prisoners to serve their sentence there.[545] The tribunals therefore have to conclude sentence enforcement agreements with third States where witnesses and acquitted persons can be relocated safely. In practice, this has, however, been difficult, and relatively few States have been willing to enter into sentence enforcement and relocation agreements.[546] Furthermore, it is not only the establishment and operation of international tribunals which pose challenges, but also the need for a residual mechanism to carry out necessary functions after the tribunal has completed its work, such as protection of witnesses, monitoring of sentence enforcement, review of acquittals, convictions and sentences, as well as the preservation and maintenance of archives.[547] A new judicial mechanism to address piracy and armed robbery at sea off the coast of Somalia – for which a host state would still have to be found – would also have to address a different situation compared with the existing United Nations and United Nations-assisted tribunals, as it would face ongoing criminal activity and potentially a large caseload with no predictable completion date.[548]

Quite apart from the problems outlined in connection with the creation of an international tribunal to deal with Somali pirates, the view has also been put forth that such tribunals, besides being expensive to operate, are not appropriate at all for dealing with a crime like piracy, a common crime that has existed for centuries, which is subject to universal jurisdiction and has been successfully prosecuted in national courts.[549]

---

[545] In this context, it has been pointed out that the long-term burden of prosecution is not the prosecution itself, but rather the critical issue of consequent imprisonment. It has been estimated that the imprisonment requirement, by the end of 2011, might be as high as 2000 persons, a number which is much higher than that generated by all of the existing international tribunals; see Report of the Secretary-General (note 491), para. 29.

[546] United Nations Contact Group on Piracy off the Coast of Somalia, Copenhagen, 26–27 August 2009, Factual Statement by the United Nations Office of Legal Affairs on international tribunals, para. 10 (on file with author).

[547] Id.

[548] See Report of the Secretary-General (note 491), para. 36.

[549] See Non-Paper: An International Piracy Court – Not the Right Direction (on file with author).

The UN Secretary-General, in his Report pursuant to a request by the Security Council contained in Resolution 1918 (2010), put forth seven options with respect to the prosecution and imprisonment of persons responsible for acts of piracy and armed robbery at sea off the coast of Somalia which essentially correspond to the various suggestions already referred to, except those relating to an extension of the competences of existing international tribunals. It is to be noted that the Secretary-General first of all referred to the enhancement of United Nations assistance to build capacity of regional States for prosecution and imprisonment of pirates – an option that was ongoing and had already achieved some success.[550]

The Security Council when dealing with this Report considered "that effective prosecution of suspected pirates and their supporters may deter future pirate attacks" and therefore deemed it "of utmost importance to find long-term solutions to the problem of prosecuting suspected, and imprisoning convicted, pirates". The intention of the Secretary-General to appoint a Special Adviser on Legal Issues Related to Piracy off the Coast of Somalia was welcomed.[551] No decision was taken by the Security Council with respect to any of the options outlined in the Secretary-General's report.

The Special Adviser appointed by the Secretary-General[552] subsequently submitted a report for information of the members of the Security Council.[553] This report favors the establishment of a court system comprising a specialized court in Puntland, a specialized court in Somaliland and a specialized extraterritorial Somalia Court that could be located in Arusha, Tanzania. The specialized court in Puntland and the extraterritorial Somalia court are considered priorities, given the possibility of granting them universal jurisdiction. Furthermore, the correctional capacities of Puntland and Somalia should be strengthened by the construction of two prisons both with the capacity to hold 500 prisoners and with protected status to allow for international monitoring. A third prison should later be built in Puntland.[554] The report by the Special Adviser has contributed to narrowing down the possible models for a special mechanism to secure the prosecution of suspected pirates.

The Security Council, in response to this Report adopted Resolution 1976 (2011), emphasizing the importance of finding a comprehensive solution to the problem of piracy and armed robbery at sea off the coast of Somalia. States and

---

[550] See Report of the Secretary-General (note 491), at Summary, 2–3, and para. 56.
[551] See Statement by the President of the Security Council, UN.doc.S/PRST/2010/16 of 25 August 2010.
[552] The former French Minister of Culture Jacques Lang.
[553] Report of the Special Adviser to the Secretary-General on Legal Issues related to Piracy off the Coast of Somalia, (note 379).
[554] See id., para. 9.

regional organisations are requested to support sustainable economic growth in Somalia thus contributing to a durable eradication of piracy and armed robbery at sea in that area, as well as other illegal activities connected therewith. Recognizing that piracy is a crime subject to universal jurisdiction, the Security Council reiterates its call on States to "favourably consider the prosecution of suspected, and imprisonment of convicted, pirates apprehended off the coast of Somalia, consistent with applicable international human rights law".[555] No decision was, however, taken with respect to the aforementioned specific recommendations by the Special Adviser. The Security Council only decided to urgently consider the establishment of specialized Somali courts to try suspected pirates both in Somalia and in the region, including an exterritorial Somali specialized anti-piracy court.

H. *Outlook*

As pointed out, maritime piracy has a very long history and was thought to have more or less become a matter of the past by the time the contemporary law of the sea was codified in the twentieth century. Its resurgence which threatens world trade and international security is a phenomenon of modern times that seems to have caught the international community rather by surprise. Its response to piracy and armed robbery at sea has therefore only gradually developed and is still hampered by various factors.[556] These include legislative gaps, as States have not implemented their obligations under UNCLOS with respect to the suppression of piracy – as also noted with concern by the Security Council;[557] legal complexities arising out of the need to harmonize measures against piracy and armed robbery against ships with international humanitarian and human rights instruments; as well as uncertainty regarding the extent to which warships can enforce coercive measures in order to suppress a common crime like piracy.[558]

At the same time, however, it must also be emphasized that the IMO has for years endeavored to design practical measures to deal with piracy and armed robbery against ships as well as to draft relevant new international legal rules. These efforts, together with those of regional States, have already borne fruit in the Malacca Strait[559] and have been extended to East Africa where they will

---

[555] UN Security Council Res. 1976 of 11 April 2011, op. para. 14.
[556] Tuerk, *The Resurgence of Piracy* (note 371), at 41.
[557] UN Security Council Res. 1918 (note 534), preambular para. 14.
[558] See Blanco-Bazán, *War Against Piracy? Some Misconceptions* (note 462), at 266.
[559] See Seoul Statement on Piracy off the Coast of Somalia, 10 June 2009 (on file with author), at 2.

hopefully likewise show positive results. Furthermore, the Security Council as well as individual States have been taking more robust action and an unprecedented armada is now patrolling some of the world's most strategically significant waterways. With respect to piracy off the coast of Somalia, it has rightly been emphasized that prevention is crucial: "until there is law and order on land, there will be anarchy off the coast".[560] As the UN Secretary-General has observed "in the long term, the issue of piracy and armed robbery at sea off the coast of Somalia will be resolved only through an integrated approach that addresses the conflict, lack of governance and absence of sustainable livelihoods on land in Somalia".[561]

Modern national anti-piracy legislation is certainly required, as applying to pirates the SUA Convention, which was elaborated as an anti-terrorism instrument, seems to offer only a partial remedy. Despite some recent progress in a number of countries regarding the adoption and implementation of relevant national legislation important challenges remain, in particular with regard to questions concerning the establishment and exercise of jurisdiction, the fulfilment of evidentiary requirements and the attribution of law enforcement powers to military personnel.[562] The conclusion of a special anti-piracy convention regulating the manner in which piracy may be suppressed as well as the application of the principle of universal jurisdiction would certainly seem useful, although not an absolute necessity.[563]

The ongoing discussion with respect to the prosecution and punishment of suspected pirates off the coast of Somalia seems to concentrate, first of all, on how best to improve the local capacities in the affected region rather than focusing on the establishment of an international mechanism.[564] There is

---

[560] See Costa, *Testimony, Fighting Piracy on Land and at Sea* (note 484), at 1; see also A. Lelarge, *La Somalie entre anarchie et piraterie*, Journal du Droit International, Vol. 137/2 at 449–474 (2010).

[561] Report of the Secretary-General pursuant to Security Council Res. 1846 (2008) of 16 March 2009, UN. doc. S/2009/146, para. 59. For a general overview with respect to the situation relating to Somali piracy (2008) see the Report of the Monitoring Group on Somalia pursuant to Security Council Res. 1853 of 19 December 2008, UN doc. S/2010/91. See also Council of Europe, Parliamentary Assembly, Resolution 1722 (2010) (note 529), para. 6.

[562] See Contact Group on Somali Piracy (note 538), Chairman's Conclusions.

[563] Tuerk, *The Resurgence of Piracy* (note 371), at 41.

[564] The United Nations Office on Drugs and Crime (UNODC) is providing targeted support and capacity-building to countries of the region which agree to undertake piracy prosecutions to ensure that the trials and detention are fair, humane and efficient and take place within a sound rule of law framework. The core support provided by UNODC within the framework of the EU/UNODC Counter-Piracy Programme is focused largely on Kenya. A joint EU/UNODC counter-piracy programme has also been launched in the Seychelles to assist that country in handling the additional challenges of piracy cases. See the official website of UNODC on the subject, available at: www.unodc.org. An international trust fund to support

growing recognition regarding an urgent need to pursue more forcefully, with the necessary resources, a comprehensive approach to combating piracy and the conditions from which it arises, through efforts on land as well as at sea, combining military, law enforcement, and development activity.[565] In any case, impediments regarding the prosecution and punishment of suspected pirates in national courts should be addressed as a matter of urgency and not be deferred in favor of attention to an international mechanism that may not be available anytime soon.[566] What should not happen is that pirates go free due to the lack of proper legislation or political will.

There is undoubtedly also an urgent need for a continuing robust military response to more aggressive and widespread pirate activity, as well as the need to provide sufficient military capability to sustain counter-piracy operations.[567] It should nevertheless be borne in mind that no matter how intimidating the presence of an international naval force may be, pirates will not be deterred if they know that there is no law to judge them.[568]

Initiatives of States Countering Piracy Off the Coast of Somalia was established on 27 January 2010; see Report to the Secretary-General (note 491), Annex II, para. 12.

[565] See the Communiqué of the eighth meeting of the Contact Group on Piracy off the Coast of Somalia, Summary, 21 March 2011 (on file with author).

[566] See Non-Paper: An International Piracy Court (note 549).

[567] See the Communiqué of the eighth meeting of the Contact Group on Piracy off the Coast of Somalia (note 565).

[568] See Blanco-Bazán, *War Against Piracy? Some Misconceptions* (note 462), at 270.

Chapter Six

Terrorism at Sea[569]

A. *The Legal Response to Terrorism at Sea*

While piracy and terrorism at sea have many similarities, and both are forms of violent interference with shipping,[570] there is a marked difference between the goals of pirates and terrorists: while pirates usually seek financial gain, terrorists wish to make a "political or ideological" point, most often coupled with the wanton destruction of human life.[571] Furthermore, pirates act with stealth, while terrorists seek publicity with their actions.[572] There is no authoritative definition of terrorism but all definitions have several elements in common: first, there must be actual or threatened violence; second, a political motive is necessary; finally, the acts must be directed at, and intended to influence, a targeted audience. The overall facet of these common elements is arguably that an act is not terrorism unless it possesses a deliberate political motive.[573]

One of the first genuine acts of maritime terrorism recorded in modern history[574] was the seizure on October 7, 1985 of the *Achille Lauro*, an Italian-flag cruise ship, while sailing from Alexandria to Port Said.[575] The passengers held hostage by Palestinian hijackers hailed from a number of different countries, including Italy, the United States and Austria. The outrage that resulted

---

[569] For this chapter see in particular H. Tuerk, *Combating Terrorism at Sea – The Suppression of Unlawful Acts against the Safety of Maritime Navigation*, 15 University of Miami International and Comparative Law Review, Special Issue, at 337–367 (2008); this article is also to be found in: Legal Challenges in Maritime Security, M.H. Nordquist et al. (eds.), at 41–78 (2008).

[570] See Jesus, *Protection of Foreign Ships against Piracy and Terrorism at Sea* (note 71), at 363.

[571] Tuerk, *Combating Terrorism at Sea* (note 569), at 343; see also L. Diaz & B.H. Dubner, *On the Problem of Utilizing Unilateral Action to Prevent Acts of Sea Piracy and Terrorism: A Protective Approach to the Evolution of International Law*, 32/1 Syracuse Journal of International Law and Commerce, at 1 (2004–2005); see further T. Sittnick, *State Responsibility and Maritime Terrorism in the Strait of Malacca: Persuading Indonesia and Malaysia to take Additional Steps to Secure the Strait*, 14 Pacific Rim Law & Policy Journal, at 751 (2005).

[572] See id., Sittnick.

[573] See Power, *Maritime Terrorism: A New Challenge* (note 393), at 114–115.

[574] See Balkin, *The IMO and Maritime Security* (note 470), at 5.

[575] Halberstam, *Terrorism on the High Seas* (note 418), at 269.

from this terrorist act prompted a quick response by the international community. The IMO Assembly adopted Resolution A. 584 (14) on "Measures to Prevent Unlawful Acts Which Threaten the Safety of Ships and the Security of Their Passengers and Crews"[576] which called on all governments, port authorities and administrations, shipowners, ship operators, shipmasters, and crews to review and strengthen port and onboard security, noting "the danger to passengers and crews resulting from the increasing number of incidents involving piracy, armed robbery and other unlawful acts against or on board ships".[577] The resolution also directed the IMO MSC, "to develop, on a priority basis, detailed and practical technical measures to ensure the security of passengers and crews on board ships".[578]

The actions taken by the IMO had the full support of the UN General Assembly which in Resolution 40/61 adopted by consensus,[579] unequivocally condemned "as criminal, all acts, methods and practices of terrorism wherever and by whomever committed," and requested that the IMO "study the problem of terrorism aboard or against ships with a view to making recommendations on appropriate measures".[580] The insertion of this request in the resolution was proposed by Austria and Italy in order to reflect the concern of the international community at the seizure of the *Achille Lauro* and to endorse any steps taken in connection with the framework of the IMO. In 1986, in response to the directive of the IMO Assembly and the request by the UN General Assembly, the MSC adopted measures aimed at minimizing the risk of terrorist acts directed against ships and their crews.[581] These recommendations specifically applied to passenger ships engaged on international voyages of twenty-four hours or more, as well as the port facilities that serviced such ships.[582]

It was, however, obvious that besides practical measures to counter the threat of international terrorism against international shipping, legal measures

[576] IMO, Measures to Prevent Unlawful Acts Which Threaten the Safety of Ships and the Security of Their Passengers and Crews, IMO Assembly Resolution A.584 (14) of 20 November 1985, available at: www.imo.org/includes/blastDataOnly.asp/data_id%3D22374/A584%2814%29.pdf (last visited 1 July 2011).

[577] Id.

[578] Id.; see also Balkin, The IMO and Maritime Security (note 470), at 6.

[579] UN General Assembly Res. 40/61 of 9 December 1985, Measures to prevent international terrorism which endangers or takes innocent human lives or jeopardizes fundamental freedoms and study of the underlying causes of those forms of terrorism and acts of violence which lie in misery, frustration, grievance and despair and which cause some people to sacrifice human lives, including their own, in an attempt to effect radical changes.

[580] Id.

[581] IMO, Measures to Prevent Unlawful Acts Which Threaten the Safety of Ships and the Security of Their Passengers and Crews, IMO doc. MSC 52/INF. 9 of 15 January 1986.

[582] Balkin, The IMO and Maritime Security (note 470), at 6.

were necessary to ensure that the perpetrators of terrorist acts were made duly accountable. Because these acts are committed on the high seas and the perpetrators as well as the victims hail from various countries that may not include that of the ship's flag, new international rules were necessary. More specifically, there was a need for rules relating to the arrest, prosecution, and subsequent detention of those responsible for acts of maritime terrorism.[583] The existing legal framework seemed inadequate to deal with such situations as it appeared doubtful whether the concept of piracy could be applied to terrorism at sea. The hijacking of the Achille Lauro had been characterized as piracy by some, in particular the United States, which issued arrest warrants charging the hijackers with hostage taking, conspiracy and "piracy on the high seas".[584]

In examining this question, the Legal Advisors of the Foreign Ministries of Austria,[585] Italy and Egypt concluded that the seizure of the *Achille Lauro* could not be considered an act of piracy as defined in the 1958 Convention on the High Seas and UNCLOS because the hijackers did not act for "private ends" and the seizure did not meet the "two-vessel" requirement.[586] There was an obvious legal lacuna which would have to be filled by creating a specific convention relating to maritime terrorism because the development of international law regarding unlawful acts against ships had not yet reached the same stage as it had with respect to civil aviation. In aviation, the 1963 Tokyo Convention on Offences and Certain Other Acts Committed on Board Aircraft, the 1970 Hague Convention for the Suppression of Unlawful Seizure of Aircraft and the 1971 Montreal Convention for the Suppression of Unlawful Acts Against the Safety of Civil Aviation – elaborated within the framework of ICAO – were already in force.[587] However, no specific international legal rules existed with respect to maritime terrorism which had never before been a serious international problem.

---

[583] Id., at 7.

[584] See Halberstam, *Terrorism on the High Seas* (note 418), at 270.

[585] At that time the author.

[586] Tuerk, *Combating Terrorism at Sea* (note 569), at 343; see also Jesus, Protection of Foreign Ships against Piracy and Terrorism at Sea (note 71), at 388; see further C. Tiribelli, Time to Update the 1988 Rome Convention for the Suppression of Unlawful Acts Against the Safety of Maritime Navigation, 8 Oregon Review of International Law, at 144 (2006).

[587] See Convention on Offences and Certain Other Acts Committed on Board Aircraft, 22 December 1969, 704 UNTS 219; Convention for the Suppression of Unlawful Seizure of Aircraft, 8 March 1973, 860 UNTS 105; Convention for the Suppression of Unlawful Acts Against the Safety of Civil Aviation, 23 September 1971, 974 UNTS 177; IMO, Consideration of a Draft Protocol to the Convention For The Suppression of Unlawful Acts Against the Safety of Maritime Navigation, at Annex 2, C. 57/25 of 1 October 1986.

As a consequence, Austria, Italy and Egypt proposed to elaborate a new international convention to deal specifically with the issue of maritime terrorism modelled on existing anti-terrorism conventions, particularly the Hague and Montreal Conventions, as well as the 1979 UN Convention Against the Taking of Hostages.[588] Following the title of the Montreal Convention, the three sponsoring countries called their draft "Convention for the Suppression of Unlawful Acts Against the Safety of Maritime Navigation".[589] In this connexion the need was underlined to make a clear distinction between the cases covered by the proposed new convention and piracy, since the latter was governed by a different regime that is internationally codified, and the customary law of the sea.[590]

The Convention for the Suppression of Unlawful Acts Against the Safety of Maritime Navigation (SUA) and the Protocol relating to Fixed Platforms Located on the Continental Shelf were adopted by consensus on March 10, 1988 by a Diplomatic Conference held in Rome.[591] The Convention which had entered into force on 1 March 1992[592] had only been ratified by 67 States until September 11, 2001. It has, however, since then found overwhelming support by the international community.[593] As of 1 July 2011, there are 157 Contracting States party to the Convention accounting for 94.73 percent of world tonnage and the Protocol has been adhered to by 146 States accounting for 89.72 percent of world tonnage.[594] This development reflects the seriousness with which the international community has in recent years taken the threat of international terrorism, and its possible effects at sea.[595]

---

[588] International Convention Against the Taking of Hostages, 17 December 1979, 1316 UNTS 205.

[589] See generally IMO, Adoption of the Final Act and Any Instruments, Recommendations and Resolutions Resulting from the Work of the Conference: Convention for the Suppression of Unlawful Acts Against the Safety of Maritime Navigation (note 14).

[590] Tuerk, *Combating Terrorism at Sea* (note 569), at 345.

[591] SUA Convention (note 14).

[592] Id.

[593] B. Kieserman, *Preventing and Defeating Terrorism at Sea: Practical Considerations for the Implementation of the Draft Protocol to the Convention for the Suppression of Unlawful Acts Against the Safety of Maritime Navigation (SUA)*, in: Recent Developments in the Law of the Sea and China, J. Norton Moore, M.H. Nordquist, K. Fu (eds.), at 434 (2005).

[594] See IMO, Summary of status of Conventions as at 28 June 2011, available at: www.imo.org/About/Conventions/StatusOfConventions/Documents/Status%20-%202011.pdf (last visited July 1 2011).

[595] Kieserman, *Preventing and Defeating Terrorism at Sea* (note 593), at 434.

B. *The 1988 Convention for the Suppression of Unlawful Acts Against the Safety of Maritime Navigation (SUA) and Protocol*[596]

As already stated, the SUA Convention in substance is based on previously existing anti-terrorism conventions by adapting their provisions to the maritime field. However, it is also a "genuine" anti-terrorism convention because its Preamble expresses deep concern about "the world-wide escalation of acts of terrorism in all its forms, the occurrence of which is considered a matter of grave concern to the international community as a whole".[597] Furthermore, the Preamble quotes from the aforementioned General Assembly Resolution 40/61 concerning the unequivocal condemnation as criminal of all acts, methods and practices of terrorism.[598] There are no such references to be found in the Hague, Tokyo and Montreal Conventions. In order to achieve the necessary political compromise and secure the adoption of the Convention by consensus, the Preamble quotes another paragraph of Resolution 40/61 which refers to the need that "all States contribute to the progressive elimination of causes underlying international terrorism".[599] There is, however, no authoritative definition of this term and no attempt was made to create such a definition at the Rome Conference as this would certainly have led to insurmountable political difficulties.[600]

The SUA Convention applies to ships on an international voyage operating or scheduled to operate seaward of any State's territorial sea. The covered territory is a potentially vast geographic area into which many States would find it difficult to project an enforcement presence much beyond their respective littorals.[601] Ships engaged in cabotage that takes place exclusively within the territorial sea of a coastal State – so-called short range cabotage – are thus excluded and any unlawful act directed against them is governed solely by national law.[602] In conformity with general international law of sovereign immunities, warships or government vessels used for naval, customs or police purposes are excluded from the ambit of the Convention.[603]

---

[596] See G. Plant, *The Convention for the Suppression of Unlawful Acts Against the Safety of Maritime Navigation* (containing a detailed analysis of the provisions of the SUA Convention), 39 International and Comparative Law Quarterly, at 27–56 (1990).

[597] See id., 32–34.

[598] See id., at 32; UN General Assembly Res. 40/61 (note 579).

[599] See Plant, *The SUA Convention* (note 596), at 32; UN General Assembly Res. 40/61 (note 579).

[600] See Tuerk, *Combating Terrorism at Sea* (note 569), at 347.

[601] Kieserman, *Preventing and Defeating Terrorism at Sea* (note 593), at 427.

[602] Balkin, *The IMO and Maritime Security* (note 470), at 9.

[603] See D. Freestone, *The 1988 International Convention for the Suppression of Unlawful Acts Against the Safety of Maritime Navigation*, 3 International Journal of Estuarine & Coastal Law, at 308 (1988); id. Balkin, at 8.

Although entitled "Convention for the *Suppression* of Unlawful Acts Against the Safety of Maritime Navigation", the SUA's operative provisions deal primarily with events after illegal acts have taken place; that is the apprehension, conviction and punishment of those who commit such acts, as opposed to the prevention or suppression of those acts.[604] Only one provision directly addresses the problem of prevention or suppression: Article 13 requires States parties to cooperate in the prevention of offenses by taking all practical measures to prevent preparations in their respective territories for the commission of the offences within or outside their territories as well as to exchange information and to coordinate measures to prevent the commission of those offences. Furthermore, there is a duty for States parties that have a reason to believe that an offense set forth in the Convention will be committed to furnish as promptly as possible any relevant information to those States having established jurisdiction over such offenses.[605]

Similar to most international anti-terrorism conventions, the core provision of the SUA Convention, enshrined in Article 10, is the requirement for States to "extradite or prosecute".[606] This provision is substantially the same as the corresponding provision of the Convention Against the Taking of Hostages. There is no absolute obligation to extradite and there is furthermore no absolute duty to punish. The State in whose territory the offender is found is only required "to submit the case without delay to its competent authorities for the purpose of prosecution," which "shall take their decision in the same manner as in the case of any other offence of a grave nature under the law of that State".[607] This provision, although it corresponds to other anti-terrorism conventions, has been called a deficiency of the SUA Convention since it arguably allows terrorists to escape punishment.[608] People are left to trust the independence and efficiency of the judiciary systems called upon to deal with such offenders.[609]

In support of the framework – *dedere aut iudicare* – States parties are required to establish their jurisdiction over specified offenses and make these offenses punishable by appropriate penalties which take into account their grave nature. The idea behind such a provision is to ensure that terrorists will not find a safe haven in any territories of those States that are parties to the Convention.[610] There is, however, no binding obligation, but only a discretion, to extradite to

---

[604] Sittnick, *State Responsibility and Maritime Terrorism in the Strait of Malacca* (note 571), at 760–761; Kieserman, *Preventing and Defeating Terrorism at Sea* (note 593), at 427.
[605] See id. Kieserman.
[606] See id.
[607] T. Treves, *The Convention for the Suppression of Unlawful Acts against the Safety of Maritime Navigation*, 2 Singapore Journal of International and Comparative Law, at 542 (1998).
[608] See Id.
[609] Tuerk, *Combating Terrorism at Sea* (note 569), at 349–350.
[610] See id., at 553; see also Balkin, *The IMO and Maritime Security* (note 470), at 9.

the flag State rather than another State because only "due regard" is to be paid to the interests and responsibilities of the State party whose flag the ship was flying at the time of the commission of the offense. A clear priority in favor of the flag State proved unacceptable to many States at the Diplomatic Conference in view of difficulties with domestic legislation.[611]

The offenses covered by the Convention are listed in Article 3 and substantially reproduce *mutatis mutandis* those provided for in the aviation precedents.[612] At the initiative of the United States, a new offense was added for injuring or killing a person in connection with the commission, or attempted commission, of any of the other offenses.[613]

The SUA Convention established extraditable offenses of direct involvement, or complicity, in the intentional and unlawful threatened, attempted or actual endangerment of the safe navigation of a ship by: the commission or attempt of seizure or exercise of control over a ship by any form of intimidation; violence against a person on board a ship; destruction of a ship; the causing of damage to a ship or to its cargo; placement on a ship of a device or substance which is likely to destroy or cause damage to that ship or its cargo; destruction of, serious damaging of, or interference with maritime navigational facilities; knowing communication of false information; and injury to or murder of any person in connection with any of the preceding acts.[614] These offenses are also deemed to be includable as extraditable offenses in any extradition treaty existing between any of the States parties.

Article 6 established two types of jurisdiction; namely, obligatory and discretionary.[615] A State party is obliged to establish domestic law jurisdiction over those offenses committed against, or on board, a ship flying the flag of the State at the time the offense is committed, or in the territory of that State, including its territorial sea, or by a national of that State. Furthermore, a State party may establish jurisdiction over any such offense, when: it is committed by a stateless person whose habitual residence is in that State; or during its commission a national of that State is seized, threatened, injured or killed; or it is committed in an attempt to compel that State to do or abstain from doing any act. The inclusion of discretionary jurisdiction represented a compromise between the States that supported obligatory jurisdiction, derived from the

---

[611] See Plant, *The SUA Convention* (note 596), at 50, 55.
[612] Id., at 40.
[613] See P. Kirsch, *The 1988 ICAO and IMO Conferences: An International Consensus against Terrorism*, 12 Dalhousie Law Journal, at 18 (1989–1990).
[614] Kieserman, *Preventing and Defeating Terrorism at Sea* (note 593), at 427–428.
[615] Plant, *The SUA Convention* (note 596), at 44.

nationality of the victim or from coercion of a State, and those who opposed any sort of jurisdiction on these grounds.[616]

Furthermore, Article 6 contains the important obligation for a State party to establish its jurisdiction over the offenses in question in cases where the alleged offender is present in its territory and the State does not extradite him to any of the States parties having established their jurisdiction in accordance with the aforementioned provisions.[617] This rule underlines the fact that the punishment of the offences covered by the SUA Convention is a common goal of the international community even though it does not contain a specific provision on universal jurisdiction.[618]

Article 8 permits the master of a ship to deliver to the authorities of any other State party any person who he has reasonable grounds to believe has committed one of the offences set forth in Article 3 and all pertinent evidence in the master's possession.[619] This provision was included in the Convention in order to address those cases where the ship is navigating far from the flag State, flying a flag of convenience, or of a landlocked State, since few ships are equipped to keep alleged offenders on board for long periods of time.[620] This right of a master of a ship has been criticized as placing the potentially politically sensitive decision to choose the State of delivery in the hands of a private citizen.[621] It seems, however, highly unlikely that the master of a vessel would take such a decision without previously consulting his competent authorities. In addition, the practical effect of that provision appears rather limited as it is difficult to imagine that the crew of a commercial vessel or a passenger ship would be in a position to overpower and detain terrorists.[622]

The elaboration of the "Protocol for the Suppression of Unlawful Acts Against the Safety of Fixed Platforms Located on the Continental Shelf" was motivated by the possibility of a terrorist seizure of an oil or gas platform.[623] The Protocol aims to provide a similar regime for fixed platforms located on the continental shelf as most of the articles of the Convention are applied *mutatis mutandis.*

---

[616] Id., at 46.

[617] See id., at 44.

[618] See Freestone, *The 1988 SUA Convention* (note 603), at 310.

[619] Kieserman, *Preventing and Defeating Terrorism at Sea* (note 593), at 428; Plant, *The SUA Convention* (note 596), at 48.

[620] Id.

[621] Id., see also Freestone, *The 1988 SUA Convention* (note 603), at 314–315.

[622] Tuerk, *Combating Terrorism at Sea* (note 569), at 352.

[623] See IMO, Adoption of the Final Act and Any Instruments, Recommendations and Resolutions Resulting From the Work of the Conference, Protocol of 2005 to the Protocol for the Suppression of Unlawful Acts Against Safety of Fixed Platforms Located on the Continental Shelf, IMO doc. LEG/CONF.15/22 of 1 November 2005, available at: www.state.gov/documents/organization/58425.pdf (last visited 1 July 2011).

A fixed platform is defined as "an artificial island, installation or structure permanently attached to the sea-bed for the purpose of exploration or exploitation of resources or for other economic purposes".[624] Military style or defence installations are thus *de facto* excluded.[625]

C. *The Updating of the SUA Convention and Protocol*[626]

Since the SUA Convention and Protocol entered into effect in 1992, terrorism and the proliferation of weapons of mass destruction have increasingly plagued global security with transnational networks of terrorists having global reach and making common cause, thus posing a threat to all nations.[627] In a number of resolutions, the UN General Assembly and the Security Council have emphasized the duty of States to prevent terrorism and deny all forms of support and safe haven to terrorists, as well as those supporting terrorism. A link has also been developed between terrorism and the proliferation of weapons of mass destruction.[628]

The traumatic events of September 11, 2001 have exposed the vulnerability of the global transport infrastructure both as a potential target for terrorist activity and a potential weapon of mass destruction.[629] The shift towards containerization in the transportation of general cargo has reduced transparency in the shipping industry and greatly enhanced the potential risk of terrorist attack. The efficiency of containerized systems makes containers a potential security threat because the emphasis on speed means that cargo is rarely inspected.[630] Actual and planned acts of terrorism against shipping have targeted vessels either in port or close to the shore.[631] Furthermore, the perils to commercial shipping have been heightened by an increased danger of possible coordinated efforts by terrorists and pirates, especially in important areas of international maritime

---

[624] Id.

[625] See Freestone, *The 1988 SUA Convention* (note 603), at 315–316.

[626] See generally C. Young, *Balancing Maritime Security and Freedom of Navigation on the High Seas: A Study of the Multilateral Negotiation Process in Action* (containing a detailed description of the negotiating process), 24/2 University of Queensland Law Journal, at 355 (2005).

[627] Report by the UN Secretary-General, UN doc. A/59/2005 (2005), in: Larger Freedom: Towards Development, Security and Human Rights for All, at 87.

[628] See J.S.C. Mellor, *Missing the Boat: The Legal and Practical Problems of the Prevention of Maritime Terrorism, 18 American University International Law Review*, at 367 (2002–2003); see Wolfrum, *Fighting Terrorism at Sea* (note 426), at 664–665.

[629] Balkin, *The IMO and Maritime Security* (note 470), at 16.

[630] Mellor, *Missing the Boat: Problems of the Prevention of Maritime Terrorism* (note 628), at 348.

[631] Smarttraveler.gov, *Shipping and Ports*, available at: www.smarttraveller.gov.au/zw-cgi/view/Advice/shipping_and_ports (last visited 1 July 2011).

transportation.[632] As already mentioned, more than 90% of world trade is carried by sea, terrorist incidents, particularly when occurring in vulnerable and strategic sea routes, have the potential for a severe disruption of international trade.[633]

It was evident that the previous work of the IMO to combat terrorism at sea was insufficient to prevent this new kind of terrorist activity from posing a serious threat to the safety of international shipping.[634] In 2001, the IMO Assembly therefore adopted Resolution A.924 (22) calling for "a review of the existing international legal and technical measures to prevent and suppress terrorist acts against ships at sea and in port and to improve security aboard and ashore, in order to reduce any associated risk to passengers, crews and port personnel on board ships and in port areas and to the vessels and their cargoes".[635] The competent committees were given the task "to review, on a high priority basis, the instruments under their purview to determine whether they should be updated and whether there was a need to adopt other maritime security measures".

As a consequence, a Diplomatic Conference held in December 2002 adopted a series of wide-ranging new security measures.[636] Amendments were added to the 1974 Convention on the Safety of Life at Sea (SOLAS) addressing special measures to enhance maritime security. In addition, the International Ship and Port Facility Security Code (ISPS) was adopted and made in part mandatory under the amended SOLAS Convention.[637] This new comprehensive maritime security regime for international shipping entered into force on July 1, 2004.[638]

---

[632] Sittnick, *State Responsibility and Maritime Terrorism in the Strait of Malacca* (note 571), at 744; see also E. Barrios, *Note: Casting a Wider Net: Addressing the Maritime Piracy Problem in Southeast Asia*, 28/1 Boston College International and Comparative Law Review, at 149, 151 (2005).

[633] Balkin, *The IMO and Maritime Security* (note 470), at 2.

[634] Id., at 16.

[635] IMO, Renewal of Measures and Procedures to Prevent Acts of Terrorism Which Threaten the Security of Passengers and Crews and the Safety of Ships, IMO Assembly Resolution A.924 (22) of 20 November 2001, available at: www.imo.org/OurWork/Security/docs/TEST/A.924(22).pdf (last visited 1 July 2011); see Balkin, *The IMO and Maritime Security* (note 470), at 16.

[636] See id. Balkin, at 17.

[637] The ISPS Code is a comprehensive set of measures designed to enhance the security of ships and port facilities. It contains detailed mandatory security requirements for governments, port authorities and the shipping companies as well as a series of non-mandatory guidelines regarding the implementation of these requirements. The Code covers both passenger ships and cargo ships, including tankers, weighing 500 gross tonnage or more as well as port facilities serving ships on international voyages and mobile offshore drilling units. See also Tiribelli, *Time to Update the 1988 SUA Convention* (note 586), at 148, footnote 39; see further P. DeCaro, *Safety Among Dragons: East Asia and Maritime Security*, 33 Transport Law Journal, at 234 (2005–2006).

[638] See id. Tiribelli, at 147.

Furthermore, the IMO Legal Committee began re-examining the provisions of the 1988 SUA Convention and Protocol.[639] The conclusion was that the categories of unlawful acts set forth in these legal instruments were too narrow and would require expansion in order to cope with modern day terrorist threats, including threats from biological, chemical and nuclear weapons or material.[640] It was further acknowledged that these instruments did not include provisions that would allow law enforcement officials to board foreign flag ships on the high seas, either to search for alleged terrorists or their weapons, or to render assistance to a vessel suspected of being under attack.[641] The drafting of such provisions became one of the main focuses of the revision exercise,[642] while also seeking to ensure that freedom of navigation, the right of innocent passage, and the basic principles of international law and the operation of international commercial shipping would not be jeopardized.[643] With respect to the question of whether the titles of the SUA Convention and Protocol should be amended to include the term "terrorist acts" it was considered that such an amendment would not be appropriate since the amending instruments were merely proto- cols to an existing Convention and Protocol. Although the treaties retained the term "unlawful acts" it was nevertheless understood that the object and purpose of these treaties was to deal with acts of terrorism and to provide a legal frame- work for the apprehension and prosecution of alleged terrorists.[644]

On October 14, 2005[645] the International Conference on the Revision of the SUA Treaties – one of the most politically charged conferences in the history of the IMO[646] – adopted the proposed amendments by consensus. By decision of the Conference, the original 1988 SUA Convention and Protocol, and the

---

[639] See Balkin, *The IMO and Maritime Security* (note 470), at 25; see also Young, *Balancing Maritime Security and Freedom of Navigation on the High Seas* (note 626), at 358; T.A. Mensah, *Suppression of Terrorism at Sea: Developments in the Wake of the Events of 11 September 2001*, in: Verhandeln für den Frieden – Negotiation for Peace, Liber Amicorum Tono Eitel, J. Frowein et al. (eds.), at 640 (2003).

[640] Balkin, *The IMO and Maritime Security* (note 470), at 23.

[641] Id.

[642] Id.

[643] Tiribelli, *Time to Update the 1988 SUA Convention*, at 147 (note 586).

[644] Balkin, *The IMO and Maritime Security* (note 470), at 24.

[645] IMO doc. LEG/CONF.15/22 (note 623). Three delegations – India, Pakistan, and Russia – however, made statements regarding provisions in the Protocol, such as concern over refer- ences to rights and responsibilities under the Non-Proliferation Treaties and their possible application to State parties which are not also a party to these instruments in Arts 2bis and 3bis, and concern over the "dual use" provisions in Art. 3bis. See Young, Balancing Maritime Security and Freedom of Navigation on the High Seas (note 626), at 384.

[646] IMO, International Conference on the Revision of the SUA Treaties: Closing Statement by the Secretary-General, As Delivered, IMO doc. LEG/CONF.15/RD/2 of 14 October 2005, available at: www.sjofartsverket.se/upload/5143/15-RD-2.pdf (last visited 1 July 2011).

amending Protocols constitute single instruments now called the "Convention for the Suppression of Unlawful Acts against the Safety of Maritime Navigation, 2005 (the 2005 SUA Convention)" and the "Protocol for the Suppression of Unlawful Acts against the Safety of fixed Platforms located on the Continental Shelf, 2005 (2005 SUA Fixed Platforms Protocol)".[647] As of 1 July 2011 the amended SUA Convention has been adhered to by 20 and the amended Protocol by 16 States. Both instruments entered into force on 28 July 2010.[648]

D. *The Protocols of 2005 to the SUA Convention and Protocol*

The core provisions of the 2005 Protocol to the 1988 SUA Convention are Article 3bis, which substantially enlarges the offenses covered by the Convention and Article 8bis, which relates to ship boarding and provides a mechanism through which the international community may enforce the provisions.[649] The amendments to the 1988 Protocol for the Suppression of Unlawful Acts against the Safety of Fixed Platforms Located on the Continental Shelf reflect those in the 2005 Protocol to the SUA Convention.[650]

In its Preamble, the amending Protocol to the SUA Convention acknowledges that terrorist acts threaten international peace and security. It does, not however, contain a definition of terrorism, but a terrorist-purposes provision instead – Article 3bis (1)a – based on the definition found in the 1999 International Convention for the Suppression of the Financing of Terrorism.[651] An act is thus criminalized under the Protocol when its purpose, by its nature or context, is to intimidate a population or to compel a Government or an international organization to do or to abstain from doing any act.[652]

---

[647] A. Blanco-Bazán, *Suppressing Unlawful Acts: IMO Incursion in the Field of Criminal Law*, in *Law of the Sea, Environmental Law and Settlement of Disputes*, T.M. Ndiaye & R. Wolfrum (eds.), at 720 (2007).

[648] See Summary of status of Conventions, available at: www.imo.org/About/Conventions/Status OfConventions/Documents/Status%20-%202011.pdf (last visited 1 July 2011).

[649] C.A. Harrington, *Heightened Security: The need to Incorporate Arts 3bis(1)(A) and 8bis(5)(E) of the 2005 Draft SUA Protocol into Part VII of the United Nations Convention on the Law of the Sea*, 16 Pacific Rim Law & Policy Journal, at 122 (2007).

[650] Tuerk, *Combating Terrorism at Sea* (note 569), at 364.

[651] Art. 2 (1) (b) International Convention for the Suppression of the Financing of Terrorism, 9 December 1999, 2178 UNTS 197, "Any (...) act intended to cause death or serious bodily injury to a civilian, or to any other person not taking an active part in the hostilities in a situation of armed conflict, when the purpose of such act, by its nature or context, is to intimidate a population or to compel a government or an international organization to do or to abstain from doing any act."; see Wolfrum, *Fighting Terrorism at Sea* (note 426), at 650, footnote 2.

[652] See id., Art. 2 (1)(b).

According to Article 3bis(1)a an offense within the meaning of the Convention is committed if a person for the purpose referred to unlawfully and intentionally:

(i) uses against or on a ship or discharging from a ship any explosive, radioactive material or BCN – biological, chemical, nuclear – weapon and other nuclear explosive devices – in a manner that causes or is likely to cause death or serious injury or damage;
(ii) discharges, from a ship, oil, liquefied natural gas, or other hazardous or noxious substance, in such quantity or concentration that causes or is likely to cause death or serious injury or damage;
(iii) uses a ship in a manner that causes death or serious injury or damage;
(iv) threatens to commit any of these offences.[653]

Article 3bis (1)b focuses on the transportation of materials that could be used in a terrorist attack.[654] It prohibits the shipping of BCN weapons, source material not covered under the International Atomic Energy Agency's comprehensive safeguards agreement, other explosive or radioactive material to be used in a terrorist attack or such a threatened attack, and any equipment, materials or software or related technology that is intended to contribute to the design, manufacture or delivery of a BCN weapon.[655] The provision relating to dual-use goods may give rise to problems for determining whether such goods found on board a ship point to an offense under the Convention. In most situations, a seafarer would not have the requisite general knowledge and intent. Furthermore, a typical seafarer would not know what is in a container ordinarily sealed and loaded at port.[656]

In addition, the transportation of nuclear material is not considered an offense if, subject to specific conditions, such item or material is transported to or from the territory of, or is otherwise transported under the control of, a State party to the Treaty on the Non-Proliferation of Nuclear Weapons.[657] The fact that the Protocol further grants recognized nuclear weapon States a privileged position with respect to other States encountered opposition during the

---

[653] IMO doc. LEG/CONF.15/22 (note 623), Art. 3bis (1)a.
[654] Harrington, *Heightened Security: The Need to Incorporate Articles of the 2005 Draft SUA Protocol into UNCLOS* (note 649), at 123.
[655] Id.
[656] Consideration of a Draft Protocol to the Convention For The Suppression of Unlawful Acts Against the Safety of Maritime Navigation; Comments on the Protections Afforded to the Shipping Industry, U.S.-ICFTU, IMO doc. LEG/CONF.15/14, No. 11 of 20 September 2005, available at: www.sjofartsverket.se/upload/5143/15-14.pdf (last visited 1 July 2011).
[657] See generally Blanco-Bazán, *Suppressing Unlawful Acts* (note 647), at 719.

negotiations and may well prevent certain countries from adhering to the amended Convention in the future.[658]

Under the Protocol, a person also commits an offense within the meaning of the Convention if that person unlawfully and intentionally transports another person on board a ship knowing that the person has committed an act that constitutes an offense under the SUA Convention or an offense set forth in the nine anti-terrorism conventions listed in the Annex.[659] When adhering to the Protocol, if a State is not a party to a treaty listed in the Annex, it may, however, declare that the treaty in question shall be deemed not to be included in that provision.

An important innovation is the new article 8bis covering co-operation and procedures to be followed if a State party desires to board a ship flying the flag of another State party when the requesting State party has reasonable grounds to suspect that the ship or a person on board the ship is, has been, or is about to be involved in, the commission of an offense under the Convention.[660] However, before boarding, the express authorization and co-operation of the flag State is required. Such authorization may be given in general or ad hoc.[661] A flag State may further authorize the boarding State to exercise powers of, or in relation to arrest, detention, forfeiture and prosecution.[662] A State party may notify the IMO Secretary-General that it would allow authorization to board and search a ship flying its flag, its cargo and persons on board if there is no response within four hours.[663] A State party can also notify that it authorizes a State party to board and search the ship, its cargo and persons on board, and to question the persons on board to determine if an offence has been, or is about to be, committed.[664] Finally, a State party may grant the authorization to board a ship under its flag when requested.[665] During negotiations on the amendments, no agreement could be reached that a flag State would automatically be

---

[658] See Balkin, *The IMO and Maritime Security* (note 470), at 23; see generally Harrington, *Heightened Security: The Need to Incorporate Articles of the 2005 Draft SUA Protocol into UNCLOS* (note 649), at 123.

[659] See IMO, Background Information on the 2005 Protocols to the SUA Treaties, 10–14 October 2005, available at: www.imo.org/Newsroom/mainframe.asp?topic_id=1018&doc_id=5334 (last visited 1 July 2011).

[660] Id., IMO, Revised Treaties to Address Unlawful Acts at Sea Adopted at International Conference, available at: www.imo.org/Newsroom/mainframe.asp?topic_id=1018&doc_id=5334 (last visited 1 July 2011).

[661] Wolfrum, *Fighting Terrorism at Sea* (note 426), at 20.

[662] See id.

[663] Id.

[664] IMO, Background Information on the 2005 Protocols to the SUA Treaties (note 659), Boarding Provisions.

[665] Id.

deemed to have authorized a boarding when it fails to respond to a request by another State to board within a certain timeframe – as had been advocated by the United States.[666]

In addition, Article 8bis includes important safeguards for innocent seafarers and carriers when a State party takes measures against a ship, including boarding.[667] These safeguards include: not endangering the safety of life at sea; ensuring that all persons on board are treated in a manner which preserves human dignity and in keeping with human rights law; taking due account of safety and security of the ship and its cargo; ensuring that measures taken are environmentally sound; and taking reasonable efforts to avoid a ship being unduly detained or delayed.[668] When carrying out the authorized actions under this provision, the use of force is to be avoided except when necessary to ensure the safety of officials and persons on board, or where the officials are obstructed in the execution of these actions.[669] Any use of force shall not exceed the minimum degree necessary and reasonable in the circumstances. These use of force provisions are consistent with current practice on the use of force in international law.[670] States parties shall also be liable for any damage, harm or loss attributable to them arising from measures taken pursuant to this Article when the grounds for such measures prove to be unfounded, or unlawful, or exceed those reasonably required in light of available information.[671] This provision concerning liability of States for an illegal or unfounded boarding constitutes an important safeguard ensuring that vessels are not stopped and searched without reasonable grounds.[672]

The new Article 11bis states that, for the purposes of extradition, none of the offenses shall be regarded as a political offense or as an offense connected therewith or inspired by political motives.[673] This provision directly follows the model of the 1997 International Convention for the Suppression of Terrorist Bombings.[674] According to the new Article 11ter, the obligation to extradite

---

[666] See generally the International Convention for the Suppression of the Financing of Terrorism (note 651).

[667] IMO, Background Information on the 2005 Protocols to the SUA Treaties (note 659), Boarding Provisions.

[668] Id.

[669] Id.

[670] See IMO doc. LEG/CONF.15/14 (note 656), at 22.

[671] IMO doc. LEG/CONF.15/22 (note 623), at 8bis 10(b).

[672] G. Witschel, *Mare Liberum and Maritime Security: Contradiction or Complementarity?*, Keynote address, in: Legal Challenges in Maritime Security, M.H. Nordquist et al. (eds.), 112 (2008).

[673] IMO, Revised Treaties to Address Unlawful Acts at Sea (note 660), at Extradition.

[674] See Balkin, *The IMO and Maritime Security* (note 470), at 30–31; International Convention for the Suppression of Terrorist Bombings, 15 December 1997, 2149 UNTS 256.

or afford mutual legal assistance need not apply if the requested State party has substantial grounds for believing that the request for extradition has been made for the purpose of prosecuting or punishing a person on account of that person's race, religion, nationality, ethnic origin, political opinion or gender, or that compliance with the request would cause prejudice to that person's position for any of these reasons.[675]

In line with the most recent United Nations anti-terrorism conventions, the Protocol also contains a savings clause – Article 2bis: nothing in the Convention shall affect other rights, obligations and responsibilities of States and individuals under international law, nor does it apply to the activities of armed forces during armed conflict or the activities undertaken by military forces of a State in the exercise of their official duties.[676]

E. *The SUA Convention and Piracy*[677]

As the SUA Convention was meant to be an anti-terrorism convention, the view has been put forth that it only applies to acts committed by terrorists as well as "unlawful acts other than piracy". It has also been pointed out that to expand the notion of piracy to include terrorist acts would undermine the anti-piracy regime since the strategies to combat each crime are "poles apart". The offences should therefore continue to be treated separately.[678] The drafters of the SUA Convention undoubtedly departed from the premise that piracy was a crime already legislated in an international treaty, namely UNCLOS. They certainly did not take into account that so many States parties to UNCLOS would see no need to enact appropriate anti-piracy legislation in compliance with that framework Convention.[679] In view of the lack of such legislation in many countries, it has been suggested that the SUA Convention could also be used to detain pirates, as the motive of the person committing any of the offences listed therein was not relevant.[680]

---

[675] IMO, Revised Treaties to Address Unlawful Acts at Sea (note 660), at Extradition.

[676] IMO doc. LEG/CONF.15/22 (note 623), at Art. 2bis.

[677] See also Tuerk, *The Resurgence of Piracy* (note 371), at 26–32.

[678] See Collins & Hassan, *Combating Piracy: A South East Asian Perspective* (note 435), at 100. The Annotated Supplement to the Commander's Handbook on the Law of Naval Operations states that terrorist attacks on shipping "for the sole purpose of achieving some political end are arguably not piracy under current international law", available at: www.nuclear weaponslaw.com/Annotated_Supplement_to_the_Commanders_Handbook_All.pdf (last visited 1 July 2011); see Bahar, Attaining Optimal Deterrence at Sea (note 401), at 27.

[679] See Blanco-Bazán, *Suppressing Unlawful Acts* (note 647), at 265.

[680] See Beckman, *The 1988 SUA Convention and 2005 SUA Protocol* (note 436), at 330; see also Collins & Hassan, *Combating Piracy: A South East Asian Perspective* (note 435), at 106.

In this connection, it is to be recalled that at the time of the elaboration of the original SUA Convention the Special Representative of the UN Secretary-General had already pointed out that although the rules on piracy were inapplicable to maritime terrorism, it would seem that acts of piracy or armed robbery at sea could also qualify as unlawful acts under the Convention if they met the definition of the offences set forth therein.[681] In the same vein, the Security Council, in Resolution 1846 (2008)[682] for the first time established a link between the SUA Convention and piracy by noting that this Convention "provides for parties to create criminal offences, establish jurisdiction, and exercise delivery of persons responsible for or suspected of seizing or exercising control over a ship by force or threat thereof or any other form of intimidation".[683] Furthermore, States parties to the Convention are urged to fully implement their respective obligations and cooperate with the Secretary-General and the IMO to build judicial capacity for the successful prosecution of persons suspected of piracy and armed robbery at sea off the coast of Somalia.[684]

It has, however, also been stated that applying the SUA Convention to piracy may help in some situations but that this remained a defective remedy because it did not reflect the clear distinctions between piracy and maritime terrorism established by the drafters of the two basic treaties addressing crimes at sea. Although there may be States that have piracy legislation not conforming to those distinctions as many States party to UNCLOS have not in fact updated their nineteenth century legislation in this regard, the use of the SUA Convention in order to suppress piracy did nevertheless not reflect sound legal policy.[685] It has thus been recommended that States modernize their piracy legislation in accordance with UNCLOS, which should include the obligation to exercise jurisdiction not only in connection with piracy incidents against the country's own ships, but also in connection with ships flying the flag of other countries affected by piracy. Once uniform piracy legislation would be in place worldwide, clear distinctions could be established between piracy as a crime subject to universal jurisdiction on the one hand, and unlawful acts under the

---

[681] N.D. Korolyova, *International Legal Issues of Cooperation Between States in Suppressing Piracy and Terrorism: Some Aspects*, Moscow Symposium on the Law of the Sea, T.A. Clingan, Jr. & A.L. Kolodkin (eds.), at 177 (1988); see also Treves, *The SUA Convention* (note 607), at 544. The IMO considers the SUA Convention to be a "relevant treaty" for the suppression of piracy; see Virginia Commentary, Vol. III (note 273), at 185.

[682] UN Security Council Res. 1846 (note 505).

[683] Id. op. para. 15. See also Kraska & Wilson, *Piracy Repression, Partnering and the Law* (note 386), at 56. The use of the SUA Convention for prosecuting pirates was affirmed by UN Security Council Res. 1851 of 16 December 2008, op. para. 5.

[684] See UN Security Council Res. 1846 (note 505), op. para. 15.

[685] See Blanco-Bazán, *Suppressing Unlawful Acts* (note 647), at 267.

SUA Convention on the other, to be counteracted not through universal, but through multiple jurisdiction.[686]

F. *Current Situation*

While piracy is an age-old phenomenon plaguing mankind, terrorism at sea has only manifested itself in recent times with the hijacking of the Italian cruise ship *Achille Lauro* in 1985 serving as a wake-up call. Because the rules of international law relating to piracy are not applicable *mutatis mutandis* to maritime terrorism, the international community has since been striving to adopt a series of legal as well as practical measures in order to prevent the recurrence of such a terrorist act in the future. The 1988 SUA Convention and Protocol addressed the danger of terrorism at sea for the first time, constituting an important milestone in the development of an international anti-terrorist legislation. These instruments were a continuation of the "sectoral" approach of dealing with international terrorism. Additionally, they represented an important extension of a cooperative law enforcement regime into a wholly new area[687] because they contained a finely balanced *aut dedere aut iudicare* scheme and gave preference to the specific enumeration of offenses over any attempt to define terrorism or terrorist acts.[688] These instruments, however, faced the criticism that they were of a reactive rather than a preventative nature.[689]

The terrorist attacks of September 11, 2001 were a gruesome demonstration that means of transport can be used as a weapon of mass destruction.[690] As a result, it became obvious that the 1988 SUA Convention and Protocol required revision and updating in order to be rendered more effective. The 2005 Protocols to these instruments significantly expanded their scope by providing for the first time an international treaty framework for combating and prosecuting individuals who use ships as weapons or as a means of committing a terrorist attack or transporting terrorists or cargo intended for use in connection with weapons of mass destruction programs. It is also no longer possible for a State party to refuse a request for extradition or for mutual legal assistance on the

---

[686] See id.

[687] See Freestone, *The 1988 SUA Convention* (note 603), at 316.

[688] Plant, *The SUA Convention* (note 596), at 56.

[689] See Mellor, *Missing the Boat: Problems of the Prevention of Maritime Terrorism* (note 628), at 384; Sittnick, *State Responsibility and Maritime Terrorism in the Strait of Malacca* (note 571), at 760–761.

[690] N. Khalid, *A Rush of Blood to the Head? Some Reflections on Post-9/11 Maritime Security Measures*, 21 Ocean Yearbook, at 523 (2007).

grounds that the offense may be characterized as politically inspired or motivated.[691]

As long as the 2005 SUA Convention and Protocol have not been more widely ratified, the Proliferation-Security-Initiative (PSI) announced by the United States in 2003,[692] which has since been endorsed by 97 nations,[693] will remain the most important tool to fight the proliferation of weapons of mass destruction using maritime transportation.[694] The PSI is a multilateral initiative with the objective to interdict the "transfer or transport of weapons of mass destruction, their delivery systems, and related materials to and from States and non-State actors of proliferation concern."[695] It furthermore explicitly contemplates boarding ships and, if necessary, using armed forces to seize weapons and the materials used to make them.[696] The PSI is not based on an international agreement, but constitutes a political alliance[697] which has been endorsed by the UN Secretary-General as well as to a large extent also by the Security Council in resolutions adopted under Chapter VII of the Charter.[698]

The United States has further negotiated a number of bilateral PSI ship boarding agreements, particularly with countries having the largest ship registries[699] in the world, whose regulations contain more stringent restrictions of

---

[691] Balkin, *The IMO and Maritime Security* (note 470), at 31.

[692] Remarks by President George W. Bush to the People of Poland, 31 May 2003, available at: georgewbush-whitehouse.archives.gov/news/releases/2003/05/20030531-3.html (last visited 1 July 2011); see also C.C. Joyner, *The Proliferation Security Initiative: Nonproliferation, Counterproliferation, and International Law*, 30 Yale Journal of International Law, at 508 (2005).

[693] See US Department of State, Proliferation Security Initiative, Participants, available at, www.state.gov/t/isn/c27732.htm (last visited 1 July 2011). See also Statement of Admiral Patrick M. Walsh (note 89). See further T.V. Thomas, *The Proliferation Security Initiative: Towards Relegation of Navigational Freedom in UNCLOS? An Indian Perspective*, 8/3 Chinese Journal of International Law, at 657 (2009).

[694] Witschel, Mare *Liberum and Maritime Security: Contradiction or Complementarity?* (note 672), at 114.

[695] Wolfrum, *Fighting Terrorism at Sea* (note 426), at 21.

[696] M.R. Shulman, *The Proliferation Security Initiative and the Evolution of the Law on the Use of Force*, 28 Houston Journal of International Law, at 774–75 (2006).

[697] Witschel, *Mare Liberum and Maritime Security: Contradiction or Complementarity?* (note 672), at 112.

[698] Thomas, *The Proliferation Security Initiative: An Indian Perspective* (note 693), at 1; UN Security Council Res. 1540 of 28 April 2004 on Non-proliferation of weapons of mass destruction, adopted unanimously, called on all States to take cooperative action to prevent trafficking in weapons of mass destruction; see further on the Proliferation Security Initiative: www.state.gov/t/isn/c10390.htm (last visited 1 July 2011).

[699] W. Boese, *Proliferation Security Initiative: A Piece of the Arms Control Puzzle*, 6 Georgetown Journal of International Affairs, at 64 (2005); S.E. Logan, *The Proliferation Security Initiative: Navigating the Legal Challenges*, 14 Journal of Transnational Law & Policy, at 273 (2004–2005); see also Chatham House, *Ship-Boarding: An Effective Measure Against Terrorism and*

the flag State principle in connection with ship boarding than the revised SUA Convention.[700] Each such boarding agreement conveys the willingness of the governments involved to allow their ships to be stopped and searched on a case-by-case basis if they are suspected of transporting weapons of mass destruction or related materials. These agreements further establish an expedited process to ask for boarding permission. A failure to respond to the request within two, respectively four hours will be treated as a green light to board the ship.[701]

Taking into account the changing nature of the terrorist threat, which has grown more urgent in recent years, international law is slowly adapting to become a more efficient means for fighting terrorism at sea. The interdependent nature of the world's economies also means that a successful terrorist attack on the international transport system might well trigger a chain reaction that could affect the entire world.[702] Nevertheless, whatever the legal and practical measures devised by the international community in order to combat maritime terrorism may be, no one can ever say with certainty that these will be sufficient or effective to deter a terrorist attack.[703] These measures could only prove their true value in the face of a planned, imminent or actual attack. No one would, however, wish that we have to face that test.[704]

WMD Proliferation?, available at: www.chathamhouse.org.uk/publications/papers/view/-/id/318/ (last visited 1 July 2011). The United States has entered into bilateral ship-boarding agreements with the Bahamas, Belize, Croatia, Cyprus, Liberia, Malta, the Marshall Islands, Mongolia, Panama, Antigua and Barbuda and St. Vincent and the Grenadines, available at: www.state.gov/t/isn/c27733.htm (last visited 1 July 2011); see also Thomas, *The Proliferation Security Initiative: An Indian Perspective* (note 693), at 652, footnote 37.

[700] See Shulman, *The Proliferation Security Initiative and the Evolution of the Law on the Use of Force* (note 696), at 691.

[701] Boese, *Proliferation Security Initiative: A Piece of the Arms Control Puzzle* (note 699), at 64. The time allowed for a response is, for instance, two hours for Belize, Liberia and Panama; and four hours for Cyprus and the Marshall Islands; see Klein, *The Right of Visit and the 2005 SUA Protocol* (note 70), at 312–313.

[702] See Balkin, *The IMO and Maritime Security* (note 470), at 34.

[703] See Khalid, *A Rush of Blood to the Head? Post-9/11 Maritime Security Measures* (note 690), at 523.

[704] See also Tuerk, *Combating Terrorism at Sea* (note 569), at 367.

Chapter Seven

The International Tribunal for the Law of the Sea (ITLOS)[705]

A. *UNCLOS and the Settlement of Disputes*

Since its entry into force, UNCLOS has undoubtedly played a major role in bringing order to the oceans and eliminating the causes for many maritime disputes between States. This is facilitated by the fact that the Convention, as already mentioned, contains quite an innovative system for the settlement of disputes, perhaps one of the most far-reaching and complex systems of dispute settlement to be found anywhere in international law. There can be no doubt that the underlying rationale for the creation of such a system was the wish to safeguard the many delicate compromises enshrined in that instrument and to secure its uniform interpretation and application.[706] The negotiators at the Third United Nations Conference on the Law of the Sea strongly believed that compulsory third-party dispute settlement should be an essential feature of

---

[705] For this chapter see in particular H. Tuerk, *The Work of the International Tribunal for the Law of the Sea*, 26 Ocean Yearbook, A. Chircop, S. Coffen-Smout and M. McConnel (eds.), Brill Publishers (2012), forthcoming; see also H. Tuerk, *The Contribution of ITLOS to International Law*, 26/2 Penn State International Law Review, 289–316 (2007); see further the article on the same topic in: Maritime Boundary Disputes, Settlement Processes, and the Law of the Sea, S.-Y. Hong & J.M. Van Dyke (eds.), 253–275 (2009); see also Tuerk, *The Contribution of ITLOS to International Law, in: The International Legal Regime of Areas Beyond National Jurisdiction: Current and Future Developments*, A.G. Oude Elferink and E.J. Molenaar (eds.), 217–230 (2010); see further H. Tuerk, *Zwölf Jahre Internationaler Seegerichtshof*, in: Die Welt im Spannungsfeld zwischen Regionalisierung und Globalisierung – Festschrift für Heribert Franz Köck, P. Fischer et al. (eds.), 479–498 (2009); see further R. Wolfrum, *The Settlement of Disputes before the International Tribunal for the Law of the Sea-A Progressive Development of International Law or Relying on Traditional Mechanisms?*, in: 51 Japanese Yearbook of International Law, 140–163 (2008); see also R. Mackenzie, et al., *The International Tribunal for the Law of the Sea*, Manual on International Courts and Tribunals, I Global Courts, 40–71 (2010); see further Z. Keyuan, *The International Tribunal for the Law of the Sea: Procedures, Practices, and Asian States*, 41 Ocean Development & International Law, 131–151 (2010).

[706] R.R. Churchill, *Some Reflections on the Operation of the Dispute Settlement System of the UN Convention on the Law of the Sea During its First Decade*, in: Law of the Sea – Progress and Prospects, D. Freestone, R. Barnes & D.M. Ong, (eds.), at 388 (2006).

the new Convention.[707] While compulsory dispute settlement is integral to the effective operation of UNCLOS, the emphasis is nevertheless on consent-based modes of dispute settlement and choice of procedures.[708]

The settlement of disputes is dealt with in Part XV of UNCLOS,[709] which imposes an obligation on States parties to settle disputes by peaceful means and in its Section 2 provides for compulsory procedures with binding decisions.[710] Prior to the resort to such procedures, States parties must have recourse to alternative methods of dispute settlement. Section 1 of Part XV permits them to utilize a wide range of peaceful methods, including settlement under separate agreements. Negotiation and settlement through diplomatic channels is emphasized through the obligation to exchange views. The use of conciliation is also encouraged through the inclusion of a separate procedure in Annex V to UNCLOS. Furthermore, States have the possibility to utilize procedures entailing binding decisions, under general, regional or bilateral agreements instead of those enshrined in Part XV.[711] States parties are thus accorded a great deal of flexibility in choosing methods for dispute resolution, and remain complete masters regarding the manner of settling their disputes peacefully.[712]

Annex VI to the Convention contains the Statute of ITLOS which is, however, only one of four means for the settlement of disputes entailing binding decisions. The alternative means are the ICJ, an arbitral tribunal constituted in accordance with Annex VII and a special arbitral tribunal under Annex VIII for certain categories of disputes – fisheries, protection and preservation of the marine environment, marine scientific research or navigation, including pollution from vessels and dumping.[713] Such flexibility as to the choice of fora

---

[707] J.E. Noyes, *Judicial and Arbitral Proceedings and the Outer Limit of the Continental Shelf* (note 207), at 3; see also Noyes, *Compulsory Third-Party Adjudication and the 1982 United Nations Convention on the Law of the Sea*, 4 Connecticut Journal of International Law, at 677–679 (1988–1989); see further Noyes, *The International Tribunal for the Law of the Sea*, 32 Cornell International Law Journal, at 115–116 (1999).

[708] N. Klein, Dispute Settlement in the UN Convention on the Law of the Sea, at 30 (2005).

[709] See Arts. 279–299 UNCLOS.

[710] See also T. Treves, *The Exclusive Economic Zone and the Settlement of Disputes*, in: The Exclusive Economic Zone and the United Nations Convention on the Law of the Sea, 1982–2000: A Preliminary Assessment of State Practice, E. Franckx & P. Gautier (eds.), at 79 (2003). Treves underlines the fact that compared to the provisions concerning the settlement of disputes "contained in other 'codification conventions', the system for the settlement of disputes in the United Nations Convention on the Law of the Sea is remarkably different, because it provides, as a rule, the possibility of compulsory settlement".

[711] See Klein, Dispute Settlement in UNCLOS (note 708), at 31.

[712] Id., at 32.

[713] See Art. 287 (1) UNCLOS. To date there have been no instances of disputes being referred to arbitration in accordance with Annex VIII. Given that only nine States parties to UNCLOS have so far selected Annex VIII arbitration as one of their preferred means of settlement,

available to States parties was indispensable in order to achieve consensus on compulsory dispute settlement at the Conference on the Law of the Sea.[714] It has rightly been pointed out that this user-friendly mechanism is the distinctive feature of the dispute settlement system under UNCLOS, reflecting the trend of modern international law with its diversity and flexibility of response in terms of the peaceful settlement of disputes tailored to meet the needs of present-day international society.[715]

The question of the establishment of a special tribunal within the framework of UNCLOS was originally dealt with in the context of the creation of the ISA to be entrusted with the task of administering the resources of the deep seabed beyond the limits of national jurisdiction as the "common heritage of mankind". This new tribunal was to be one of the principal organs of the Authority, following the example of the ICJ – the "principal judicial organ of the United Nations".[716] In the course of the negotiations this approach was, however, abandoned in favor of establishing a full-fledged Tribunal for the settlement of all law of the sea disputes as an autonomous international organization, not part of any other organ set up by UNCLOS, with a special Seabed Disputes Chamber.[717] The term "Tribunal", which may lead to some confusion in particular with respect to *ad hoc* tribunals, was used in order to distinguish this new institution from the ICJ.

A major reason for the establishment of a Tribunal with full competence concerning law of the sea disputes was the reluctance of a considerable number of States to have such disputes decided solely by the ICJ or by arbitral tribunals. Whereas the ICJ is a world court in general, the Tribunal is a world court on the law of the sea.[718] Even States that are not parties to UNCLOS may become parties to cases before it.[719] In view of the vast expanse of the world's oceans

---

the chances of a dispute being referred to such arbitration are currently rather small. See R.R. Churchill, *Dispute Settlement under the UN Convention on the Law of the Sea: Survey for 2008*, 24/4 The International Journal of Marine and Coastal Law, at 614 (2009).

[714] Klein, Dispute Settlement in UNCLOS (note 708), at 54.

[715] L.D.M. Nelson, *The Settlement of Disputes Arising from Conflicting Outer Continental Shelf Claims*, 24/2 The International Journal of Marine and Coastal Law, at 410 (2009).

[716] Art. 1 of the Statute of the ICJ.

[717] A.O. Adede, *The System for Settlement of Disputes under the United Nations Convention on the Law of the Sea – A Drafting History and a Commentary*, 10 Publications on Ocean Development, at 173–174 (1987); see also A.K. Escher, *Release of Vessels and Crews before the International Tribunal for the Law of the Sea*, 3/2 The Law and Practice of International Courts and Tribunals: A Practitioner's Journal, E. Valencia-Ospina (ed.), at 237–238 (2004).

[718] P. Chandrasekhara Rao, *ITLOS: The Conception of the Judicial Function*, in: Coexistence, Cooperation and Solidarity, Liber Amicorum Rüdiger Wolfrum, Holger P. Hestermeyer/ D. Koenig et al. (eds.), vol. 2, at 1087 (2012).

[719] Id., at 4.

and seas ITLOS has the largest geographical jurisdiction in the world, besides the ICJ.[720]

The principal provision of Part XV is Article 287, which outlines various procedures available to parties to settle their disputes peacefully through the compulsory mechanisms established by it.[721] This Article provides that a State party, when signing, ratifying or acceding to the Convention or at any time thereupon, is free to choose one or more of the aforementioned four means for the settlement of disputes, by submission of a written declaration to the UN Secretary-General. So far only 45 States have made such a declaration – 32 of which have chosen ITLOS as preferred procedure or as one possibility.[722] In the absence of such a declaration or if the parties have not accepted the same procedure under Article 287, they are deemed to have accepted arbitration under Annex VII to UNCLOS, which is thus the default procedure. It might have been preferable to provide for a residual competence of ITLOS but such a solution was not within reach during the negotiations at the Conference on the Law of the Sea.

B. *Composition and Structure of ITLOS*[723]

ITLOS, which became operational on October 1, 1996, is the specialized international judicial body established for the settlement of disputes concerning the interpretation or application of UNCLOS, and for rendering advisory opinions.[724] It is the largest world-wide judicial body, composed of 21 judges "with recognized competence in the field of the law of the sea".[725] The judges are elected by the States parties to the Convention for a term of nine years,

---

[720] See Tuerk, *The Contribution of ITLOS to International Law* (note 705), at 291.

[721] D.R. Rothwell, *The International Tribunal for the Law of the Sea and Marine Environmental Protection: Expanding the Horizons of International Ocean Governance*, 17 Ocean Yearbook, at 32 (2003).

[722] For a list of these Declarations see: www.un.org/Depts/los/convention_agreements/convention_declarations.htm (last visited 1 July 2011). The Russian Federation, Ukraine and Belarus have recognized ITLOS only for prompt release cases and St. Vincent and the Grenadines only for the arrest and detention of vessels. The declarations of Bangladesh and Myanmar are restricted to a specific dispute and are thus not being counted.

[723] See Annex VI to UNCLOS, which contains the Statute of the International Tribunal for the Law of the Sea. See also the ITLOS publication "A Guide to Proceedings before the Tribunal" (2009/1), in particular at 3–9, available at the official ITLOS website www.itlos.org.

[724] See also P. Chandrasekhara Rao, *ITLOS: The First Six Years*, 6 *Max Planck Yearbook of United Nations Law*, A. von Bogdandy and R. Wolfrum (eds.), at 185 (2002), and L. Dolliver M. Nelson, *Reflections on the 1982 Convention on the Law of the Sea*, in: Law of the Sea: Progress and Prospects, D. Freestone, R. Barnes, D. Ong (eds.), at 35 (2006).

[725] See Art. 2 Annex VI to UNCLOS.

whereby the term of one third of the members of the Tribunal expires every three years, following the system of the ICJ. Experience has shown that these regular changes in the composition of the Tribunal have not altered the legal perspective of the judges.[726] The composition of ITLOS must ensure adequate representation of the principal legal systems of the world, and an equitable geographical distribution. In comparison with the ICJ, added weight has been given to developing countries in the composition of the Tribunal.[727] So far, the geographical origin of the judges, however, seems to have had little influence, if any at all, on the decisions of ITLOS.[728]

The States parties to the Convention had originally agreed to elect five judges each from Africa and Asia, four each from Latin American and Caribbean States as well as from Western European and Other States and three from the Eastern European States Group.[729] This arrangement was, however, subsequently changed upon the insistence of the African and the Asian Group. As of 2011 there is thus one seat previously assigned to the Western and Other States, floating between that Group and the African and the Asian Group.[730] If the Tribunal does not include upon the bench a judge of the nationality of a party to a dispute, that party may designate a person of its choice to sit as a judge *ad hoc*[731] which has become prevailing practice.

The President and the Vice-President of ITLOS are elected by secret ballot by a majority of the members for a period of three years and may be re-elected.[732] Re-election has so far not happened in practice as the Tribunal has strictly adhered to the system of rotation among the different regional groups. The President chairs all the meetings of the Tribunal, directs its work, supervises its administration and represents it in its relations with States and other entities. In the event of an equality of votes, the President has a casting vote. The administrative organ of ITLOS is the Registry, headed by the Registrar, and is composed of a small international staff. The Registrar and his deputy are elected by the judges for a term of five years.[733]

---

[726] See P. Chandrasekhara Rao, *ITLOS: The Conception of the Judicial Function* (note 718), at 1101.
[727] A.E. Boyle, *The International Tribunal for the Law of the Sea and the Settlement of Disputes*, in: The Changing World of International Law in the Twenty-First Century, J.J. Norton et al. (eds.), at 118 (1998).
[728] See also R. Wolfrum, *Der Internationale Seegerichtshof*, in: Handbuch des Seerechts, W. Graf Vitzthum (ed.), at 476 (2006).
[729] Id.
[730] See P. Gautier, *The International Tribunal for the Law of the Sea: Activities in 2009*, 9/4 Chinese Journal of International Law, at 786 (2010).
[731] See Art. 17 (2) and (3) Annex VI to UNCLOS.
[732] Art. 12 (3), Annex VI to UNCLOS.
[733] Tuerk, *Zwölf Jahre Internationaler Seegerichtshof* (note 705), at 485.

The Statute of ITLOS provides that the President and the Registrar shall reside at its seat[734] while the other judges only travel to Hamburg for sessions. The reason for such a provision is that the negotiators of the Convention believed that the low workload during the first years of the existence of the Tribunal would not justify a permanent presence of the judges at its seat.[735] Although this system may make sense from a economic point of view, it would nevertheless have been more conducive to enhancing the international standing of this new judicial institution to provide for the presence in Hamburg not only of the President, but also of the Vice-President and a judge from each one of the five geographical regions. In such a manner, a court permanently in session could have been created with justifiable expenditure.[736]

The Statute of ITLOS contains a provision for the establishment of the Seabed Disputes Chamber as well as special chambers for dealing with particular disputes or categories of disputes.[737] The Seabed Disputes Chamber, which is a "tribunal within a tribunal", consists of 11 judges, each of whom is selected every three years by a majority of the members of the Tribunal. With respect to the election of the members of this Chamber the Assembly of the ISA may adopt recommendations of a general nature regarding the representation of the principal legal systems of the world and equitable geographical distribution.[738] To date, no such recommendations have been made.

Following a similar system of the ICJ, ITLOS established several special chambers. These are the Chamber of Summary Procedure, composed of the President, the Vice-President, acting *ex officio,* three other members and two alternates, the Chamber for Fisheries Disputes and the Chamber for Marine Environment Disputes, each consisting of seven members of the Tribunal, and the Chamber for Maritime Delimitation Disputes comprising eight judges. A judgment given by any of the special chambers is considered to have been rendered by the full Tribunal.[739]

More important in practice, however, seems to be the possibility to form an *ad hoc* special chamber, which consists of at least three members, who may be chosen from among the members of the Tribunal; the parties may also designate *ad hoc* judges.[740] That system should be of particular interest to parties considering arbitration, since, as in arbitration, parties are given substantial

---

[734] Art. 2 (3), Annex VI to UNCLOS.
[735] Wolfrum, *Der Internationale Seegerichtshof* (note 728), at 418.
[736] See also Tuerk, *Zwölf Jahre Internationaler Seegerichtshof* (note 705), at 137.
[737] See Art. 14 respectively 15, Annex VI to UNCLOS.
[738] See Art. 35 paras. 1 and 2 of Annex VI to UNCLOS.
[739] See Art. 15, Annex VI to UNCLOS.
[740] See Arts. 19–22 Rules of the Tribunal, ITLOS doc. ITLOS/8, 17 March 2009, available at: www.itlos.org.

freedom to choose the judges who are to sit in such a chamber, and may even propose modifications to the Tribunal's rules of procedure for the chamber to apply. Thus, the parties can enjoy all the benefits of arbitration, without being required to bear the expenses of the chamber.[741]

So far, the system of special chambers – apart from *ad hoc* chambers – has not proven particularly successful. Until now, the cases dealt with by ITLOS, with one exception of an ad hoc chamber and one case – a request for an advisory opinion submitted to the Seabed Disputes Chamber on the basis of its exclusive jurisdiction – have been submitted to the full Tribunal. This reflects the reality that chambers do not deliver their orders or judgments any more quickly than does the full Tribunal, nor are the costs for the parties significantly lower. Parties to a dispute might even consider that the judgment of a full Tribunal stands on a higher footing than a judgment of a chamber – although the legally binding nature of the decision rendered is exactly the same in both cases.[742] Likewise, recourse to the system of chambers offered by the ICJ has been made in only a modest number of cases.

Recourse to ITLOS involves no costs for the States parties to UNCLOS. When a dispute involves an entity that is neither a State party nor the ISA, the Tribunal fixes the amount which that party must contribute towards the expenses of the Tribunal.[743] Other costs, notably the fees for legal representation, are borne by the party incurring them, unless decided otherwise by the Tribunal.[744] A trust fund to assist developing States to settle their disputes through the Tribunal has been established by the UN Secretary-General, following a decision of the General Assembly.[745] So far, this fund has not been made use of.

C. *The Jurisdiction of ITLOS*

The jurisdiction of ITLOS, in principle, includes any dispute relating to the law of the sea, such as disputes relating to maritime boundaries, fisheries, sea pollution or marine scientific research. Its jurisdiction is, however, subject to limitations spelled out in Article 297 of UNCLOS that relates to the exercise of certain discretionary powers by the coastal State, in particular, disputes relating to its sovereign rights in respect of fisheries in the EEZ. Furthermore, according

---

[741] See Chandrasekhara Rao, *ITLOS: The First Six Years* (note 724), at 194.
[742] Id., at 195.
[743] See Art. 19 Annex VI to UNCLOS.
[744] See Art. 34 Annex VI to UNCLOS.
[745] See UN General Assembly Resolution 55/7 of 30 October 2000. For further information see www.un.org/Depts/los/ITLOS/itlos_trust_fund.htm (last visited 1 July 2011).

to Article 298, exceptions to the compulsory procedures may also be made by virtue of written declarations for matters concerning sea boundary delimitations, historic bays or titles, military activities, certain enforcement activities in the exercise of sovereign rights in the EEZ and disputes in which the UN Security Council is exercising its functions under Chapter VII of the Charter. States parties have so far used article 298 of the Convention rather restrictively as to date only 33 such declarations have been made.[746]

In two instances, ITLOS has compulsory jurisdiction: Article 290(5) regarding provisional measures, and Article 292 concerning the prompt release of vessels and/or crews, independently of the choice of procedure mechanism under Article 287. These particular instances of compulsory jurisdiction have been entrusted to the Tribunal because they concern functions that cannot properly be performed by an arbitral tribunal.[747] The drafters of UNCLOS therefore considered that such matters should be resolved by a permanently established body. Furthermore, it should be borne in mind that only permanent tribunals are institutions that allow the development of a corpus of jurisprudence as they have the capacity and the obligation to create a body of decisional law that will serve the long-term interests of all States.[748]

It is important to note that a State party is supposed to have accepted compulsory procedure by the mere fact of having ratified or adhered to UNCLOS in respect of any dispute arising hereunder, unless it expressly excludes the application of this type of procedure. There is thus no need to make a separate declaration to accept the compulsory procedure, a declaration being required only to exclude such procedure. This is a significant innovation with respect to the traditional compulsory jurisdiction system, which requires separate consent, as is the case with Article 36(2) of the Statute of the ICJ.

Submissions to ITLOS may also be made on a consensual basis through an ad hoc special agreement, a traditional possibility referred to in Article 24(1) of the Statute. A variant thereof is the *forum prorogatum* where one party makes a unilateral application and the other party to the dispute consents. A consensual submission does, however, not necessarily exclude disputes regarding the jurisdiction of the Tribunal.[749] Article 22 of the Statute further allows ITLOS to exercise jurisdiction over disputes relating to the interpretation or application of

---

[746] See: treaties.un.org/Pages/ViewDetailsIII.aspx?&src=TREATY&mtdsg_no=XXI-6&chapter=21&Temp=mtdsg3&lang=en (last visited 1 July 2011).

[747] T. Treves, *The Jurisdiction of the International Tribunal for the Law of the Sea*, 37 Indian Journal of International Law, at 400 (1997).

[748] Judge R. Wolfrum, President of ITLOS, Statement to the Sixth Committee of the UN General Assembly, 20 October 2006, at 6, available at: www.itlos.org.

[749] Wolfrum, *The Settlement of Disputes Before the ITLOS: Progressive or Traditional?* (note 705), at 148.

treaties already in force, and concern the subject-matter covered by the Convention, provided that all the parties to that treaty so agree.[750]

The jurisdiction of ITLOS may furthermore derive from relevant clauses included in international agreements relating to the law of the sea.[751] At present, there are ten international agreements – six of which are fisheries-related – containing provisions making specific reference to the dispute settlement procedures of Part XV of UNCLOS and conferring therewith jurisdiction on the Tribunal.[752] The best known are the 1995 Fish Stocks Agreement,[753] the 2001 UNESCO Convention on the Protection of the Underwater Cultural Heritage[754] and the 2007 Nairobi International Convention on the Removal of Wrecks.[755] With respect to these agreements, the procedures of Part XV apply, whether a party to the agreement is a State party to UNCLOS or not. The inclusion of such jurisdictional clauses has thus become an established practice and it can only be of benefit to the parties if such clauses are included in every new maritime agreement that is being negotiated.[756] In this connection it has to be borne in mind that the ICJ is already referred to as the dispute settlement mechanism in more than 150 international agreements, most of which have been concluded long before the establishment of ITLOS. This is undoubtedly an important reason why the Court is being used more often for the settling of maritime disputes than the Tribunal.[757]

UNCLOS does not contain any provision conferring advisory jurisdiction on the Tribunal as such, which may, however, on the basis of Article 21 of its Statute give an advisory opinion on a legal question if this is provided for by an international agreement related to the purposes of the Convention conferring

---

[750] Id., at 8.

[751] See Guide to Proceedings before the Tribunal (note 723), at 6.

[752] See id., Annex 1, at 39, listing these agreements; see also Statement by Mr. Doo-young Kim, Deputy Registrar of ITLOS, reproduced as Appendix G to the Report of the First Meeting of Regional Fishery Body Secretariats Network, at 4, FAO doc. FIEL/R837 (12–13 March 2007).

[753] Fish Stocks Agreement (note 12).

[754] UNESCO Convention on the Protection of the Underwater Cultural Heritage, 2 November 2001, 41 ILM 40 (2002), available at: unesdoc.unesco.org/images/0014/001430/143085e.pdf (last visited 1 July 2011).

[755] Nairobi International Convention on the Removal of Wrecks, 18 May 2007, IMO doc. LEG/CONF.16/19 (23 May 2007), available at: www.basel.int/ships/abandonment/wrc.pdf (last visited 1 July 2011).

[756] Judge R. Wolfrum, President of ITLOS, Statement on the Report of the Tribunal to the Sixteenth Meeting of States parties to UNCLOS, 19 June 2006, at 7, available at: www.itlos.org.

[757] Judge R. Wolfrum, President of ITLOS, Statement on 'The Value for Hamburg of the International Tribunal for the Law of the Sea – Profile, Expectations and Reality' at the Übersee-Club, Hamburg, 27 February 2008, at 13, available at: www.itlos.org.

jurisdiction on it.[758] Although no request for advisory opinions has so far been made, the advisory function of ITLOS as a full court could provide a flexible mechanism for those seeking to clarify points of law or legal questions concerning the interpretation or application of the provisions of UNCLOS.[759] This might constitute a useful tool for States seeking to reconcile differences relating thereto without wishing to engage in a controversial procedure.[760]

The law to be applied by ITLOS comprises the Convention, and other rules of international law not incompatible with it,[761] while there is no such hierarchy of norms to be taken into account by the ICJ.[762] This does not, however, preclude the Tribunal from holding jurisdiction to determine a matter *ex aequo et bono*,[763] if the parties so agree. As a general rule, the judgments and orders of ITLOS, like those of the ICJ, contain compromise elements.[764] More than half of the decisions so far rendered by the Tribunal have been adopted unanimously which is strengthening its authority. Decisions are final and the parties to the dispute are required to comply with them, which has thus far always been the case. The decisions, however, have no binding force beyond the parties to the dispute,[765] although they may be quite significant for the development of the law of the sea in general, and may, in addition, influence the future inter-

---

[758] The respective Article 138 of the Rules of the Tribunal is based on Article 21 of its Statute, which states that the jurisdiction of the Tribunal comprises "all disputes and all applications submitted to it in accordance with this Convention and all matters specifically provided for in any other agreement which confers jurisdiction on the Tribunal". See generally H. Tuerk, *Advisory Opinions and the Law of the Sea*, in: The Challenges of Contemporary International Law and International Relations – Liber Amicorum Dr. Ernest Petrič, M. Pogačnik et al. (eds.). European Law Faculty of Nova Gorica (2011), forthcoming; see also H. Caminos, *The International Tribunal for the Law of the Sea: An Overview of its Jurisdictional Procedure*, in: New International Tribunals and New International Proceedings, A. Del Vecchio (ed.), at 22 (2006).

[759] See R. Wolfrum, *The Tenth Anniversary of the International Tribunal for the Law of the Sea*, 2/3 Romanian Journal of International Law, at 76–77 (2006). Wolfrum points out that the advisory function of the Tribunal is a significant innovation in the international judicial system and may offer a potential alternative for those seeking a non-binding opinion on a legal question or an indication as to how a particular dispute may be solved through direct negotiations. Such proceedings could be of particular assistance to parties to a dispute in the process of reaching a solution by negotiation, for example in maritime delimitation cases.

[760] Statement by Judge J.L. Jesus, President of ITLOS, at the OLDEPESCA XX Conference of Ministers, La Paz, Bolivia, 2 September 2009, at 6, available at: www.itlos.org.

[761] See Art. 293 UNCLOS.

[762] R. Wolfrum, *Advisory Opinions: Are They a Suitable Alternative for the Settlement of International Disputes?* (to be published, on file with author), at 61 (2011).

[763] Rothwell, *ITLOS and Marine Environmental Protection* (note 721), at 33.

[764] P. Chandrasekhara Rao, *ITLOS: The Conception of the Judicial Function* (note 718), at 1100.

[765] See Art. 296 UNCLOS.

pretation of this body of law. It should also be noted that the parties have no recourse to appeal against a decision of the Tribunal.[766]

ITLOS is open to States parties to UNCLOS, other States, as well as other entities, such as international organizations and natural or legal persons in any case expressly provided for in Part XI of UNCLOS – relating to the exploration and exploitation of the international seabed "Area" – or in any case submitted pursuant to any other agreement conferring jurisdiction on the Tribunal that is accepted by all the parties to that case.[767] This procedural development broadening the jurisdiction of ITLOS *ratione personae* in a way that has not been done before, responds to the need to recognize the increasing role of international organizations and also to provide the operators and investors involved in deep seabed mining with an international judicial means to settle potential disputes.[768] It has been pointed out that the fact that the European Community – now the European Union – can be a party before ITLOS renders it the Community's preferred choice when it comes to disputes with third countries relating to the law of the sea.[769] Although the jurisdiction of ITLOS is not as broad *ratione materiae* as that of the ICJ, being confined to matters provided for in the Convention and related instruments, it is certainly more comprehensive *ratione personae*, as in cases before the Court only States may be parties.[770] Access is probably the most significant difference between the Tribunal and the ICJ.[771]

The Seabed Disputes Chamber has been granted exclusive and compulsory jurisdiction over disputes arising out of the exploration and exploitation of the "Area", independent of any choice of procedure made under Article 287 of UNCLOS.[772] The particular categories of disputes over which that Chamber has

---

[766] Rothwell, *ITLOS and Marine Environmental Protection* (note 721), at 34.

[767] See Art. 20, Annex VI to UNCLOS.

[768] Statement by Judge J.L. Jesus, President of ITLOS, The Gilberto Amado Memorial Lecture, held during the 61st Session of the ILC, Geneva, 15 July 2009, p. 6, available at www.itlos.org.

[769] Statement by Dr. Joe Borg, Commissioner for Fisheries and Maritime Affairs of the European Union on the occasion of his visit to the Tribunal on 2 September 2005, as quoted in the Speech by Judge R. Wolfrum, President of ITLOS, on the occasion of the Information Session organized by the Tribunal for the Diplomatic Corps, 6 October 2005, at 6, available at www.itlos.org.

[770] See Art. 34 (1) of the Statute of the International Court of Justice, available at www.icj-cij.org.

[771] A.E. Boyle, *Dispute Settlement and the Law of the Sea Convention: Problems of Fragmentation and Jurisdiction*, 46/1 International & Comparative Law Quarterly, at 51 (1997); see also R. Wolfrum, *Verfahren zur Freigabe von Schiffen vor dem Internationalen Seegerichtshof*, in: Seehandelsrecht und Seerecht: Festschrift für Rolf Herber zum 70. Geburtstag, R. Lagoni & M. Paschke (eds.), at 568 (1999).

[772] See also Presentation by Judge H. Tuerk, Vice-President of ITLOS, at the Seminar on Exploration and Exploitation of Deep Seabed Mineral Resources in the Area: Challenges for Africa, and Opportunities for Collaborative Research in the South Atlantic Ocean, Abuja, Nigeria, 24 March 2009, at 9–10, available at: www.itlos.org.

jurisdiction are listed in Article 187. A first category includes disputes between States parties concerning the interpretation of application of Part XI and the Annexes relating thereto. In such cases, the dispute may at the request of the parties, be submitted to a special chamber of the Tribunal, but it may also be submitted to an *ad hoc* chamber of the Seabed Disputes Chamber at the request of any party.[773] In addition, disputes between a State party and the ISA also fall within the scope of jurisdiction of the Seabed Disputes Chamber. These disputes may concern acts or omissions of the Authority or of a State party alleged to be in violation of Part XI and its Annexes or of rules, regulations and procedures of the Authority. They may also relate to acts of the Authority alleged to be in excess of jurisdiction or to be a misuse of power. Finally, there are the disputes between the ISA and a prospective contractor concerning the refusal of a contract or a legal issue arising in the negotiation of the contract as well as disputes involving the alleged liability of the Authority for any damage arising out of wrongful acts.

An arbitral tribunal dealing with a commercial dispute concerning activities in the "Area" must refer any question of the interpretation of Part XI of UNCLOS and the Annexes relating thereto to the Seabed Disputes Chamber, either at the request of any party to the dispute, or *proprio motu*.[774] The objective of this procedure is to ensure that the monopoly of the Chamber to interpret the deep seabed regime is not infringed upon.[775]

UNCLOS also sets some limitations on the jurisdiction of the Seabed Disputes Chamber designed to protect the Assembly and the Council of ISA from too much interference by a judicial organ.[776] The Chamber thus has no jurisdiction with regard to the exercise by the Authority of its discretionary powers. Nor does it have competence to pronounce itself on the question of whether any rules, regulations and procedures of the Authority are in conformity with the Convention, or to declare such rules, regulations and procedures invalid.[777] The Seabed Disputes Chamber may, however, give advisory opinions at the request of the Assembly or the Council of the ISA "on legal questions arising within the scope of their activities." Such opinions are to be given as a matter of urgency.[778] The Chamber may also be requested by the Assembly of the Authority to give an opinion as to the conformity with the Convention of a

---

[773] Art. 188 UNCLOS.

[774] Art. 188(2) UNCLOS.

[775] Wolfrum, *Advisory Opinions: Are They a Suitable Alternative for the Settlement of International Disputes?* (note 762), at 18.

[776] Virginia Commentary, Vol. VI, M. Nordquist, S. Nandan, S. Rosenne, M.W. Lodge (eds.), at 635 (1989).

[777] Art. 189 UNCLOS.

[778] Art. 191 UNCLOS.

proposal on any matter before it.[779] While the Council has already submitted one request for an advisory opinion, the Assembly has so far not made use of that possibility.

It is to be noted that the decisions of the Seabed Disputes Chamber are enforceable in the territories of the State parties in the same manner as judgments or orders of the highest court of the State party in whose territory the enforcement is sought.[780] This provision – which makes these decisions enforceable as a domestic matter[781] – has given rise to constitutional difficulties in certain countries as such direct enforcement of international judgments is rather exceptional. This rule, however, clearly reflects the intention of the framers of UNCLOS to make that Chamber the guarantor for upholding the rule of law regarding deep seabed activities on a worldwide scale. In that respect the functions of the Seabed Disputes Chamber might well be compared to that of a constitutional court.[782]

D. *The Jurisprudence of ITLOS*

1. *Provisional Measures*

ITLOS may be requested to prescribe provisional measures in two situations, first according to Article 290 (1) where a dispute on the merits has been submitted to it, and second on the basis of Article 290 (5) when such a dispute has been submitted to an arbitral tribunal, pending its constitution.[783] When provisional measures have been requested by a party to a dispute that has been submitted to an arbitral tribunal, ITLOS is empowered, pursuant to Article 290(5) UNCLOS, to grant such measures pending the constitution of the arbitral tribunal, unless the parties have agreed to seize another court or tribunal within two weeks from the date of the request for provisional measures. Thus, ITLOS may, at the request of a State party, prescribe provisional measures against another State party pending the final decision to be given not by the

---

[779] Art. 159, para. 10 UNCLOS.

[780] Art. 39 of the Statute of the Tribunal (note 21).

[781] Virginia Commentary, Vol. V, M.H. Nordquist, S. Rosenne & L.B. Sohn (eds.), at 414 (1989).

[782] Wolfrum, *Advisory Opinions: Are They a Suitable Alternative for the Settlement of International Disputes?* (note 762), at 16.

[783] Judge R. Wolfrum, President of ITLOS, Statement to the Sixth Committee of UNGA, 20 October 2006, at 5; available at www.itlos.org. According to Judge Wolfrum it is also of interest to note that under the Straddling Fish Stocks Agreement of 1995 the Tribunal is empowered to prescribe provisional measures to protect the rights of the parties as well as to prevent damage to the fish stocks in question.

Tribunal itself, but by an arbitral tribunal that is yet to be constituted. In order to prescribe provisional measures, ITLOS must consider that the measures are required by the urgency of the situation and that, *prima facie*, the arbitral tribunal to be constituted would have jurisdiction.

It is interesting to note in this regard important innovations introduced by UNCLOS. First, the measures prescribed by ITLOS are binding upon the parties to the dispute. Second, the Tribunal may prescribe provisional measures not only to preserve the respective rights of the parties to the dispute, but also to "prevent serious harm to the marine environment". This ground for provisional measures does not require the risk of irreparable harm which should make such measures under Article 290 particularly attractive in environmental cases.[784] Given the fact that it is not exceptional for States to grant oil or gas concessions or exploration permits or to conduct scientific activities in disputed maritime areas, recourse to provisional measures may serve very practical purposes, not only to prevent armed incidents in the area, but also to preserve the *status quo* pending a judicial decision.[785] In addition, ITLOS may follow up the measures it has prescribed by requesting the parties to submit reports on compliance.[786] In order to strengthen the pressure of public opinion on the parties with respect to provisional measures, the Tribunal also has the possibility to send the notices relating to the prescription, modification, or revocation of provisional measures,[787] not only to the parties to the dispute, but also to such other States parties to UNCLOS it considers appropriate. The Tribunal has so far made use of this possibility only once.[788]

The competence of ITLOS to prescribe provisional measures also reflects the importance the Convention attaches to the protection of the environment. Furthermore, provisional measures may also be prescribed to prevent damage to fish stocks regulated by the Fish Stocks Agreement. Such justifications for provisional measures add a new element to their general objective which is not directly linked to the interests of the parties to the dispute and thus makes the tribunal or court a mechanism working not only in the interest of the parties

---

[784] P. Gautier, *Urgent Proceedings before the International Tribunal for the Law of the Sea*, 8/1 Issues in Legal Scholarship, at 13 (2009).

[785] Id., at 17.

[786] Judge R. Wolfrum, President of ITLOS, Statement to the Informal Meeting of Legal Advisers of Ministries of Foreign Affairs, 24 October 2005, at 5, available at www.itlos.org.

[787] To date there are no cases where provisional measures prescribed by the Tribunal have been modified or revoked by the Tribunal or Annex VII tribunals.

[788] Only the Order of 27 August 1999 in the *Southern Bluefin Tuna* Cases made reference to the relevant Article 290 (4) of the Convention and Article 94 of the Rules of the Tribunal. The Tribunal decided that the provisional measures prescribed in this Order shall forthwith be notified by the Registrar through appropriate means to all States parties to the Convention participating in the fishery for southern bluefin tuna.

involved but also in that of the community of States. This reflects the change of international law from a mechanism providing for the coordination of States' activities to one recognizing and preserving common values of the international community.[789]

The Tribunal has to date been seized with requests for provisional measures in five cases: the *M/V Louisa Case* in connection with an application on the merits, the other four, pending the constitution of an arbitral tribunal, relating to the protection of the marine environment – the *Southern Bluefin Tuna Cases*, the *MOX Plant Case*, and the *Case concerning Land Reclamation by Singapore in and around the Straits of Johor*. No cases requesting provisional measures under Article 290 have so far been submitted to any other court or tribunal having jurisdiction under UNCLOS.

In the *M/V Louisa Case*,[790] *Saint Vincent and the Grenadines v. Spain*, ITLOS was seized with an application relating to the merits together with a request for provisional measures. The applicant requested the Tribunal, in particular, to order the release of the vessel and its tender – held by Spain since 1 February 2006 for alleged violation of Spain's historical patrimony – the return of scientific research, information and property, and to order the respondent to pay the costs incurred in connection with the request. In its Order of 23 December 2010, the Tribunal found that it had *prima facie* jurisdiction over the dispute and that there was no "real and imminent risk" that irreparable prejudice may be caused to the rights of the parties or to the marine environment on account of degradation of the vessel, considering the assurances given in this respect by Spain. In the circumstance of the case, the Tribunal saw no requirement to prescribe provisional measures, without in any way prejudging the question of its jurisdiction to deal with the merits and the merits themselves.

In the *Southern Bluefin Tuna Cases*,[791] the applicants, Australia and New Zealand, sought relief from ITLOS in relation to Japan's unilateral decision to conduct an experimental fishing program, which was planned for a duration of three years. The Tribunal was requested to prescribe provisional measures to the effect that Japan immediately cease its unilateral experimental fishing of

---

[789] Wolfrum, *The Settlement of Disputes Before ITLOS: Progressive or Traditional?* (note 705), at 155.

[790] *Louisa* (Saint Vincent and the Grenadines v. Spain), Provisional Measures, Order of 23 December 2010, ITLOS Press Releases No. 154, 24 November 2010, 156, 8 December 2010, 157, 20 December 2010, available at www.itlos.org.

[791] ITLOS, *Southern Bluefin Tuna* (New Zealand v. Japan; Australia v. Japan), Provisional Measures, Order of 27 August 1999, 3 ITLOS Reports (1999), at 280–336, reprinted in 38 ILM 1624 (1999); ITLOS Press Releases No. 27, 26 August 1999, and No. 28, 27 August 1999, available at: www.itlos.org.

southern bluefin tuna, restrict its catch to the national quotum as last agreed,[792] and require all parties to act consistently with the precautionary principle – caution and vigilance – in fishing for southern bluefin tuna pending final settlement of the dispute. In its Order of August 27, 1999, ITLOS considered that the parties should, in the circumstances, act with "prudence and caution" to ensure that effective conservation measures were taken to prevent serious harm to stock of southern bluefin tuna. It also ordered, *inter alia*, that the parties should resume negotiations without delay, with a view to reaching agreement on measures for the conservation and management of these fish stocks, and that the parties should restrict their catches.

What may be considered quite striking was the fact that ITLOS decided that all of the parties had to adhere to the annual national allocation that had last been agreed upon unless the parties were able to agree otherwise. The prescription of fish catch totals is normally an exercise of authority taking place on a national basis, or cooperatively between the relevant States.[793] Although there is no express reference in the Order to the precautionary principle itself, the Tribunal nevertheless prescribed de facto precautionary measures and seems at least implicitly to have relied on that principle.[794] It has also been observed that the Tribunal's intervention at the stage of provisional measures played a very significant role in bringing the parties – Australia, New Zealand and Japan – back to negotiations with each other, with the eventual result that the Southern Bluefin Tuna Commission was revitalized and is now functioning well.[795]

In the *MOX Plant Case*,[796] ITLOS heard a dispute between Ireland and the United Kingdom regarding the potentially harmful impact on the marine environment of the operation of a MOX plant situated at Sellafield, United Kingdom, on the coast of the Irish Sea. Such a plant recycles material from nuclear reactors and converts it into a new fuel called MOX – mixed oxide fuel – intended for use as an energy source in nuclear power stations. Ireland requested that the dispute be submitted to an arbitral tribunal to be established

---

[792] See Convention for the Conservation of Southern Bluefin Tuna, 10 May 1993, 1819 UNTS 359.

[793] Klein, Dispute Settlement in UNCLOS (note 708), at 81.

[794] G. Rashbrooke, *The International Tribunal for the Law of the Sea: A Forum for the Development of Principles of International Environmental Law*, 19/4 International Journal of Marine and Coastal Law, at 523 (2004); R. Rayfuse, *The Future of Compulsory Dispute Settlement Under the Law of the Sea Convention*, 36 Victoria University of Wellington Law Review, at 698 (2005).

[795] See Statement by Professor J. Crawford, Counsel in the *Southern Bluefin Tuna Cases*, as quoted in the Statement by Judge R. Wolfrum, President of ITLOS, to the Informal Meeting of Legal Advisers, 24 October 2005 (note 786), at 5.

[796] ITLOS, *MOX Plant* (Ireland v. United Kingdom), Provisional Measures, Order of 3 December 2001, 5 ITLOS Reports (2001), at 89–112, reprinted in 41 ILM 405 (2002); ITLOS Press Releases No. 61, 29 November 2001, and No. 62, 3 December 2001.

under Annex VII to UNCLOS, and furthermore submitted a request to the Tribunal for the prescription of provisional measures pending the constitution of the arbitral tribunal. In its Order of December 3, 2001, the Tribunal found that the urgency of the situation did not, in the short period before the constitution of the Annex VII arbitral tribunal, require the prescription of provisional measures as requested by Ireland. However, it did consider that the duty to co-operate is a fundamental principle in the prevention of pollution of the marine environment under Part XII of UNCLOS, as well as under general international law, and that rights arise therefrom which the Tribunal may consider appropriate to conserve under article 290 UNCLOS. The litigants were therefore ordered – pending a decision by the arbitral tribunal – to co-operate and enter into consultations in order to exchange further information regarding the possible consequences for the Irish Sea arising from the commissioning of the MOX plant, and to devise, as appropriate, measures to prevent pollution of the marine environment which might result from the plant's operation.

In its judgment of May 30, 2006, in the case *Commission of the European Communities v. Ireland*,[797] the European Court of Justice stated that it had exclusive jurisdiction to rule on disputes concerning the interpretation and application of provisions of UNCLOS which form part of the Community legal order. By bringing proceedings under the dispute settlement procedure laid down in the Convention, Ireland had failed to comply with its duty of cooperation under the European Community and Euratom Treaties, and accordingly was in breach of Community Law. This judgement clearly cannot please the Tribunal[798] as the position taken by the European Court of Justice may seriously affect the future possibility of Member States of the European Union to make use of the dispute settlement mechanism of UNCLOS in cases of disputes among them. It may in practice limit the competence of ITLOS to delimitation disputes among these States.[799] Some concerns may also be voiced from the viewpoint of non-EU parties to UNCLOS, relating, in particular, to the possible development of case-law on the Convention by the European Court.[800]

---

[797] Case C-459/03, Commission of the European Communities v. Ireland, 2006 ECR I-04635; see also N. Lavranos, *The MOX Plant judgment of the ECJ: How exclusive is the jurisdiction of the ECJ?*, 15/10 European Environmental Law Review, at 291–296 (2006).

[798] See also Churchill, *Some Reflections on the Dispute Settlement System of UNCLOS During its First Decade* (note 706), at 397.

[799] See Judge R. Wolfrum, President of ITLOS, Statement on 'The Value for Hamburg of ITLOS – Profile, Expectations and Reality' (note 757), at 7.

[800] See T. Treves, *The European Community and the European Union and the Law of the Sea: Recent developments*, 48 Indian Journal of International Law, at 19 (2008).

The Case of *Land Reclamation by Singapore in and around the Straits of Johor*[801] concerned a dispute between Malaysia and Singapore relating to land reclamation activities carried out by Singapore which, according to Malaysia, impinged upon its rights in and around the Straits of Johor, the body of water separating Malaysia from the island of Singapore. Malaysia claimed that Singapore's actions were in breach of its duties under international law, including, *inter alia*, its duties to preserve and protect the marine environment. In its Order of October 8, 2003, ITLOS prescribed provisional measures, pending a decision by an Annex VII arbitral tribunal, requiring Malaysia and Singapore to cooperate and enter into consultation to establish promptly a group of independent experts to study the effects of Singapore's land reclamation. Singapore was, furthermore, directed not to conduct its land reclamation in ways that might cause irreparable prejudice to the rights of Malaysia or serious harm to the marine environment. On April 26, 2005, Malaysia and Singapore settled their dispute by signing an agreement to this effect. On September 1, 2005, a final arbitral award was made in the case in accordance with the terms specified therein. The provisional measures ordered by ITLOS in 2003 were obviously instrumental in bringing the parties together and providing a successful diplomatic solution to the dispute.[802]

The record of ITLOS on environmental disputes is thus a positive one, despite the absence of any opportunity to decide such a case on the merits.[803] The aforementioned cases have enabled the Tribunal to contribute to the development of international environmental law, in particular by emphasizing the duty of cooperation,[804] the notion of prudence and caution, and the importance of procedural rights, as essential components of environmental obligations. In its orders for provisional measures, the Tribunal followed the line of adopting a pragmatic approach and prescribing measures which, in its view, would assist the parties to find a solution.[805] It should also be noted that these cooperation

---

[801] *Case concerning Land Reclamation by Singapore in and around the Straits of Johor* (Malaysia v. Singapore), Provisional Measures, Order of 8 October 2003, 7 ITLOS Reports (2003), at 10–64, available at: www.itlos.org; ITLOS Press Release No. 83, 6 October 2003 and No. 84, 8 October 2003, available at: www.itlos.org.

[802] Judge R. Wolfrum, President of ITLOS, Statement on the occasion of the Tenth Anniversary Ceremony at the Vertretung der Freien und Hansestadt Hamburg, Berlin, 18 September 2006, available at: www.itlos.org.

[803] A. Boyle, *The Environmental Jurisprudence of the International Tribunal for the Law of the Sea*, 22/3 The International Journal of Marine and Coastal Law, at 380 (2007).

[804] See also P. Weckel, *Les premières applications de l'article 290 de la Convention sur le droit de la mer relatif a la prescription de mesures conservatoires*, 109/4 Revue Générale de Droit International Public, at 838 (2005).

[805] Wolfrum, *The Tenth Anniversary of ITLOS* (note 759), at 76.

orders were made notwithstanding findings that the evidence failed to show that irreparable harm was either imminent or likely.[806]

2. *Prompt Release of Vessels and Crews*[807]

As already mentioned, the compulsory jurisdiction of ITLOS encompasses cases in which it is alleged that by detaining a vessel flying the flag of another State and/or its crew for certain offences – for instance in respect of illegal fishing or pollution – a State has violated the provisions of the Convention for the prompt release of the vessel and its crew upon the posting of a reasonable bond or other financial security. UNCLOS permits coastal States to exercise enforcement jurisdiction through the seizure of vessels and crews in certain limited circumstances.[808] Since its adoption, coastal States have with increasing urgency addressed the problem of illegal, unregulated and unreported fishing in their maritime zones. According to Article 73(1) of UNCLOS, referred to above, coastal States are entitled to board and inspect any vessel within their 200 nautical mile EEZs – where around 90% of commercial fishing takes place[809] – in order to enforce their laws and regulations in respect of the living resources of that area.[810] Article 73(2) requires arrested vessels and their crews to be promptly released upon the posting of a reasonable bond or other security.

Whenever it is alleged that the detaining State has not complied with that duty, the flag State of the vessel is entitled under Article 292 – a provision which constitutes a counterpart to the rights granted to coastal States – to request the release of the vessel before any court or tribunal agreed upon by the parties or, failing such agreement within 10 days from the time of the detention, before a court or tribunal accepted by the detaining State under Article 287 or before ITLOS, unless the parties otherwise agree.[811]

The question of release may be submitted not only by the flag State, but also "on its behalf."[812] In six prompt release cases, out of nine in total dealt with by the Tribunal, the proceedings were instituted "on behalf" of the flag State. What is interesting in these proceedings, is that the possibility of a State

---

[806] Boyle, *The Environmental Jurisprudence of ITLOS* (note 803), at 378.

[807] See also Escher, *Release of vessels and crews before ITLOS* (note 717).

[808] See Arts. 73, 220 and 226 UNCLOS.

[809] R.R Churchill, *The Jurisprudence of the International Tribunal for the Law of the Sea Relating to Fisheries: Is There Much In The Net?*, 22/3 The International Journal of Marine and Coastal Law, at 386 (2007), and Summary of the Symposium on the Jurisprudence of the International Tribunal for Law of the Sea: Assessments and Prospects, Hamburg, Germany, 29–30 September, 2006, available at: www.itlos.org.

[810] Klein, Dispute Settlement in UNCLOS (note 708), at 86.

[811] Art. 292 (1) UNCLOS.

[812] See also Wolfrum, *Verfahren zur Freigabe von Schiffen vor dem ISGH* (note 771), at 577–578.

authorizing another person to act on its behalf is expressly provided for in the Convention.[813] Under the Rules of the Tribunal, such authorization may even be given prior to the existence of any dispute by notification from the competent authority.[814] This permits States either once and for all, or on a case-by-case basis, to entrust the interested ship-owners, or for instance, associations of such ship-owners with the power to act on their behalf. In this way, in practice even though not in principle, private parties may be allowed to further their interests directly before ITLOS, the flag States nevertheless remaining party to the procedure.[815] In this context, it has been suggested that owners who register their ships with flag States should, in the negotiations prior to registration, already obtain the right to act on behalf of the flag State in the event of a dispute with a coastal State regarding prompt release of vessels and crew.

The prompt release cases ITLOS has thus far been seized with, nearly all of them connected with fisheries, were based on Article 73(2) UNCLOS. No State has, however, yet made use of one of the two other provisions of UNCLOS which provide for the release of the vessel upon the posting of a bond when the vessel has been detained for alleged pollution offences, that is Article 220 (6) and (7) and Article 226 (1) (b) and (c). The reason therefore might be that in the first case there is a clear wording of the release provision while in the second instance regarding pollution the provisions are drafted in a very intricate way, which may discourage State parties from submitting cases to ITLOS on that basis.[816] Although the provisions cited do not expressly refer to the crew members of detained ships, these are nevertheless covered by such prompt release proceedings since they are part of the vessel as a unit.[817] It is also important to note that in any prompt release proceedings, ITLOS may deal only with the question of the release of the vessel without prejudice to the merits of any case before the appropriate domestic forum in respect of the vessel, its owner

---

[813] Art. 292 (2) UNCLOS.

[814] Gautier, *Urgent Proceedings before ITLOS* (note 784), at 4.

[815] Treves, *The Jurisdiction of ITLOS* (note 747), at 401–402. Normal practice has been for the application to be submitted on behalf of the flag State. In the Volga case, for instance, the submission was made directly by the flag State, as the agent of the Russian Federation was a member of the Foreign Ministry. See P. Gautier, *Les affaires de 'prompte mainlevée' devant le Tribunal international du droit de la mer*, 3/d Global Community Yearbook of International Law and Jurisprudence, at 85 (2003).

[816] Gautier, *Urgent Proceedings before ITLOS* (note 784), at 4–5.

[817] See *id.* at 6; see also Judge J.L. Jesus, President of ITLOS, Statement to the Informal Meeting of Legal Advisors of Ministries of Foreign Affairs, 27 October 2009, at 6, available at: www .itlos.org.

or its crew.[818] In its jurisprudence, the Tribunal has strictly applied this requirement of the Convention.[819]

The first prompt release case concerned an application by Saint Vincent and the Grenadines for the prompt release of the oil tanker *M/V Saiga* and its crew from detention in Conakry, Guinea,[820] which had been arrested for alleged smuggling activities off that country's coast. ITLOS on 4 December 1997 ordered the prompt release of the vessel and its crew from detention upon the deposit of a bond of US$ 400,000.[821] It also held that a State may make an application under article 292 UNCLOS not only where no bond has been set but also where it considers that the bond set by the detaining State is unreasonable.

In the case of *Panama v. France*, concerning the fishing vessel *Camouco*,[822] ITLOS was requested to order the prompt release of the vessel and its Master, which had been arrested for alleged unlawful fishing in the EEZ of the Crozet Islands – French Southern and Antarctic Territories. In its judgment of 7 February 2000, the Tribunal ordered the prompt release of the vessel on the deposit of a financial security of French Francs (FF) 8 million (approximately US$ 1.2 million) although France had sought that the bond be no less than FF 20 million. The Tribunal also observed that Article 292 UNCLOS provides for a quick, independent remedy during which local remedies – as France had argued – could normally not be exhausted.

A prompt release case brought by the Seychelles against France concerned the vessel *Monte Confurco*,[823] registered in the Republic of the Seychelles, and licensed by it to fish in international waters. The vessel was apprehended for alleged illegal fishing and failure to announce its presence in the EEZ of the Kerguelen Island. ITLOS in its judgment of 18 December 2000 ordered the prompt release of the vessel and its Master by France upon the furnishing of

---

[818] See Art. 292(3) UNCLOS.

[819] Judge R. Wolfrum, President of ITLOS, Statement to the Informal Meeting of Legal Advisers, 24 October 2005 (note 786), at 3.

[820] *M/V Saiga I* (Saint Vincent and the Grenadines v. Guinea), Prompt Release, Judgment of 4 December 1997, 1 ITLOS Reports (1997), at 16–38, reprinted in 37 ILM 360 (1999); ITLOS Press Release No. 9, 21 November 1997, available at: www.itlos.org.

[821] ITLOS Press Releases No. 10, 4 December 1997, No. 13, 28 February 1998, and No. 14, 6 March 1998, available at www.itlos.org.

[822] *Camouco* (Panama v. France), Prompt Release, Judgment of 7 February 2000, 4 ITLOS Reports (2000), at 10–37, available at: www.itlos.org; ITLOS Press Release No. 35, 7 February 2000, available at: www.itlos.org.

[823] *Monte Confurco* (Seychelles v. France), Prompt Release, Judgment of 18 December 2000, 4 ITLOS Reports (2000), at 86–117; ITLOS Press Releases No. 41, 15 December 2000, and No. 42, 18 December 2000, available at: www.itlos.org.

a security of 18 million French Francs by the Seychelles, as the bond set by the national French court – 56.4 million French Francs – was not considered reasonable.

The fishing trawler *Grand Prince*,[824] at that time flying the flag of Belize, was arrested by the French authorities in the EEZ of the Kerguelen Islands for alleged illegal fishing. The competent French court fixed a bond for its release in the amount of 11 million French Francs, which was later followed by a confiscation order. ITLOS in its judgment of April 20, 2001 found that it had no jurisdiction under Article 292 UNCLOS to entertain the application as the documentary evidence submitted by the applicant failed to establish that Belize was the flag State of the vessel when the application was made; a decision that underlines the importance the Tribunal attaches to the matter of registration of ships.

The proceedings in the *"Chaisiri Reefer 2" Case*[825] were instituted by Panama against Yemen for the prompt release of that detained vessel, its crew and cargo. Following an agreement between Panama and Yemen on July 13, 2001 – after the release of the vessel and its cargo and crew – the case was removed from the Tribunal's List of cases. The availability of the relief provided by ITLOS certainly helped in reaching an out-of-court settlement.

In the *Volga*[826] case, that Russian vessel had been arrested for alleged illegal fishing in the Australian fishing zone. The Russian Federation requested the release of the *Volga* and its crew, the conditions for release imposed by Australia being neither permissible nor reasonable under the Convention. In its judgment of December 23, 2002, ITLOS took note of the concern of Australia with regard to the depletion of stocks of Patagonian Toothfish in the Southern Ocean and also stated that the amount of 1,920,000 Australian Dollars sought for the release of the vessel was reasonable in terms of article 292 UNCLOS. It, however, considered that the non-financial conditions laid down by Australia could not be considered as components of the bond or other financial security for the purposes of that provision of the Convention.

---

[824] *Grand Prince* (Belize v. France), Prompt Release, Judgment of 20 April 2001, 5 ITLOS Reports (2001), at 17–46, available at www.itlos.org; ITLOS Press Releases No. 47, 19 April 2001, and No. 48, 20 April 2001, available at: www.itlos.org.

[825] *Chaisiri Reefer 2* (Panama v. Yemen), Prompt Release, Order of 13 July 2001, 5 ITLOS Reports (2001), at 82–84, available at: www.itlos.org; ITLOS Press Releases No. 51, 5 July 2001, and No. 52, 16 July 2001, available at www.itlos.org.

[826] *Volga* (Russia v. Australia), Prompt Release, Judgment of 23 December 2002, 6 ITLOS Reports (2002), at 10–41, available at: www.itlos.org; ITLOS Press Releases No. 74, 20 December 2001, and No. 75, 23 December 2002, available at: www.itlos.org.

The *"Juno Trader" Case*[827] was submitted on behalf of Saint Vincent and the Grenadines against Guinea-Bissau concerning the detention of that vessel and its crew for alleged infringement of national fisheries legislation in that country's EEZ. Guinea-Bissau objected to the jurisdiction of ITLOS on the grounds that, according to its national legislation, the ownership of the vessel *Juno Trader* had reverted to the State of Guinea-Bissau and that therefore, Saint Vincent and the Grenadines could not any more be considered the flag State. The Tribunal, however, held that, whatever may be the effect of a definitive change in the ownership of a vessel upon its nationality, there was no basis in the particular circumstances of the case, for holding that there had been such a definitive change. In its judgment of December 18, 2004, ITLOS thus ordered the prompt release of the vessel *Juno Trader*, upon the posting of a bond of Euro 300.000. It also declared that all members of the crew should be free to leave Guinea-Bissau without any conditions.

The *"Hoshinmaru" Case*[828] concerned a dispute submitted by Japan regarding the detention of that fishing vessel by the authorities of the Russian Federation for the alleged infringement of national fisheries legislation in its EEZ. Russia had set a bond of 25,000,000 roubles (approximately US$ 980,000), later reduced to 22,000,000, which Japan considered to be unreasonable and not meeting the requirements of article 292 UNCLOS. In its judgment of August 6, 2007 ITLOS *inter alia* stated that it did not consider it reasonable for a bond to be set on the basis of the maximum penalties applicable to the owner and the Master, nor that a bond be set on the basis of the confiscation of the vessel given the circumstances of the case. The amount of the bond should be proportionate to the gravity of the alleged offences. ITLOS thus considered the amount of the bond fixed by the Russian Federation not to be reasonable and decided that the *Hoshinmaru* including its catch on board should be promptly released upon the posting of a bond or other security as determined by the Tribunal and that the Master and the crew should be free to leave without any conditions. It further determined that the bond should amount to 10,000,000 roubles (approximately US$ 390,000). On August 16, 2007 the bond was received by the Russian Federation and the vessel and crew were released on the same day.[829] This is an excellent example as to the efficiency of the prompt release procedure provided for in the Convention.

---

[827] *Juno Trader* (Saint Vincent and the Grenadines v. Guinea-Bissau), Prompt Release, Judgment of 18 December 2004, 8 ITLOS Reports (2004), at 17–92; ITLOS Press Releases No. 92 Corr. 1, 1 December 2004, and No. 95, 18 December 2004, available at: www.itlos.org.

[828] ITLOS Press Releases No. 110, 6 July 2007, No. 111, 2 August 2007, and No. 112, 6 August 2007, available at: www.itlos.org.

[829] ITLOS Press Release No. 114, 17 August 2007, available at: www.itlos.org.

The *"Tomimaru" Case*[830] was submitted by Japan on the same day as the *Hoshinmaru* case and also concerned the detention of that fishing vessel by the authorities of the Russian Federation for the alleged infringement of national fisheries legislation in its EEZ. The *Tomimaru* had already been detained eight months earlier and the crew had been allowed to leave the Russian Federation long before the application was submitted by Japan. The competent Russian courts had decided to confiscate the vessel and Russia thus maintained that the application by Japan had been rendered without object. In its judgment of August 6, 2007 ITLOS expressed the view that the decision to confiscate eliminates the provisional character of the detention of the vessel rendering the procedure for its prompt release without object. It, however, also noted that confiscation decided in "unjustified haste" would jeopardize the implementation of Article 292. Such a decision should furthermore not be taken in such a way as to prevent the ship owner from having recourse to available domestic judicial remedies, or as to prevent the flag State from resorting to the prompt release procedure set forth in the Convention.

In that case ITLOS also underscored that a decision to confiscate the vessel did not prevent it from considering an application for prompt release while proceedings are still before the domestic courts of the detaining State. As the decision by the Supreme Court of the Russian Federation – which confirmed the decision of the lower courts to confiscate the *Tomimaru* – had brought to an end the procedures before the domestic courts, ITLOS found that the application of Japan no longer had any object and that it was therefore not called upon to give a decision thereon. What makes this judgement notable is its assessment of the interplay between national and international rules as well as its consideration of the relevance of national judicial decisions to the Tribunal.[831]

In respect of the six cases in which ITLOS ordered the release of the vessel and/or its crew upon the posting of a reasonable bond, it can fairly be said that it has developed a coherent jurisprudence, particularly as regards the relevant factors for determining the reasonableness of bonds or other financial security. These factors – which by no means constitute a complete list – include the gravity of the alleged offences, the penalties imposed or imposable under the laws of the detaining State, the value of the detained vessel and of the cargo seized, the amount of the bond imposed by the detaining State and its form. The assessment of the relevant factors by the Tribunal is an objective one, taking into account all information provided by the parties and having regard to

---

[830] ITLOS Press Releases No. 110, No. 111, and No. 113, 6 August 2007, available at: www .itlos.org.

[831] Wolfrum, *The Settlement of Disputes Before ITLOS: Progressive or Traditional?* (note 705), at 152.

all the circumstances of the particular case.[832] It is to be emphasized that it is ITLOS that ultimately determines the reasonableness of the bond.[833]

The procedure for the prompt release of vessels and crews, with the possibility for private parties, if properly authorized by the flag State, to appear before ITLOS, is certainly a significant innovation provided by UNCLOS, if not the most important novel feature of its entire dispute settlement mechanism.[834] This procedure which constitutes an appropriate and cost-effective mechanism for parties faced with the arrest of vessels and crews is also characterized by its swiftness. The Tribunal, according to its Rules, shall give priority to such applications over all other proceedings.[835] The hearing must take place within a period of fifteen days commencing with the first working day following the date on which the application is received and the judgment must not be read later than 14 days after the closure of the hearing.[836] In its practice, ITLOS has acted in prompt release proceedings with remarkable efficiency and speed, having delivered its decisions within the timeframe of approximately one month. The urgency of these proceedings is justified in view of the financial burden resulting from the detention of a vessel as well as humanitarian considerations regarding detained crews.[837] This procedure thus enables shipowners to avoid that their detained vessels remain idle for long periods of time pending a decision on the merits by the competent domestic court, and furthermore provides a mechanism for a swift release of crew members from detention that otherwise might last for a considerable time.[838]

The prompt release procedure is also a good example of the balanced approach enshrined in UNCLOS. To protect the interests of the detaining State, it ensures the viability of sufficient financial security to ensure the payment of penalties that may be imposable by the domestic court of the detaining State, whereas to protect the interests of the flag State and the ship owner, it facilitates

---

[832] See 4 ITLOS Reports (2000), at 31, para. 67, 6 ITLOS Reports (2002), at 32, para. 65, and 8 ITLOS Reports (2004), at 41, para. 85. See also T.A. Mensah, *Provisional Measures in the International Tribunal for the Law of the Sea*, 62 1/2 Zeitschrift für ausländisches öffentliches Recht und Völkerrecht, at 46 (2002).

[833] Judge J.L. Jesus, President of ITLOS, Statement at the OLDEPESCA XX Conference of Ministers (note 760), at 5.

[834] See also V.P. Bantz, *Views from Hamburg: The Juno Trader Case or How to Make Sense of the Coastal State's Rights in Light of its Duty of Prompt Release*, 24/2 University of Queensland Law Journal, at 436–437 (2005).

[835] Art. 112 of the Rules of the Tribunal (note 740).

[836] Bantz, *Views from Hamburg: The Juno Trader Case* (note 834), at 418.

[837] Judge R. Wolfrum, President of ITLOS, Statement to the Informal Meeting of Legal Advisers, 24 October 2005 (note 786), at 4; see also Wolfrum, *The Tenth Anniversary of ITLOS* (note 759), at 74.

[838] Id., Wolfrum.

an expeditious return of vessel and crew to service.[839] It seems, however, that the possibility to institute such proceedings is not yet known well enough neither by shipowners nor by flag States. In this connection, it has not without some reason been said that the existence of ITLOS is one of the better-guarded secrets of the United Nations system. Flag States may also sometimes hesitate to have recourse to the Tribunal. It has therefore been suggested that owners who register their ships with flag States should, in the negotiations prior to registration, obtain the right to act on behalf of the flag State in the event of a dispute with a coastal State regarding prompt release of vessels and crew.[840]

3. *Cases relating to the Merits*

The parties may also submit a particular dispute to ITLOS at any time by means of a special agreement which to date has been done on at least three occasions. In the *M/V "SAIGA" (No. 2) Case*,[841] Saint Vincent and the Grenadines and Guinea agreed to submit to the Tribunal the merits of the dispute relating to the arrest and detention of the vessel *M/V Saiga*. The second case concerned the Conservation and Sustainable Exploitation of Swordfish Stocks in the South-Eastern Pacific Ocean, a dispute between Chile and the European Community.[842] More recently, one more case has been submitted to ITLOS on that basis: the dispute between Panama and Guinea-Bissau concerning a damage claim for the arrest of the vessel *M/V Virginia G.*[843]

In the *M/V "SAIGA" (No. 2) Case*, ITLOS had to deal with both the merits and the request for the prescription of provisional measures. The vessel and its crew continued to be held by Guinea even after the Tribunal had prescribed their prompt release. Guinea had not only arrested the tanker *M/V Saiga*, but also its master for providing fishing vessels with gasoil – bunkering – off the coast of Guinea, which it alleged was an offence under its customs laws. Saint Vincent and the Grenadines claimed, however, that the bunkering of vessels is within the freedom of navigation in the EEZ. The arrest of the *Saiga* took place at a point outside Guinea's EEZ, with Guinea claiming that the arrest

---

[839] Statement by Judge J.L. Jesus, President of ITLOS, at the OLDEPESCA XX Conference of Ministers (note 760), at 5.

[840] Tuerk, *The Contribution of ITLOS to International Law* (note 705), at 312.

[841] *M/V Saiga II* (note 511), at 10–78.

[842] See *Case concerning the Conservation and Sustainable Exploitation of Swordfish Stocks in the South-Eastern Pacific Ocean* (Chile v. European Community), Order of 29 December 2005, 9 ITLOS Reports (2005), Order of 20 December 2000, available at: www.itlos.org.

[843] See ITLOS Press Release No. 168, 5 July 2011, available at: www.itlos.org. The prevailing view is that the *Dispute concerning delimitation of the maritime boundary between Bangladesh and Myanmar in the Bay of Bengal* (Bangladesh v. Myanmar) does not belong to the category of "special agreements"; see also ITLOS Press Release No. 140, 16 December 2009, available at: www.itlos.org.

followed its right of "hot pursuit". On March 11, 1998, ITLOS ordered[844] that Guinea should refrain from taking or enforcing any judicial or administrative measures against the *Saiga*, its master and the other members of the crew, its owners or operators, in connection with the incidents leading to the arrest and detention of the vessel and to the subsequent prosecution and conviction of the master. The vessel, its captain and its crew had in fact already been released shortly before in compliance by Guinea with the judgment of the Tribunal of December 4, 1997.

ITLOS delivered its judgment on the merits of that case on July 1, 1999, within fifteen months of the proceedings being instituted. Compared with other judicial bodies, this can certainly be considered a reasonable period of time.[845] The Tribunal declared that Guinea had violated the rights of Saint Vincent and the Grenadines in arresting the *Saiga*, and awarded Saint Vincent and the Grenadines US$ 2,123,357 with interest as compensation. In that judgment, ITLOS made several important pronouncements concerning issues such as freedom of navigation, enforcement of customs laws, nationality of claims, reparation, use of force in law enforcement activities, hot pursuit and the question of the genuine link between the vessel and its flag State,[846] thereby making an important contribution to the development of international law regarding these aspects.

With respect to the question of the genuine link between the *Saiga* and Saint Vincent and the Grenadines, ITLOS concluded that the purpose of the provision of the Convention requiring such a link between a ship and its flag is to secure more effective implementation of the duties of the flag State, and not to establish criteria by reference to which the validity of the registration of ships in a flag State may be challenged by other States. In examining the question whether certain claims could be entertained because they related to violations of the rights of persons who were not nationals of Saint Vincent and the Grenadines, ITLOS declared that the relevant provisions of the Convention consider the ship as a unit, as regards the rights and obligations of the flag State with respect thereto. Thus the ship, everything on it, and every person involved or interested in its operations are treated as an entity linked to the flag State. The nationalities of these persons are not relevant. If each person that sustained

---

[844] *M/V Saiga II* (Saint Vincent and the Grenadines v. Guinea), Provisional Measures, Order of 11 March 1998, 2 ITLOS Reports (1998), at 24–40; ITLOS Press Release No. 15, 11 March 1998, available at: www.itlos.org.

[845] Judge R. Wolfrum, President of ITLOS, Statement to the Informal Meeting of Legal Advisers, 24 October 2005 (note 786), at 8.

[846] Judge R. Wolfrum, President of ITLOS, Statement to the Sixteenth Meeting of States parties (note 756), at 6.

damage were obliged to look for protection to the State from which such person is a national, undue hardship would ensue.

In the *Case concerning the Conservation and Sustainable Exploitation of Swordfish Stocks in the South-Eastern Pacific Ocean,*[847] *Chile v. European Community,* ITLOS, at the request of the parties, on 20 December, 2000 formed a Special Chamber to deal with the dispute, consisting of four judges of the Tribunal and one judge *ad hoc.*[848] This has so far been the only case where one of the parties to the dispute was an international organization. The Order of the Special Chamber of 16 December 2009 placed on record the discontinuance of the proceedings by agreement of the parties which, *inter alia,* provides for a definitive commitment to cooperate in the long term conservation and management of the swordfish stocks in the South-Eastern Pacific. The outcome of the case is a classic example of how ITLOS can contribute to the settlement of disputes by peaceful means chosen by the parties, bringing a dispute that had divided Chile and the European Union for about twenty years to a satisfactory conclusion.[849]

In the *Dispute concerning delimitation of the maritime boundary between Bangladesh and Myanmar in the Bay of Bengal, Bangladesh v. Myanmar,* both parties accepted the jurisdiction of ITLOS for its settlement. The dispute had initially been submitted to an arbitral tribunal to be constituted under Annex VII to UNCLOS. In light of the subsequent agreement of the parties to submit this delimitation dispute to ITLOS, the case was entered into its List of cases on 14 December 2009.[850] Bangladesh has requested ITLOS to delimit the boundary between the two States in the territorial sea, the exclusive economic zone and the continental shelf as well as to "confirm" that the territorial sea boundary is that set out in the Agreed Minutes between delegations of the two countries in 1974.[851] Myanmar maintains that ITLOS does not have jurisdiction with regard to the continental shelf beyond 200 nautical miles, as the delimitation line terminates well before reaching that limit. The "alleged existence" of an "agreement" concerning the delimitation of the territorial sea is "firmly" denied.[852] Both parties are, however, in agreement to ask the Tribunal to draw

---

[847] *Swordfish Stocks in the South-Eastern Pacific Ocean* (Chile v. European Community), Order of 20 December 2000, Order of 29 December 2005, 9 ITLOS Reports (2005), Order of 16 December 2009, ITLOS Press Releases 43, 21 December 2000, 45, 21 March 2001, 87, 7 January 2004, 102, 29 December 2005, 117, 30 November 2007, 129, 11 December 2008, 141, 17 December 2009, available at: www.itlos.org.

[848] ITLOS Press Release No. 43, 21 December 2000, available at: www.itlos.org.

[849] See remark by the President of the Special Chamber, Judge Chandrasekhara Rao; ITLOS Press Release 141, 17 December 2009, at 2, available at: www.itlos.org.

[850] ITLOS Press Release 140, 16 December 2009, available at: www.itlos.org.

[851] Bangladesh v. Myanmar, see Memorial of Bangladesh, Vol I, 1 July 2011, at 49, 50.

[852] Bangladesh v. Myanmar, Counter-Memorial of the Union of Myanmar, Volume I, 1 December 2010, at 5, 6 and 12.

a single maritime boundary for the seabed and the superjacent waters – that is for the continental shelf and the exclusive economic zones.[853] The written phase of the proceedings concluded on 1 July 2011 and the oral procedure took place in September 2011. Both parties have chosen ad hoc judges to sit in the case. A judgement may be expected in March of 2012.

The *M/V Louisa Case, Saint Vincent and the Grenadines v. Spain*, remains on the docket of ITLOS as far as its merits are concerned. The Tribunal had also reserved for consideration in its final decision the submissions made by both parties for costs in the proceedings. The President of ITLOS in his Orders of 12 January and 28 April 2011, upon consultation with the parties, set the time-limits for the filing of the Memorial by Saint Vincent and the Grenadines and the Counter-Memorial by Spain. As the parties wish to file a reply and a rejoinder the written procedure will conclude in early 2012.[854] The oral procedure may thus take place later in the year.

In the *M/V Virginia G. Case, Panama v. Guinea-Bissau*, proceedings were instituted on the basis of a special agreement on 4 July 2011. The dispute had initially been submitted to arbitration pursuant to Annex VII to UNCLOS. It concerns a damage claim submitted by Panama for the arrest of that vessel in the EEZ of Guinea-Bissau. According to the statement of claim the oil tanker Virginia G. was arrested on 21 August 2009 when carrying out refueling operations for fishing vessels. Panama maintains that while the tanker was released without the imposition of any penalty after fourteen months of detention, it suffered serious damages.[855] The written procedure in that Case may well last until the end of 2012.

4. *Advisory Opinion*

On 6 May 2010, the Council of the ISA decided – by consensus – to submit to the Seabed Disputes Chamber a request for an advisory opinion pursuant to Article 191 UNCLOS.[856] It was the first time ever that an advisory opinion was sought from the Chamber. The request had originally been proposed by

---

[853] Id., at 9.
[854] ITLOS Press Releases, No. 159, 13 January 2011, No. 165, 5 May 2011, available at: www.itlos.org.
[855] ITLOS Press Release, No. 168 (note 843).
[856] See Decision by the Council of the ISA, ISA doc. ISBA/16/C/13, 6 May 2010, available at: www.isa.org.jm/files/documents/EN/Press/Press10/SB-16–19.pdf (last visited 1 July 2011); see also Seabed Disputes Chamber of the International Tribunal for the Law of the Sea, Responsibilities and Obligations of States Sponsoring Persons and Entities with Respect to Activities in the Area, Advisory Opinion, 1 February 2011, at para. 1; ITLOS Press Releases No. 147, 14 May 2007, No. 148, 19 May 2007, No. 150, 29 July 2010, No. 151, 20 August

the government of Nauru to the Council which decided to reformulate the relevant questions in a more general manner.[857] The request related to the legal responsibilities and obligations of States parties to the Convention with respect to the sponsorship of activities in the "Area", the extent of liability of a State party for any failure to comply with the provisions of the Convention, in particular Part XI, and the 1994 Implementation Agreement, by an entity whom it has sponsored, and the necessary and appropriate measures that a sponsoring State must take in order to fulfill its responsibility under the relevant provisions of these instruments.[858] The background to this request was the fact that Nauru in 2008 sponsored an application by a private company for a plan of work to explore for polymetallic nodules in the "Area". It was pointed out that the potential liabilities or costs arising from this sponsorship could, in some circumstances, far exceed the financial capacities of Nauru, as well as those of many other developing countries.[859]

The President of the Seabed Disputes Chamber on 18 May 2010 adopted an Order regarding the conduct of this Case and decided that the ISA and those organizations invited as intergovernmental organizations to participate as observers in the Assembly of the Authority are considered likely to be able to furnish information on the questions submitted to the Seabed Disputes Chamber for an advisory opinion. He invited the States parties to the Convention, the ISA and the afore-mentioned organizations to present written statements on the questions contained in the Request.[860] Fifteen States as well as the ISA and other international organizations participated in the written and oral procedure, which took place in September 2010.[861]

The request was dealt with by the Seabed Disputes Chamber in a most expeditious manner as advisory opinions must be given as a matter of urgency. On 1 February 2011, the Chamber unanimously rendered its opinion in which it stated with respect to the obligations of sponsoring States under UNCLOS and

---

2010, No. 152, 6 September 2010, No. 160, 19 January 2011, No. 161, 1 February 2011, available at: www.itlos.org.

[857] See id., Advisory Opinion, at para. 4.

[858] According to Article 139, para. 1 UNCLOS States parties have the responsibility to ensure that activities in the Area, whether carried out by States parties, or state enterprises or natural or juridical persons which possess the nationality of States parties are effectively controlled by them or their nationals, are carried out in conformity with Part XI of the Convention. Annex III sets forth the basic conditions of prospecting, exploration and exploitation; for the full text of the request see Advisory Opinion (note 856), at para. 1.

[859] See Advisory Opinion (note 856), at para. 4.

[860] ITLOS List of Cases No. 17, Order 2010/3, 18 May 2010; see also ITLOS Press Release No. 148, 19 May 2010.

[861] See Advisory Opinion (note 856), at paras. 11–19.

related instruments that there is an obligation of "due diligence" and that these States are bound to make "best possible efforts" to secure compliance by the sponsored contractors. There are, *inter alia*, also obligations of the sponsoring States to assist the Authority, to apply a precautionary approach as well as the "best environmental practices", and to provide recourse for compensation. It is to be noted that these obligations apply equally to developed and developing States, unless specifically provided otherwise in the applicable provisions. The Chamber further found that the liability of the sponsoring State arises from its failure to fulfill its obligations under the Convention and related instruments, and that liability shall be for the actual amount of the damage. Finally, it held that the Convention requires the sponsoring State to adopt, within its legal system, laws and regulations and to take administrative measures that have two distinct functions, namely, to ensure compliance by the contractor with its obligations and to exempt the sponsoring State from liability.[862]

This advisory opinion given by the Seabed Disputes Chamber is certain to constitute an important guideline for States parties to UNCLOS intending to engage in or to sponsor deep seabed mining as well as for the ISA itself. The Chamber has undoubtedly accomplished its task to assist the Authority with independent and impartial judicial interpretation of UNCLOS and related instruments.[863] It has furthermore been underlined that this unanimously adopted advisory opinion is also a historic ruling, as it sets the highest standards of due diligence and endorses a legal obligation to apply precaution and best environmental practices.[864]

E. *Assessment*

ITLOS has already established a reputation for the expeditious and efficient management of cases,[865] and has made a substantial contribution to the development of international law,[866] in particular environmental law. The Tribunal

---

[862] Id., at para. 242.

[863] D.K. Anton, R.A. Makgill, C.R. Payne, *ITLOS/Case No. 17, Seabed Mining, Advisory Opinion on Responsibility and Liability*, 41/2 Environmental Policy and Law, at 65 (2011).

[864] See D. Freestone, *Advisory Opinion of the Seabed Disputes Chamber of ITLOS on "Responsibilities and Obligations of States Sponsoring Persons and Entities with respect to Activities in the Area"*, 15/7 American Society International Law, Insights, Final Thoughts (2011); available at: www.asil.org/insights110309.cfm (last visited 1 July 2011).

[865] Judge R. Wolfrum, President of ITLOS, Statement to the Sixteenth Meeting of States Parties to UNCLOS (note 756), at 5.

[866] See also M. Kamto, *Regard sur la jurisprudence du tribunal international du droit de la mer depuis son entrée en fonctionnement (1997–2004)*, 109/4 Revue générale de droit international public, at 828 (2005); see further Wolfrum, *The Tenth Anniversary of ITLOS* (note 759), at 76.

has the competence and means, under UNCLOS, to deal with a wide range of disputes, and is well equipped to discharge its functions speedily, efficiently and cost-effectively. It has, when appropriate, adopted a pragmatic approach in order to assist the parties to find a satisfactory solution to their dispute. Areas of particular concern of ITLOS have consistently been the safeguarding of human rights and the protection of the environment. The continued and significant contribution of the Tribunal to the settlement of disputes by peaceful means in accordance with Part XV of UNCLOS is regularly being noted with satisfaction by the UN General Assembly.[867]

Since it received the first case in 1998, altogether 19 cases have been submitted to ITLOS – of which 12 were fisheries related and 14 were introduced on the basis of its compulsory jurisdiction. This record does not compare unfavorably to that of other international judicial bodies in the initial stages of their existence.[868] As has been pointed out, the experience of most international courts is to start slowly and steadily build their docket.[869] To date, the Tribunal has resolved 14 cases and discontinued two at the request of the parties, one of them before it could deal with it.[870] The fact that the great majority of these cases related to urgent proceedings shows that these proceedings respond to the needs of the international community.[871] It should also be borne in mind that ITLOS is still a relatively new judicial body which is only gradually realizing its potential as the specialized judicial organ of the international community for the settlement of law of the sea disputes.[872] Efforts are constantly being undertaken to make the Tribunal and its possibilities better known to the international community, also through the organization of regional workshops, particularly in developing countries.[873]

The relative paucity of cases brought before ITLOS is certainly a matter of concern for the judges, but one over which they have little or no control.[874] It

---

[867] See for instance UN General Assembly Resolution 65/37 (note 250), op. para. 37.

[868] See also Speech by Judge L.D.M. Nelson, President of ITLOS, on the occasion of the visit to the Tribunal by Mr. Horst Köhler, President of the Federal Republic of Germany, 1 September 2004, at 4, available at: www.itlos.org.

[869] Dame Rosalyn Higgins, President of the ICJ, Speech at the 10th anniversary of ITLOS, Hamburg, 29 September 2006, available at: www.icj-cij.org/presscom/index.php?pr=1872&p1=6&p2=1&search=%22tenth%22&PHPSESSID=bcfa3b651b5fd723504d2966d1b5028c (last visited 1 July 2011).

[870] See Judge J.L. Jesus, President of ITLOS, Statement to the Informal Meeting of Legal Advisers of Ministries of Foreign Affairs, 25 October 2010, at 2, 3, available at: www.itlos.org.

[871] P. Gautier, *Urgent Proceedings before ITLOS* (note 784), at 1.

[872] Wolfrum, *The Tenth Anniversary of ITLOS* (note 759), at 76.

[873] Tuerk, *Zwölf Jahre Internationaler Seegerichtshof* (note 705), at 498.

[874] J. Seymour, *The International Tribunal for the Law of the Sea: A Great Mistake?*, 13/1 Indiana Journal of Global Legal Studies, at 35 (2006).

is a well-known fact that States are often reluctant to submit maritime disputes, which are frequently politically quite sensitive, to binding international adjudication. Thus, since the entry into force of UNCLOS in 1994 only six cases, including three maritime boundary delimitation cases, have been dealt with by arbitral tribunals constituted under Annex VII to the Convention.[875] Eight cases relating to the law of the sea, also counting two cases concerning sovereignty over islands, have been submitted to the ICJ, although not under the dispute settlement mechanism contained in Part XV of UNCLOS.[876] The undeniable underutilization of ITLOS – which has nevertheless received more cases concerning maritime disputes than any other court or tribunal referred to in the Convention – should also be seen in that context.[877] It is, however, to be noted that there has been a marked increase in the number of cases relating to the law of the sea submitted to international adjudication after the entry into force of UNCLOS, largely due to the compulsory mechanism provided thereunder for the settlement of disputes.[878] The limited number of maritime disputes brought before international courts and tribunals could also be seen as an indication that UNCLOS is operating with relative effectiveness[879] and thus as a compliment to the work of the negotiators of the Convention.[880]

The creation of ITLOS has from the very beginning been subject to a certain degree of criticism as being unnecessary and risking a fragmentation of international law.[881] It has even been suggested that its establishment has been a "great mistake".[882] It is certainly true that States, under UNCLOS, have a wide choice of forum for the settlement of disputes, which has been significantly expanded

---

[875] See list of cases at the official website of the Permanent Court of Arbitration, available at: www.pca-cpa.org/showpage.asp?pag_id=1029 (last visited 1 July 2011).

[876] See list of cases at the official website of the International Court of Justice, available at: www.icj-cij.org/docket/index.php?p1=3&p2=2 (last visited 1 July 2011).

[877] See also P. Gautier, *Le Règlement Obligatoire des Différends Relatifs au Droit de la Mer et la Pratique des Etats*, The Global Community Yearbook of International Law & Jurisprudence (I), at 109 (2009).

[878] P. Gautier, *The International Tribunal for the Law of the Sea: Activities in 2009*, (note 730), at 791.

[879] See also D.R. Rothwell and T. Stephens, *The International Law of the Sea*, Hart Publishing, Oxford and Portland, Oregon, at 459 (2010).

[880] See also, A. Serdy, *The paradoxical Success of UNCLOS Part XV: A Half-hearted Reply to Rosemary Rayfuse*, 36 Victoria University of Wellington Law Review, at 717, 721 (2005).

[881] See also Boyle, *ITLOS and the Settlement of Disputes* (note 727), at 120; see also Boyle, *Dispute Settlement and UNCLOS: Problems of Fragmentation and Jurisdiction* (note 771), at 37; see further Klein, Dispute Settlement in UNCLOS (note 708), at 55; see also Rayfuse, *The Future of Compulsory Dispute Settlement Under UNCLOS* (note 794), at 686; see further Churchill, *Some Reflections on the Dispute Settlement System of UNCLOS During its First Decade* (note 706), at 416.

[882] See also Seymour, *ITLOS: A Great Mistake?* (note 874) at 35.

by the creation of the Tribunal. The evidence so far nevertheless suggests that a choice of forum is more beneficial than harmful[883] and that the danger of conflicting jurisdiction has been widely overestimated.[884] Fragmentation of the law of the sea has thus far not occurred, and ITLOS also makes every effort to keep abreast of the developments that take place in other international judicial fora, in particular the ICJ.[885] The Tribunal is regularly referring to the judgments of the ICJ with respect to questions of international law and procedure and the Court is closely following the work of ITLOS and especially its already well-developed jurisprudence on provisional measures.[886] It has rightly been pointed out that it is important to see the range of courts and tribunals acting under the Part XV of UNCLOS as contributing to a coherent body of law.[887]

While the Convention does not grant ITLOS the privilege of being the default procedure, some of its provisions nevertheless accord it a more favorable treatment. These relate to the exclusive jurisdiction of the Seabed Disputes Chamber regarding the international seabed "Area", the residual jurisdiction of the Tribunal in prompt release cases, the special and unique jurisdiction conferred upon it to entertain requests for provisional measures pending the constitution of an arbitral tribunal under Annex VII to the Convention, and the authority, granted to the President of ITLOS by Annex VII, to appoint members of an arbitral tribunal at the request of one of the parties and in consultation with both of them.[888] It has been stated that ITLOS as a new permanent institution dedicated to resolving law of the sea disputes is rightly regarded as being at the centre of the dispute resolution system of Part XV of UNCLOS.[889]

The dispute concerning the maritime boundary between Bangladesh and Myanmar in the Bay of Bengal is the first delimitation case brought before ITLOS which underlines the confidence in the Tribunal regarding the adjudication of a politically sensitive issue. The resolution of that dispute might well

---

[883] Boyle, *Dispute Settlement and UNCLOS: Problems of Fragmentation and Jurisdiction* (note 771), at 54.

[884] Klein, Dispute Settlement in UNCLOS (note 708), at 59; see also Churchill, *Some Reflections on the Dispute Settlement System of UNCLOS During its First Decade* (note 706), at 416; see further Rayfuse, *The Future of Compulsory Dispute Settlement Under UNCLOS* (note 794), at 686.

[885] Statement by Judge R. Wolfrum, President of ITLOS, on Agenda Item 71(a) at the Plenary of the 61st Session of the UN General Assembly, 8 December 2006, at 9, available at: www.itlos.org.

[886] Dame Higgins, President of the ICJ, Speech at the 10th anniversary of ITLOS (note 869).

[887] M. Wood, *The International Tribunal for the Law of the Sea and General International Law*, 22/3 The International Journal of Marine and Coastal Law, at 353 (2007).

[888] Judge J.L. Jesus, President of ITLOS, Keynote Speech on "The Role of ITLOS in the Settlement of Law of the Sea Disputes", Globalization and the Law of the Sea, Washington D.C., 2 December 2010, at 6, available at: www.itlos.org. This authority has already been made use of on several occasions.

[889] Rothwell and Stephens, *The International Law of the Sea* (note 879), at 457.

constitute a breakthrough, leading to the submission of similar cases to ITLOS in the future. The same may also hold true for requests for an advisory opinion by the Seabed Disputes Chamber, which by most effectively dealing with the first case has set an important precedent that might encourage the Assembly and the Council of the ISA to submit further such requests. The more exploration – and in due course perhaps also exploitation – activities will take place in the international seabed "Area", the greater the likelihood that disputes will arise that can only be brought before that Chamber.[890]

The advisory jurisdiction of ITLOS as a full court is an important innovation for international judicial procedures[891] and might even offer an interesting alternative to contentious proceedings, in particular, in view of its non-binding nature. This could be advantageous in cases where legal guidance is sought as to how a particular dispute could be settled through direct negotiations.[892] Besides dispute resolution, advisory proceedings before ITLOS may prove to be of particular value in the years to come as the international community will be facing ever new challenges in ocean activities.[893]

---

[890] Judge J.L. Jesus, President of ITLOS, Keynote Speech on "The Role of ITLOS in the Settlement of Law of the Sea Disputes" (note 888), at 9.

[891] S. Rosenne, *International Tribunal for the Law of the Sea: 1996–97 Survey*, 13/4 The International Journal of Marine and Coastal Law, at 507 (1998); see also Judge R. Wolfrum, President of ITLOS, Statement at the Plenary of the Sixtieth Session of the United Nations General Assembly, 28 November 2005, para. 15, available at: www.itlos.org.

[892] Judge R. Wolfrum, President of ITLOS, Statement to the Informal Meeting of Legal Advisers of Ministries of Foreign Affairs (note 783), at 7, 8.

[893] Judge J.L. Jesus, President of ITLOS, Statement at the Plenary of the Sixty-third Session of the United Nations General Assembly, 5 December 2008, at 4, available at: www.itlos.org.

Chapter Eight

The Waning Freedom of the Seas[894]

A. The "Territorial Temptation" of Coastal States

More than fifteen years after the entry into force of UNCLOS it seems appropriate to analyze its implementation by the States parties and to consider further in which direction State practice with respect to the law of the sea is generally evolving.[895] Although UNCLOS has put a certain halt to the process of territorial expansion of coastal States sovereignty, sovereign rights and jurisdiction over the seas, some of its provisions lend themselves nevertheless to an extensive interpretation which has quite liberally been made use of. Furthermore, coastal States have a tendency to expand the reach of their regulations beyond 200 nautical miles – once again the old problem of "creeping jurisdiction". Even more important, however, is the trend towards a continual functional expansion of coastal State jurisdiction by an ever more stringent regulation of a wider range of activities within their maritime zones – the rather new phenomenon of "thickening jurisdiction".[896] All of these trends together have been subsumed under the notion of "territorial temptation" of coastal States.[897]

Already the determination of the baselines from which the seaward extent of the territorial sea, the contiguous zone and the EEZ is measured may give rise to certain problems.[898] As straight baselines had – in limited geographical – circumstances been declared permissible by the ICJ in 1951, this method found its way also into Article 7 UNCLOS. It is therefore not surprising that almost all coastal States which are parties to the Convention provide for that possibility in

---

[894] For this chapter see in particular Tuerk, *The Waning Freedom of the Seas* (note 15).

[895] See also S. Kaye, *State Practice and Maritime Claims: Assessing the Normative Impact of the Law of the Sea Convention*, in: The Future of Ocean Regime-building: Essays in Tribute to Douglas M. Johnston, A. Chircop et al. (eds.), at 133–158 (2009).

[896] Bateman, Rothwell & VanderZwaag, *Navigational Rights and Freedoms in the New Millennium: 20th Century Controversies and 21st Century Challenges* (note 64), at 323.

[897] See Oxman, *The Territorial Temptation* (note 56).

[898] See Davidson, *Law of the Sea and Freedom of Navigation in Asia Pacific* (note 79), at 134–135.

their domestic legislation, of which a large number of them has actually made use of, if no claim to archipelagic status was made in the first place.[899]

The basic requirement for drawing straight baselines is that they must not depart to any appreciable extent from the general direction of the coast and that the sea areas lying within the lines must be sufficiently closely linked to the land domain to be subject to the regime of internal waters.[900] The practical effect of a "liberal" interpretation of this requirement is, however, that the area where the coastal State enjoys varying degrees of competence is moved much further towards the high seas than this would otherwise have been the case, besides creating large areas of internal waters.[901] In some instances the baseline has been fixed at 50 nautical miles or even more from the mainland, eliciting protests from other States. The application of straight baselines in the context of ice-covered coasts seems even more problematic. In any case, the use of that method on a relatively large scale has resulted not in a major, but nevertheless noticeable diminution of the areas of the high seas and the international seabed "Area".[902]

A vexing question with substantial effects on the freedom of the high seas and the common heritage of mankind is the problem of islands. UNCLOS in Article 121 (3) provides that "rocks which cannot sustain human habitation or economic life of their own shall have no EEZ or continental shelf."[903] This exception to the rule that islands are entitled to the same maritime space as the mainland was designed to prevent a further reduction of the global commons.[904] There is considerable and unresolved controversy as to the exact meaning and scope of that provision, in particular, as to whether the term "rock" should be construed as implying specific geological features, thus not comprising islands even if they are tiny islets. It has, however, also been pointed out that the essential element of definition is the second one, namely whether such a feature can sustain human habitation or economic life of its own.[905]

Be that as it may, the fact is that coastal States have generally declared EEZs also around minuscule islands and on that basis, whenever possible, further laid claim to a continental shelf beyond 200 nautical miles, even where it is

---

[899] See table of Claims to Maritime Jurisdiction (as at 31 July 2010), available at: www.un.org/ Depts/los/LEGISLATIONANDTREATIES/PDFFILES/table_summary_of_claims.pdf (last visited 1 July 2011).

[900] Art. 7 (3) UNCLOS.

[901] See Roach & Smith, *US Responses to Excessive Maritime Claims* (note 80), at 75 ff.

[902] See also Oxman, *The Territorial Temptation* (note 56), at 837.

[903] Art. 121 (3) UNCLOS.

[904] Kwiatkowska, *Creeping Jurisdiction* (note 58), at 158.

[905] See A.G. Oude Elferink, *Clarifying Article 121(3) of the Law of the Sea Convention: The Limits Set By Nature Of International Legal Processes*, 6/2 IBRU, Boundary and Security Bulletin, at 61 (1998).

rather obvious that the requirement of human habitation or own economic life is not fulfilled. In spite of protests by some States in such cases it appears that the "rocks principle" enshrined in UNCLOS has had only a very limited effect in preventing maritime expansion by coastal States.[906] The possibility that any insular feature which can generate a territorial sea might be used as a basis for declaring an EEZ was already noted with concern by Ambassador Pardo in the course of the negotiations leading to the new law of the sea. He pointed out that the effectiveness of international administration of ocean space beyond national jurisdiction would be gravely impaired, if a 200 mile limit of jurisdiction could be founded on the possession of uninhabited, remote or very small islands.[907]

The EEZ, as mentioned, embraces approximately one third of the marine environment. It is important to emphasize that on the basis of the current law of the sea, the EEZ is not to be understood as an area of coastal State jurisdiction in a comprehensive sense, akin to the territorial sea; on the contrary, its essence is the substantive balance between the rights of the coastal State on the one hand, and those of the international community on the other.[908] It is thus not a "zone of national jurisdiction" – a notion that was not accepted at the Third United Nations Conference on the Law of the Sea – but a zone "with national jurisdiction."[909] This substantive balance is under pressure through various attempts at increasing the powers and competence of the coastal State. A tendency has manifested itself to extend coastal State legislation applicable to the territorial sea not only to the contiguous zone, but also across the entire EEZ. There is, however, no apparent basis in international law for such an expansion of jurisdiction.[910] An upsetting of the substantive balance of the EEZ, even in incremental steps, would obviously lead to a gradual territorialization of that area[911] with the traditional freedoms of the seas becoming mere exceptions to coastal State sovereignty.

---

[906] Kwiatkowska, *Creeping Jurisdiction* (note 58), at 158–159; see also Vukas, *The Law of the Sea, Selected Writings* (note 79), at 45; see further *Volga (Russia v. Australia)*, Prompt Release, Judgment of 23 December 2002, 6 ITLOS Reports (2002), Declaration of Judge Vukas, at 42–48, available at: www.itlos.org; see further id., Oude Elferink, at 58–68.

[907] UN General Assembly, Committee on the Peaceful Uses of the Sea-Bed and the Ocean Floor Beyond the Limits of National Jurisdiction, doc. A/AC. 138/SR.45–60, at 167.

[908] See Oxman, *The Territorial Temptation* (note 56), at 839; see also A. Proelss, *Ausschließliche Wirtschaftszone*, in: *Handbuch des Seerechts*, W. Graf Vitzthum (ed.), at 228–229 (2006).

[909] Tuerk, *The Waning Freedom of the Seas* (note 15), at 928.

[910] See S. Dromgoole, *Legal Protection for the Underwater Cultural Heritage: The Immediate Challenge and Methods of Response*, in: Recent Developments in the Law of the Sea and China, M.H. Nordquist, J.N. Moore, K. Fu (eds.), at 471 (2006).

[911] See also Oxman, *The Territorial Temptation* (note 56), at 839.

While the attempt by some coastal States to cast doubt on the continued application of the high seas freedom of overflight to the EEZs failed, efforts to expand the authority of coastal States in the EEZ as well as on the continental shelf to embrace marine archaeology were successful.[912] The 2001 Convention on the Protection of the Underwater Cultural Heritage[913] grants the coastal State party the right to prohibit or authorize any activity on underwater cultural heritage located in its EEZ or on its continental shelf so as to prevent interference with its sovereign rights or jurisdiction as provided for by international law, including the Convention on the Law of the Sea. This rule is also quite innovative: the right to prohibit or authorize activities directed at underwater cultural heritage accorded to the coastal State, though functionally limited to the prevention of interference with the coastal State's sovereign rights or jurisdiction, is in no way granted under UNCLOS.[914]

With regard to cases of the discovery of underwater cultural heritage in the EEZ or on the continental shelf that do not involve interference with a coastal State's sovereign rights or jurisdiction, that State plays a role unknown under the current law of the sea: it shall consult all other States parties that have declared an interest in how best to protect this heritage, and shall coordinate such consultations as "Coordinating State"; a status which it may refuse.[915] In order to take into account concerns voiced by maritime powers, the Coordinating State shall act on behalf of the States parties as a whole and not in its own interest, and any of these actions shall not in itself constitute a basis for the assertion of any preferential or jurisdictional rights not provided for in international law, including the Convention on the Law of the Sea.[916] It has also been stated that the Convention on the Protection of the Underwater Cultural Heritage can be seen as a "reasonable defence against the disastrous regime on underwater cultural heritage" set forth in UNCLOS, not allowing the State which has a cultural link with the objects "to prevent pillage of its historical heritage."[917] This Convention nevertheless reflects the view of the EEZ and the

[912] See Dromgoole, *Legal Protection for the Underwater Cultural Heritage* (note 910), at 467–477; see also G. Carducci, *New Developments in the Law of the Sea: The UNESCO Convention on the Protection of Underwater Cultural Heritage*, 96 American Journal of International Law, at 419 (2002).

[913] UNESCO Underwater Cultural Heritage Convention (note 754).

[914] Carducci, *New Developments: UNESCO Convention on Underwater Cultural Heritage* (note 912), at 430; see also Dromgoole, *Legal Protection for the Underwater Cultural Heritage* (note 910), at 471.

[915] Id.

[916] Carducci, *New Developments: UNESCO Convention on Underwater Cultural Heritage* (note 912), at 430–431.

[917] T. Scovazzi, *The entry into force of the 2001 UNESCO Convention on the Protection of the Underwater Cultural Heritage*, 1 Aegean Rev Law Sea, at 19 (2010).

continental shelf as appropriate tools for accumulating additional coastal State competences.[918]

To a certain extent the phenomenon of "thickening jurisdiction" also seems to arise with respect to marine scientific research. First of all, there can be little doubt that the regime for marine scientific research enshrined in UNCLOS has substantially increased the possibilities for coastal States to exercise control over such research. The planning and execution of marine scientific projects in areas under – limited – coastal State jurisdiction has become more difficult and more expensive, even more so in the case of such projects being conducted within such areas of several coastal States.[919]

Coastal States resort to the pertinent articles of UNCLOS to protect their proprietary interests regarding foreign marine scientific research activities that might yield data, samples and results bearing on the commercial exploitation of their natural resources because of ambiguity or suspicions concerning the true nature and objectives of such foreign activities. It has also been stated that coastal State suspicion concerning the motives underlying certain types of biological and chemical oceanography may have a potentially deleterious effect on obtaining clearance for fundamental research.[920] In any case, the domestic legislation of certain States does not reflect the balance achieved with respect to marine scientific research between the interests of coastal and other States in UNCLOS, but instead emphasizes the exclusive jurisdiction of the coastal State.[921] In general, State practice seems to evidence a restrictive trend in the application of the respective provisions of the Convention, conditions more detailed than those set out therein are sometimes prescribed or provisions attenuating the requirement of consent ignored.[922]

B. *Limitations to the Freedom of Navigation*

The right of the flag State to free navigation, an essential element of the freedom of the seas, is increasingly becoming subject to compliance with international rules drafted in reaction to the risks posed by ever changing technological progress and the increasing effect on the environment. New types of ships have brought new risks and calls for new security measures to protect persons and

---

[918] Oxman, *The Territorial Temptation* (note 56), at 840.

[919] A.H.A. Soons, *Marine Scientific Research and the Law of the Sea*, at 268 (1982).

[920] Gorina-Ysern, *An International Regime for Marine Scientific Research* (note 164), at 458–459.

[921] See Z. Keyuan, *Governing Marine Scientific Research in China*, Singapore: East Asian Institute, National University of Singapore, at 11 (2001).

[922] T. Treves, *Marine Scientific Research*, Max Planck Encyclopedia of Public International Law, online version www.mpepil.com, at 3 (2008).

goods at sea, measures which usually prevent environmental hazards as well. Protection of the environment can thus be considered a secondary benefit of the enhancement of navigational safety.[923] In the case of life at sea, search and rescue, etc., humanitarian law, of no concern at the time of Grotius, now prevails. Navigation is no longer at one's own risk, but has been regulated by a number of conventions elaborated within the framework of the IMO,[924] the most important being the International Convention for the Safety of Life at Sea (SOLAS).[925] The right to freedom of navigation is also conditioned to compliance with labor law enshrined in treaties drafted within the ILO, dealing with labor and welfare conditions on board.[926]

A further most important area entailing limitations to the freedom of navigation is the growing body of international rules and standards governing vessel-source pollution. While coastal States have a duty to take protective measures against that kind of pollution, they must do so in a manner that does not interfere unjustifiably with international navigation rights – this applies to the territorial sea, international straits and the EEZ. Any protective action to be taken must be in accordance with international rules and standards adopted through the IMO.[927] In this connection, the International Convention for the Prevention of Pollution from Ships (MARPOL) is of primary importance.[928] It

---

[923] J. Roberts, *Protecting Sensitive Marine Environments: The Role and Application of Ships Routeing Measures*, 20/1 International Journal of Marine and Coastal Law, at 136 (2005).

[924] See Blanco-Bazán, *Freedom of Navigation – outdated?* (note 27), at 5, 6.

[925] International Convention for the Safety of Life at Sea (hereinafter referred to as the SOLAS Convention), UNTS, Vol. 1184, N. I-18961 available at: www.imo.org/About/Conventions/ ListOfConventions/Pages/International-Convention-for-the-Safety-of-Life-at-Sea-(SOLAS),- 1974.aspx (last visited 1 July 2011).

[926] See in particular the Maritime Labour Convention 2006 which created a single, coherent instrument embodying as far as possible all up-to-date standards of existing international maritime labour Conventions and Recommendations, as well as the fundamental principles to be found in other international labour Conventions. As of 1 July 2011 only 13 countries have ratified the Convention; its entry into force requires 30 ratifications; see: www.ilo .org/global/about-the-ilo/press-and-media-centre/insight/WCMS_145146/lang--en/index .htm (last visited 1 July 2011).

[927] A. Chircop, *The Designation of Particularly Sensitive Sea Areas: A New Layer in the Regime for Marine Environmental Protection from International Shipping*, in: The Future of Ocean Regime-building: Essays in Tribute to Douglas M. Johnston, A. Chircop et al. (eds.), at 577 (2009).

[928] International Convention for the Prevention of Pollution from Ships 1973 as Modified by the Protocol of 1978 Relating Thereto, 1340 UNTS 61, available at: www.imo.org/ about/conventions/listofconventions/pages/international-convention-for-the-prevention-of- pollution-from-ships-(marpol).aspx (last visited 1 July 2011). While MARPOL deals with waste generated on board ships at sea, the 1989 Basel Convention on the Control of Trans- boundary Movements of Hazardous Waste and their Disposal and the 1972 London Conven- tion on the Prevention of Marine Pollution by Dumping of Wastes and Other Matter and its

applies to hazardous waste generated at sea on board ships, requiring them to be managed and disposed of in an environmentally sound manner, in order to prevent the pollution of the sea and harm to human health. Only limited amounts of wastes may be discharged into the sea; most must be discharged in ports.[929] The long practiced principle according to which freedom of navigation implies freedom to dispose of any waste generated as a consequence of navigation thus no longer exists.[930]

MARPOL also provides for a higher level of protection for certain sea areas designated as "Special Areas"[931] in which the discharge of certain types of hazardous wastes from ships is either strictly limited or prohibited, for technical reasons relating to their oceanographical and ecological condition and the amount of maritime traffic.[932] The MARPOL regime, however, did not expand the coastal States' enforcement powers, but operates within the jurisdictional framework of UNCLOS.[933] Preventive interference in the EEZ is therefore not allowed as UNCLOS presumes the occurrence of an illegal discharge as a prerequisite of coastal State intervention.[934]

The rules laid down in MARPOL are, however, being ignored by a large number of ships, including those sailing the waters of the European Union. The implementation of that Convention has therefore been harmonized at Union level and ship-source discharges of polluting substances in internal waters, the territorial sea, straits used for international navigation, the EEZ and the high seas, are under certain circumstances regarded as criminal offences, if committed with intent, recklessly or by serious negligence.[935] The respective EC-Directive sets a stricter standard than MARPOL by also criminalizing accidental pollution not only in internal waters, but also in the territorial sea by "serious

---

1996 Protocol apply only to wastes originating on land and shipped as cargo; see L.A. de La Fayette, The Sound Management of Wastes Generated at Sea – MARPOL, not Basel, 39/4–5 Environmental Policy and Law, at 208 (2009).

[929] See id.

[930] Blanco-Bazán, *Freedom of Navigation – outdated?* (note 27), at 6.

[931] As regards oil pollution these Special Areas are: Mediterranean Sea, Baltic Sea, Black Sea, Red Sea, "Gulfs" area, Gulf of Aden, Antarctic area, North West European waters, Oman area of the Arabian Sea and Southern South African waters; see Special Areas under MARPOL, as quoted by de La Fayette, The Sound Management of Waste Generated at Sea (note 928), at 210.

[932] Id.

[933] K. Hakapää, *Foreign Ships in Vulnerable Waters: Coastal Jurisdiction over Vessel-Source Pollution with Special Reference to the Baltic Sea*, 33 International Journal of Legal Information, at 267 (2005).

[934] Id., at 264.

[935] See Directive 2005/35/EC of the European Parliament and of the Council of 7 September, 2005 on Ship-source pollution and on the introduction of penalties for infringements, 2005 OJ (L 255) 11.

negligence", while in the EEZ and on the high seas the exceptions to responsibility provided for by that Convention are applicable.[936] Opinions are strongly divided whether coastal States may deviate from MARPOL-rules in the framework of their criminal jurisdiction and whether this constitutes an impediment to innocent passage through the territorial sea and thus a violation of international law.[937]

Apart from obligations emanating from international conventions, certain restrictions upon the freedom of navigation may be based upon measures taken by IMO which has the competence to designate certain areas outside the territorial sea as Particularly Sensitive Sea Areas (PSSAs).[938] These are areas that need special protection because of their significance for recognized ecological, socio-economic or scientific reasons and which may be vulnerable to damage by international shipping activities.[939] The designation of an area as a PSSA, the legal basis for which can essentially be found in UNCLOS,[940] has no binding effect as such. It requires "associated protective measures" within the purview of IMO, such as ships routeing measures and ships reporting systems near or in the area under the SOLAS Convention as well as compulsory pilotage schemes or vessel management systems,[941] and the designation of Special Areas

---

[936] See D. König, *Die EU-Meeresverschmutzungsrichtlinie – Weiterentwicklung oder Bruch des Seevölkerrechts?*, in: Meeresfreiheit und Ocean Governance – Festgabe zum 65. Geburtstag von Rainer Lagoni, P. Ehlers & M. Paschke (eds.), at 80 (2008); see also Treves, *The EC and the EU and the Law of the Sea* (note 800).

[937] See id., Treves, at 84; id. Lagoni, at 94, and H.H. Nöll, *Schifffahrtsfreiheit und Meeresumweltschutz im Seerechtsübereinkommen von 1982 – sind sie richtig austariert?*, P. Ehlers & M. Paschke (eds.), at 102 (2008). See also Case C-308/06, Intertanko and Others, 2008 ECR I-4057.

[938] In 2004 the IMO approved the designation of the Baltic Sea as a PSSA; see IMO Marine Environment Protection Committee, doc. MEPC 51/8/1 of 19 December 2003, available at: http://merchantmarine.financelaw.fju.edu.tw/data/IMO/MEPC/51/MEPC%2051-8–1 (last visited 1 July 2011); see also M.J. Kachel, *Particularly Sensitive Areas: the IMO's Role in Protecting Vulnerable Marine Areas*, 13 Hamburg Studies on Maritime Affairs, at 154–184 (2008).

[939] See in particular the IMO, Revised Guidelines for the Identification and Designation of Particularly Sensitive Sea Areas (PSSAs), IMO Assembly Resolution A.982(24) (1 December 2005), available at: www.imo.org/includes/blastDataOnly.asp/data_id%3D14373/982.pdf (last visited 1 July 2011). See also N. Ünlü, *Particularly Sensitive Areas: Past, Present and Future*, 3/2 WMU Journal of Maritime Affairs (2004), available at: www.imo.org/includes/blastDataonly.asp/data_id%3D17988/Particularly.pdf (last visited 1 July 2011).

[940] See Art. 211 (6) UNCLOS, which, however, only refers to oceanographical and ecological conditions whereas IMO Resolution 982(24) also mentions socio-economic, educational and archeological criteria.

[941] See G. Mapplebeck, *Management of Navigation through Vessel Traffic Services, Navigational Rights and Freedoms and the New Law of the Sea* (note 64), at 138; see also Judge R. Wolfrum, President of ITLOS, *Freedom of Navigation: New Challenges*, Statement made on 8 January 2008, at 6, available at: www.itlos.org; see likewise: R. Wolfrum, *Freedom of Navigation: New*

in accordance with the MARPOL Convention.[942] A request submitted to the IMO for the designation of a PSSA must thus include a proposal of the protective measures that will be associated with the area's status.[943] UNCLOS does not restrict the size of a PSSA, but only requires that it be a particularly clearly defined area of the respective EEZ.[944] In any case, the assessment of the need for a PSSA should be based on ecological criteria and not on jurisdictional notions; such an area should therefore not coincide with the EEZ.[945] In view of the perceived stakes involved – protection of the marine environment versus encroachments on international navigation – the PSSA discourse in the IMO is most likely to remain contentious.[946]

Another controversial issue is the introduction of mandatory pilotage systems in straits used for international navigation.[947] In 1998 the Baltic States did not accept a proposal by Denmark to introduce such a system with respect to the entrances to the Baltic Sea as it would not be in conformity with UNCLOS.[948] In 2005 the IMO had approved[949] the extension of the Great Barrier Reef PSSA to the Torres Strait, as proposed by Australia and Papua New Guinea. The respective Resolution also "recommended" that governments recognize the need for effective protection and inform ships flying their flag that they "should" comply with Australia's system of pilotage while navigating the Torres Strait.[950]

Challenges, in: Freedom of Seas, Passage Rights and the 1982 Law of the Sea Convention, M.H. Nordquist, T.T.B. Koh and J. Norton Moore (eds.), at 79–101 (2009).

[942] See MARPOL Annexes I (Prevention of Pollution by Oil), II (Control of Pollution by Noxious Liquid Substances), and V (Prevention of Pollution by Garbage from Ships); see also table concerning adoption, entry into force and date of taking effect of Special Areas, www.imo.org/environment/mainframe.asp?topic_id=760 (last visited 1 July 2011).

[943] See also H. Lefebvre Chalain, *Fifteen Years of Particularly Sensitive Sea Areas: A Concept in Development*, 13/1 Ocean and Coastal Law Journal, at 53 (2007).

[944] J. Roberts, M. Tsamenyi, T. Workman & L. Johnson, *The Western European PSSA proposal: "a politically sensitive sea area"*, 29 Marine Policy, at 439 (2005).

[945] Blanco-Bazán, *Freedom of Navigation – outdated?* (note 27), at 8.

[946] Chircop, *The Designation of Particularly Sensitive Sea Areas* (note 927), at 607.

[947] See R. Beckman, *Semaphore – the Newsletter of the Sea Power Centre Australia, Compulsory Pilotage in the Torres Strait*, 153 Maritime Studies at 23–26 (2007); see also S. Kaye, *Regulation of Navigation in the Torres Strait: Law of the Sea Issues*, in: Navigational Rights and Freedoms and the New Law of the Sea, D.R. Rothwell & S. Bateman (eds.), at 119–135 (2000), see further Wolfrum, *Freedom of Navigation: New Challenges* (note 941), at 7.

[948] Helsinki Commission, Baltic Marine Environment Protection Commission, Mandatory Pilotage in Certain Areas of the Baltic Sea, 11 May 2001, HELCOM EXTRA PREP 1/2001, Document No. 7 (on file with author).

[949] IMO, Marine Environmental Protection Committee Resolution, IMO doc. MEPC 133(53) (22 July 2005), available at: www.imo.org/includes/blastDataOnly.asp/data_id%3D18030/133%2853%29.pdf (last visited 1 July 2011).

[950] R. Beckman, *PSSAs and Transit Passage: Australia's Pilotage System in the Torres Strait Challenges the IMO and UNCLOS*, 38 Ocean Development & International Law, at 357 (2007).

In 2006 Australia introduced a compulsory pilotage scheme for the Strait – as an "associated protective measure" – enforceable by severe penalties; ships failing to take on a pilot would be subject to arrest the next time they voluntarily entered an Australian port within three years after the passage.[951] Several States, in particular the United States and Singapore, challenged the compulsory system as not in line with the understandings reached at IMO with respect to the afore-mentioned Resolution and as inconsistent with Part III of UNCLOS with respect to straits used for international navigation.[952]

The introduction of a compulsory pilotage system in the Torres Strait, resulting in a fee for transiting ships, raises fundamental issues regarding the powers and procedures of the IMO in adopting associated protective measures in PSSA's and the powers of littoral States under UNCLOS to adopt regulation on ships exercising the right of transit passage in a strait used for international navigation.[953] The IMO Legal Committee has remained divided on this issue and there is also a manifest disagreement whether the new system of pilotage in the Torres Strait constitutes a precedent for other straits.[954] It has, however, been pointed out that following the introduction of that system there has been 100 per cent compliance.[955] In any case, exceptional measures aimed at restricting the freedom of navigation should only be taken after proving which particular area requires a regime of exception on ecological or socio-economic grounds. There is a need to balance ecological interests with the interests of commercial navigation.[956]

The same holds true with respect to limitations of the freedom of navigation that may result from the establishment of Marine Protected Areas (MPAs) by coastal States in the EEZ on the basis of Article 211(6) UNCLOS. MPAs are linked to the concept of sustainable development, one of the highly important aspects of current environmental law;[957] they are areas of the marine ecosystem set aside for special protection and management in order to conserve biological

---

[951] Id., at 338.

[952] Id., at 326.

[953] Id., at 351; see also S. Bateman, *The Compulsory Pilotage Regime in the Torres Strait – A "Melting Pot" of Operational, Legal and Political Considerations*, in: Essays in Tribute to Douglas M. Johnston, A. Chircop et al. (eds.), at 261–286 (2009).

[954] Id. Beckman, at 333; see also S. Bateman & M. White, *Compulsory Pilotage in the Torres Strait: Overcoming Unacceptable Risks to a Sensitive Marine Environment*, 40/2 Ocean Development & International Law, at 197 (2009).

[955] See A. McCarthy, *Protecting the Environment and Promoting Safe Navigation: Australia's System of Pilotage in the Torres Strait, The Maritime Law Association of Australia and New Zealand*, 2007 Conference Paper (on file with author).

[956] Blanco-Bazán, *Freedom of Navigation – outdated?* (note 27), at 8.

[957] T. Scovazzi, *Marine Protected Areas on The High Seas: Some Legal and Policy Considerations*, 19/1 The International Journal of Marine & Coastal Law, at 2 (2004).

or also cultural resources by limiting or even prohibiting human activities within a given area. The most protective type are marine reserves which severely limit or forbid all extraction activities.[958] As the afore-mentioned provision of UNCLOS also refers to the "utilization or the protection of resources" as a criterion for the establishment of an MPA, these areas cover a broader range of measures than a Special Area under MARPOL.[959] In view of increasing evidence concerning significant harm to the world's ocean ecosystems, MPAs have become a widely accepted ocean management tool, also enshrined in multilateral treaties, to help achieve the conservation of marine biodiversity and the sustainability of fishing.[960] They are, however, also frequently viewed as an impermissible "fencing of the sea".[961] An underlying concern seems to be the fear that the establishment of an MPA would automatically exclude military activities in the respective area.[962] While numerous States have laws and regulations that do not allow them to prohibit navigation in certain environmentally sensitive areas, other States have foreseen limits not only for specific aspects of navigation, such as anchoring or speed, but have also adopted provisions regarding the prohibition of navigation in defined parts of MPAs, even if only for certain types of vessels.[963]

The legal regime of MPAs depends on the degree of powers that interested States can exercise over the marine spaces where they are established.[964] The designation of MPAs within territorial waters where most of such areas are located should, in general, not give rise to substantial legal problems; the situation may, however, be different in areas beyond, in particular the high seas.[965] Thus, a unilateral establishment of an MPA on the high seas would be in contravention of UNCLOS. The Convention, however, also obliges States parties to cooperate with respect to the protection of the environment, also on the high

---

[958] See J.L. Schorr, *The Australian Representative System of Marine Protected Areas and the Marine Zoning System: A Model for the United States?* 13 Pacific Rim Law and Policy Journal, at 673–674 (2004).

[959] R. Lagoni, *Marine Protected Areas in the Exclusive Economic Zone*, in: International Marine Environmental Law, Institutions, Implementations and Innovations, A. Kirchner (ed.), at 161 (2003).

[960] See also Marine Protected Areas – A Strategy for Canada's Pacific Coast, Discussion paper, August 1989, at 5 (on file with author).

[961] See Schorr, *The Australian Representative System of Marine Protected Areas: a Model for the US?* (note 958), at 681.

[962] K.M. Gjerde, *Current Legal Developments: High Seas Marine Protected Areas*, 16/3 The International Journal of Marine and Coastal Law, at 522 (2001).

[963] F. Spadi, *Navigation in Marine Protected Areas: National and International law*, 31/3 Ocean Development & International Law, at 291, 293 (2000).

[964] Scovazzi, *Marine Protected Areas on The High Seas* (note 957), at 5.

[965] See G. Peet & S. Gubbay, *Marine Protected Areas in the North Sea*, 5 International Journal of Estuarine and Coastal Law, at 243 (1990); see also id., Scovazzi, at 4.

seas. This obligation includes the duty set forth in Article 194(5) UNCLOS –
not limited to areas with national jurisdiction – to take the necessary measures to protect and preserve rare or fragile ecosystems as well as the habitat
of depleted, threatened or endangered species or other forms of marine life.[966]
Nevertheless, to date there is no appropriate forum to enable the establishment
of MPAs on the high seas based on an integrated approach for the protection
of the marine ecosystem.[967] The European Union has therefore suggested to
elaborate an implementation agreement to UNCLOS to remedy this situation.
Any such agreement would have to strike a balance between the applicable
rights and freedoms of the seas, in particular rights of passage and freedom of
navigation, and the obligation of all States under international conventions,
including UNCLOS, to protect and preserve the marine environment.[968] In
2002, the Plan of Implementation adopted at the World Summit on Sustainable Development at Johannesburg called on States to establish MPAs by 2012,
including representative networks.[969] The UN General Assembly when referring
to the possible establishment of MPAs has emphasized that these be consistent
with international law, as reflected in UNCLOS.[970]

As pointed out, restrictions of the freedom of the high seas due to the duty
of all States to combat piracy have for a long time been part of international law
with the right to take enforcement measures against pirates being vested in all
States and not only those which have suffered from an act of violence.[971] Measures taken by the international community in the fight against the resurgent
phenomenon of piracy and armed robbery at sea may also result in a temporary
limitation of the freedom of navigation, such as the marine interception operations undertaken by various naval units in the Indian Ocean and off the coast of
Somalia on the basis of several UN Security Council resolutions already referred
to.[972] Flag States may not object to an investigation of ships under their flag

---

[966] Gjerde, *Current Legal Developments: High Seas Marine Protected Areas* (note 962), at 524, footnote 26.
[967] Beslier, *Genetic Resources of the High Seas from the European Union's Perspective* (note 261), at 336.
[968] See also Scovazzi, *Marine Protected Areas on The High Seas* (note 957), at 5–6.
[969] See Plan of Implementation of the World Summit on Sustainable Development, para. 32 (c), available at: www.un.org/esa/sustdev/documents/WSSD_POI_PD/English/WSSD_PlanImpl.pdf (last visited 1 July 2011). See also T. Lowry, *Protecting the Mysteries of the Deep: Conserving Biodiversity in Marine Areas Beyond National Jurisdiction*, 16 Dalhousie Journal of Legal Studies, at 128 (2007).
[970] See UN General Assembly Res. 64/71 (note 250), para. 153.
[971] See Arts. 100–107 UNCLOS.
[972] UN Security Council Res. 1801 of 20 February 2008, 1816 (2008) (note 503), 1846 (2008) (note 505), 1851 (2008) (note 512) and 1897 (2009) (note 505). See also Wolfrum, *Freedom of Navigation: New Challenges* (note 941), at 10.

by warships of other States, as long as the measures taken are proportionate.[973] These temporary limitations, although expressly not to be considered as establishing customary international law and limited to Somalia, nevertheless constitute a certain precedent. The freedom of navigation may further be affected by the afore-mentioned regional agreements concluded in Asia and Africa with the object of combating piracy and armed robbery at sea.

The 1988 Vienna Convention against Illicit Traffic in Narcotic Drugs and Psychotropic Substances[974] is based on the general requirement under Article 108 UNCLOS to cooperate in the suppression of illicit drug trafficking on the high seas by allowing the interception of a ship suspected of illicit trafficking by a State other than the flag State. Suggestions that there should be consideration of arrangements for law enforcement authorities to board vessels flying foreign flags were considered "inappropriate" and left to bilateral or regional arrangements. That Convention did not ultimately provide a general grant of authority for the right to visit foreign vessels suspected of involvement in drug trafficking. Instead, its Article 17 sets up a procedure whereby a State party may request permission to board a vessel of another State party when the ship is outside the territorial sea of any State. Authorizations may be granted on an ad hoc basis, or by means of separate agreements or arrangements otherwise reached between the parties. A flag State is permitted to subject its authorization to conditions to be mutually agreed between it and the requesting party. Moreover, there is no precise timeframe for the authorization by the flag State, but a simple requirement for a party to "respond expeditiously to a request from another party" regarding the nationality of a vessel and authority to board.[975]

As stated before, the more recent problem of terrorism at sea was first addressed by the 1988 SUA Convention[976] which, however, primarily deals with the prosecution or extradition of the perpetrators of terrorist acts, rather than the prevention or suppression of such acts.[977] The 2005 Protocol to that Convention enlarges its scope by, *inter alia*, permitting the boarding of a ship flying the flag of another State party on reasonable grounds of suspicion that an offense under the Convention – which includes the proliferation of weapons of mass destruction using maritime transportation – has been or is about to be committed. As a result, freedom of navigation had to be restricted, although only with the express authorization – in general or *ad hoc* – and cooperation of

---

[973] Wolfrum, *Fighting Terrorism at Sea* (note 426), at 37.

[974] United Nations Convention against Illicit Traffic in Narcotic Drugs and Psychotropic Substances (note 13).

[975] Klein, *The Right of Visit and the 2005 SUA Protocol* (note 70), at 304–305.

[976] SUA Convention (note 14).

[977] See Tuerk, *Combating Terrorism at Sea* (note 569), at 54.

the flag State.[978] These boarding procedures do not change any rules of international law[979] since they are in conformity with the legal framework established by Articles 92 and 110 UNCLOS. Both articles allow flag States to enter international treaties granting a non-flag State the right to board their vessels on the high seas.[980] It has, however, been observed that these boarding provisions are more limited than those contained in the 1995 Fish Stocks Agreement[981] which provides for the boarding and inspection of a fishing vessel on the high seas if there are sufficient grounds to believe that it has seriously violated the rules concerning fishing.[982] No *ad hoc* authorization by the flag State is required.[983] The protection of living resources is obviously regarded as a more technical question, while the fight against terrorism is considered to have highly political aspects. Thus, States in that context are clearly more reluctant to agree to a limitation of their exclusive jurisdiction on the high seas over ships flying their flag.

The multilateral measures against the maritime transport of weapons of mass destruction are being supplemented by measures on a bilateral basis further affecting the freedom of the seas, namely the already mentioned PSI which explicitly contemplates the boarding of ships with the object to seize weapons and the materials used for their production, if necessary by armed force.[984] It has been pointed out that the PSI aims to restrict the right of innocent passage guaranteed under UNCLOS on the basis that passage of a shipment of weapons of mass destruction or related material cannot be an "innocent passage."[985] Intercepting ships suspected of carrying such weapons or material beyond internal waters without the consent of the flag State, however, raises the question of the compatibility of such action with the law of the sea, as the mere transit of cargo of that nature would not seem to be contrary to the regime of innocent passage as enshrined in the Convention.[986] It is further a matter

---

[978] IMO, Revised Treaties to Address Unlawful Acts at Sea (note 660), at 3,4; see also id., Tuerk, at 75–76.

[979] See Consideration of a Draft Protocol to the SUA Convention, IMO doc. LEG/CONF.15/14 (note 656).

[980] Harrington, Heightened Security: The Need to Incorporate Articles of the 2005 Draft SUA Protocol into UNCLOS (note 649), at 127; see also IMO, Comments on Counter-Terrorism, Non-Proliferation and Boarding Provisions Submitted by the United States, IMO doc. LEG/Conf.15/15 of 22 September 2005.

[981] Fish Stocks Agreement (note 12); see Wolfrum, *Fighting Terrorism at Sea* (note 426), at 21.

[982] Id.

[983] Id.

[984] Shulman, *The Proliferation Security Initiative and the Evolution of the Law on the Use of Force* (note 696), at 774, 775.

[985] Thomas, *The Proliferation Security Initiative: An Indian Perspective* (note 693), at 8.

[986] Wolfrum, *Freedom of Navigation: New Challenges* (note 941), at 9. In this context it has been pointed out that in the US-Soviet Joint Statement of 23 December 1989 the United States

of controversy whether ships carrying weapons of mass destruction without being targeted against a particular State may be interdicted on the high seas by warships of another State without the consent of the flag State concerned.[987] Though a political commitment that is voluntary in nature, the PSI has generated a growing State practice of bilateral or regional arrangements and agreements in support of interdictions of foreign flag ships suspected of carrying weapons of mass destruction, related delivery systems or material in spite of the lack of any respective legal authority in UNCLOS.[988]

In contrast to the multilateral endeavors of the PSI and the bilateral agreements initiated by the United States, the Australian Maritime Identification System (AMIS) announced at the end of 2004, was a unilateral declaration intended to enhance the maritime security of Australia. Its purpose is to identify vessels intending to enter Australian ports, as well as all vessels entering Australia's EEZ. The AMIS extends 1000 nautical miles from the Australian coast and thus also encompasses vast areas of the high seas. Australia's right to request information from vessels seeking to enter its ports is consistent with its rights under the SOLAS Convention and the ISPS Code.[989] However, any efforts at interdictions to enforce the information requirement on the high seas as well as any attempt to secure identification information from all vessels that enter its EEZ would likely be unlawful, particularly when those vessels are merely in transit and do not stop at an Australian port.[990]

In this context it is to be noted that on 1 January 2008 a new regulation, included in chapter V of the SOLAS Convention, relating to long range identification and tracking (LRIT) of certain categories of ships on international voyages[991] entered into force. The regulation aims at complementing the comprehensive maritime security measures contained in the ISPS Code, by detecting security threats and taking preventive measures against security incidents

---

itself has stated that the right of innocent passage may be exercised irrespective of the cargo of the vessel.

[987] Id., Wolfrum, at 10. It has been stated that PSI is a highly selective non-proliferation initiative because it does not target proliferation of weapons of mass destruction as such, but targets such proliferation only to those States or non-State actors that are deemed to be proliferation concern; a PSI activity is thus based on a unilateral determination by a PSI partner State; see Thomas, *The Proliferation Security Initiative: An Indian Perspective* (note 693), at 3.

[988] Id., Thomas, at 10.

[989] Klein, *The Right of Visit and the 2005 SUA Protocol* (note 70), at 314.

[990] Id., at 315–316.

[991] These are: passenger ships, including high-speed craft, cargo ships, including high-speed craft of 300 gross tonnage and upwards as well as mobile offshore drilling units. The LRIT system thus does not apply to smaller vessels or fishing vessels. See SOLAS Regulation V/19-1.

affecting ships or port facilities.[992] SOLAS Contracting Governments are thus entitled to receive information about ships navigating within a distance not exceeding 1000 nautical miles off their coast. The regulation establishes a multilateral agreement for sharing LRIT information for security and search and rescue purposes. It maintains the right of flag States to protect information about ships entitled to fly their flag, where appropriate, while allowing States to access the information about ships navigating off their coasts. The IMO has underlined that this SOLAS regulation does not create or affirm any new rights of States over ships beyond those existing in international law, particularly UNCLOS.[993] Mandatory ship reporting systems of which the IMO has already adopted quite a number have, however, also come under criticism as being nothing more than prior notice and consent regimes for ships transiting coastal State territorial seas and EEZs.[994]

As of 1 July 2010, Canada has implemented a mandatory reporting system – the strengthened Northern Canada Vessel Traffic Services (NORDREG) Zone – replacing a previous voluntary reporting system for tracking cargo and cruise vessels passing through the Canadian Arctic archipelago. Ships of 300 tons or more are now required to report to the Canadian Coast Guard prior to entering the zone, while navigating in the zone, and upon exiting from it. Enforcement action may include follow-up communications with the flag State of a foreign vessel, notification through Port State Control Procedures and possible prosecution in accordance with the Canada Shipping Act of 2001. The reason given for the mandatory reporting system was to enable the Canadian Coast Guard to promote the safe navigation of vessels, keep watch on vessels carrying pollutants, fuel oil and dangerous goods and respond quickly in the event of an accident. The Canadian measure, which was not previously forwarded to the IMO for evaluation, was criticized by the Baltic and International Maritime Council (BIMCO) as being in conflict with the SOLAS Convention, which stipulates that vessel traffic rules "may only be made mandatory within the territorial sea of a coastal State," while the Canadian regulations are being enforced from shore to 200 nautical miles. Concerns were also expressed regarding the risk of not being granted authorization to proceed in the case of non-compliance as

---

[992] M. Tsamenyi & M.A. Palma, *Long-Range Identification and Tracking Systems for Vessels: Legal and Technical Issues*, in: Lloyd's MIU Handbook of Maritime Security, R.H. Burns et al. (eds.), at 215 (2009).

[993] See IMO, MSC, 81st session (2006), available at www5.imo.org/SharePoint/mainframe .asp?topic_id=110&doc_id=6208#amends (last visited 1 July 2011).

[994] R. Pedrozo, *Encroachment on Navigational Freedom*, 84 International Legal Study Series, US Naval War College, at 86 (2008).

this could be seen "as effectively interfering with the right of innocent passage as ensured by UNCLOS".[995]

Recent State practice thus illustrates that in the EEZ ships must carefully limit their movements in many ways. Even military vessels which enjoy immunity must respect the many rules that have been established to protect the marine environment and the security of coastal populations. Fishing vessels are subject to the most restraints and must give notice whenever they travel through the EEZ of another country. Oil tankers, especially those with single hulls are now subject to a wide variety of restraints, and any ship with a dangerous cargo must conform to international, regional and national regulations. Ships carrying ultrahazardous nuclear cargoes have been told by many countries to avoid their EEZs, and these ships have in fact chosen routes designed to avoid most such zones.[996] The balance between navigation and other national interests continues to evolve, and navigational freedoms appear to be dwindling during this process.[997]

An important element of navigational freedom is undoubtedly the possibility of access to foreign ports, even more so for landlocked countries – already Grotius had articulated such a general right.[998] Ports are, however, located in internal waters which are under the complete sovereignty of the coastal State. The right of the coastal State to regulate access to its internal waters, including its ports, has been confirmed in Article 25 (2) UNCLOS.[999] If a ship does not meet the required conditions, it may be refused permission to enter. It is also generally accepted that under certain circumstances coastal States are entitled to close those ports which are normally open to international traffic, in particular for reasons of national security. It has rightly been pointed out – a view also expressed by the ICJ – that there is no legal obligation based on customary international law[1000] to maintain open ports, although most States enjoy the

---

[995] See www.maritimemag.com/index.php?option=com_content&view=article&id=55:bimco-slams-canada-arctic-control-measure&catid=4:news&Itemid=6 (last visited 1 July 2011); see also contemplatingsnot.blogspot.com/2010/07/bimco-objects-to-new-canadian-rules-on.html (last visited 1 July 2011). The U.S. has also expressed concerns about these new Canadian regulations; the Canadian view is that "the waters in question are within the exclusive jurisdiction of Canada and there is no legal obligation to seek approval from the IMO."

[996] Van Dyke, *The disappearing right to navigational freedom in the EEZ* (note 108), at 121.

[997] Id.

[998] V. Tasikas, *The Regime of Maritime Port Access: A Relook at Contemporary International and United States Law*, 5 Loyola Maritime Law Journal, at 6 (2007).

[999] L.M. Diaz & B. Hart Dubner, *Environmental Damage and the Destruction of Life – Problems that Add a New Balancing Dimension to International Port Access vs. Efficient Trade Under International Law*, 10 Barry Law Review, at 6 (2008).

[1000] Tasikas, *The Regime of Maritime Port Access* (note 998), at 3.

right to enter flagged merchant vessels into foreign ports under treaty law.[1001] UNCLOS itself provides a right for coastal States to block access for ships carrying hazardous materials and to impose requirements concerning vessel-source pollution as a condition to the access of a foreign-flagged vessel into port.[1002] Under the ISPS Code ships using port facilities may be subject to port State control inspections and there may be circumstances in which entry into a port could be denied. International access to ports has gone from a historic presumption that all merchant ships should be allowed to enter ports to the present day restrictions which States deem necessary in order to attempt to protect major port areas and cities from the threat of international terrorism.[1003]

C. *The Restricted Freedom of High Seas Fishing*

The most important international instrument relating to high seas fishing is the 1995 Fish Stocks Agreement, adopted to supplement the regime of UNCLOS,[1004] providing schemes to facilitate more effective coordination between coastal States and States with vessels fishing on the high seas to set sustainable and sensible allowable catch limits.[1005] Such cooperation is to be pursued either directly or through appropriate sub-regional or regional fisheries management organizations or arrangements. The Fish Stocks Agreement – the membership of which is still rather limited[1006] – expressly requires States to widely apply the precautionary approach to conservation, management and exploitation of straddling fish stocks and highly migratory fish stocks in order to protect living marine resources and preserve the marine environment.[1007] The Agreement is intended to apply primarily beyond the limits of national jurisdiction.[1008] It is generally considered to have improved the regulations that conserve and manage fish stocks for optimal utilization and sustainable growth.

The respective regulations are most often administered by Regional Fisheries Management Organizations (RFMO's), groups of States that collectively

---

[1001] Id., at 25.

[1002] Diaz & Hart Dubner, *Environmental Damage and the Destruction of Life* (note 999), at 11.

[1003] Id., at 23.

[1004] Z. Tyler, *Saving Fisheries on the High Seas: The Use of Trade Sanctions to Force Compliance with Multilateral Fisheries Agreements*, 20 Tulane Environmental Law Journal, at 7 (2006).

[1005] M.A. Becker, *The Shifting Public Order of the Oceans: Freedom of Navigation and the Interdiction of Ships at Sea*, 46/1 Harvard International Law Journal, at 198 (2005).

[1006] See status of UNCLOS (note 6), table recapitulating the status of the Convention and of the related Agreements, as of 31 May 2011. To date 77 States and the European Union have adhered to the Fish Stocks Agreement.

[1007] See Art. 6 Fish Stocks Agreement (note 12).

[1008] See Lowry, *Protecting the Mysteries of the Deep* (note 969), at 120.

manage and police the waters to which their regulations apply. In practice, this requires a kind of RFMO dominion over parts of the high seas, which might be described as a fine-tuned *mare clausum* in the limited context of fisheries regulation enforcement.[1009] RFMO regulation has restricted the freedom of fishing in certain high seas areas where States have adopted a range of voluntary and mandatory measures to protect fish stocks. It is important to note that the Fish Stocks Agreement not only permits enforcement by non-flag States against the vessels of other flag States, but also against non-parties to the RFMOs.[1010] This Agreement brings an evident "encroachment" on the principle of the freedom of the high seas, but it was considered a necessary tool to promote the conservation and sound management of living marine resources and was thus accepted by a great majority of States.[1011]

The right to fish the high seas is further tempered by the 1993 Agreement to Promote Compliance with International Conservation and Management Measures by Fishing Vessels on the High Seas and the Convention on Biological Diversity (CBD).[1012] The Compliance Agreement specifically requires each Party to "take such measures as may be necessary to ensure that fishing vessels entitled to fly its flag do not engage in any activity that undermines the effectiveness of international conservation and management measures".[1013] Parties to this Agreement shall encourage non-parties to accept it and to adopt laws and regulations consistent with its provisions.[1014] The CBD contains the obligation for each Contracting Party to regulate or manage, as far as possible, biological resources beyond national jurisdiction that are important for the conservation of biological diversity "with a view to ensuring their conservation and sustainable use".[1015] The Contracting Parties are furthermore required to cooperate to this end and on other matters of mutual interest with each other directly

---

[1009] Id., at 199; see also M. Gorina-Ysern, *World Ocean Public Trust: High Seas Fisheries after Grotius – Towards a New Ocean Ethos?*, 34/3 Golden Gate University Law Review, at 684 (2004). See also FAO, "What are Regional Fishery Bodies?, www.fao.org/fishery/topic/16800/en (last visited 1 July 2011).

[1010] See Fish Stocks Agreement (note 12). See also Tyler, *Saving Fisheries on the High Seas* (note 1004), at 7; see also M. Hayashi, *Enforcement by Non-Flag States on the High Seas under the 1995 Agreement on Straddling and Highly Migratory Fish Stocks*, 9 Georgetown International Environmental Law Review, at 27 (1996–1997).

[1011] Scovazzi, *Marine Protected Areas on The High Seas* (note 957), at 7.

[1012] Agreement to Promote Compliance with International Conservation and Management Measures by Fishing Vessels on the High Seas, 24 November 1993, 2221 UNTS 91 (hereinafter referred to as the Compliance Agreement); Convention on Biological Diversity, 1760 UNTS 79; see Pendleton, State Responsibility and the High Seas Marine Environment (note 77), at 502–504.

[1013] Id., Pendleton, at 502–503.

[1014] See Art. III (1) Compliance Agreement (note 1012).

[1015] See Pendleton, *State Responsibility and the High Seas Marine Environ*ment (note 77), at 504.

or, where appropriate, through competent international organizations.[1016] The CBD also applies to the marine environment irrespective of the legal conditions of the waters and the sea-bed concerned.[1017]

The FAO in 1995 unanimously adopted a Code of Conduct for Responsible Fisheries, consistent with the Fish Stocks Agreement and the Compliance Agreement – the latter forms an integral part of the Code – establishing, in a non-mandatory manner, principles and standards applicable to the conservation, management and development of all fisheries. The Code also recommends that States widely apply the precautionary approach.[1018] In 2008 the FAO adopted International Guidelines for the Management of Deep Sea Fisheries in the High Seas. These Guidelines set out standards and criteria for identifying vulnerable marine ecosystems (VMEs) located beyond the limits of national jurisdiction and for assessing the impacts of fishing activities on them, in order to facilitate the adoption and implementation of conservation and management measures by RFMOs and flag States. Coastal States may also apply these Guidelines within their national jurisdiction as appropriate.[1019]

The shrinking of the living resources of the seas is also in no small measure due to illegal, unreported and unregulated (IUU) fishing which has become the scourge of the oceans, taking place, on both the high seas and within EEZs.[1020] Port State measures have been identified as a key tool in the fight of the international community against IUU fishing, such measures aiming to deny port access to vessels listed as having engaged or supported IUU fishing activities having been enacted by some RFMOs.[1021] After a Model Scheme on Port State

---

[1016] Art. 5 Convention of Biological Diversity (note 1012).

[1017] Scovazzi, *Marine Protected Areas on The High Seas* (note 957), at 9.

[1018] See FAO Code of Conduct for Responsible Fisheries (note 76), Arts. 1 and 6.

[1019] See International Guidelines for the Management of Deep Sea Fisheries in the High Seas, Final Version, 29 August 2008, see in particular the Preamble and para. 10, available at: www.southpacificrfmo.org/assets/6th-Meeting-October-2008-Canberra/DW-Subgroup-VI/ SPRFMO6-SWG-INF01-FAO-Deepwater-Guidelines-Final-Sep20.pdf (last visited 1 July 2011).

[1020] IUU fishing includes a wide range of fishing activities that are prohibited under national law and international conventions. Most common violations involve fishing without license and the use of illegal gear, disregard for established fishing seasons, catching illegal or undersized species, and fishing in closed areas; see R. Daley, *Commentary: New Agreement Establishing Global Port State Measures to Combat IUU Fishing*, 2/1 Australian Journal of Maritime Affairs, at 28 (2010). The FAO has also reported difficulties relating to the number of non-reporting fishing countries, which has increased, as well as a worsening of the quality of capture statistics; see: Oceans and the law of the sea, Report of the Secretary-General, UN doc. A/66/70 of 11 April 2011, at 13.

[1021] See Commission of the European Communities Proposal for a Council Decision, COM (2009), 556 final, 16 October 2009, Explanatory Memorandum. The European Union is a member of the FAO as well as of 13 RFMOs.

measures had already been adopted in 2005, the FAO in 2009 finally approved the "Agreement on Port State Measures to Prevent, Deter and Eliminate Illegal, Unreported and Unregulated Fishing". This Agreement, which will enter into force after adherence by 25 States, is the first ever global treaty focusing specifically on the problem of IUU fishing. It was not, however, approved by consensus as a number of States considered it a limitation of their sovereignty.[1022] The Agreement nevertheless constitutes a significant achievement which highlights widespread support for a mandatory minimum standard of port and flag State enforcement.[1023] Its objective is to prevent, deter and eliminate IUU fishing through the implementation of effective port State measures and thereby to ensure the long term conservation and sustainable use of marine resources and marine ecosystems. A party to the Agreement has the obligation to prohibit entry into and use of its ports by vessels that have engaged in IUU fishing or fishing related activities in support thereof. Such a decision is to be communicated to the flag State and more widely as appropriate.[1024]

The present international fishing regime highlights some of the most interesting trends in the shifting balance of State interest over the ocean.[1025] In view of the international obligations of States to protect and conserve the high seas marine environment the right to fish the high seas has become a qualified rather than an absolute right.[1026] Conservation measures are, however, all the more necessary as global overfishing and other unsustainable fishing practices have adversely affected nearly all commercial fish populations and degraded the ecosystems that support them. According to the FAO 53% of marine fish stocks are estimated to be fully exploited, with no room for further expansion, and 33% to be either overexploited, depleted or recovering from depletion.[1027] This is not surprising in view of the fact that the global fishing fleet is already up to

---

[1022] The "Port State Measures Agreement" was approved by the FAO Governing Conference on 22 November 2009 by 106 countries in favor, 2 against and 12 abstentions. Following its adoption it was signed by the European Union and ten States – Angola, Brazil, Chile, Indonesia, Iceland, Norway, Samoa, Sierra Leone, the United States of America and Uruguay; see FAO Media Centre, "Groundbreaking treaty on illegal fishing approved", available at: www .fao.org/news/story/en/item/37627/icode/ (last visited 1 July 2011). Prior to the entry into force of the Agreement, States or regional economic integration organizations may opt to apply its provisions on a provisional basis (Article 32). The Agreement has been signed by 23 States, but so far there have only been two accessions; see www.fao.org/Legal/treaties/037s-e .htm (last visited 1 July 2011).

[1023] Daley, *Commentary: New Agreement to Combat IUU Fishing* (note 1020), at 28.

[1024] Id., at 30.

[1025] Becker, *The Shifting Public Order of the Oceans* (note 1005), at 199.

[1026] Pendleton, *State Responsibility and the High Seas Marine Environment* (note 77), at 505.

[1027] See FAO, The State of World Fisheries and Agriculture 2010, at 8, available at: www.fao .org/docrep/013/i1820e/i1820e.pdf (last visited 1 July 2011).

250% larger than is needed to catch what the ocean can sustainably produce.[1028] If current trends are not reversed all major commercial fisheries may collapse within the next fifty years.[1029] In view of that danger it has been said that the freedom of high seas fishing has outlived its legitimacy.[1030]

[1028] See: A Role for the WTO: Fisheries Subsidies and Sustainability, Oceana, Protecting World's Oceans, July 2004, Washington, D.C., at 1, available at: na.oceana.org/sites/default/files/reports/SOWF_FINAL_July071.pdf (last visited 1 July 2011).

[1029] See State of The World's Fisheries: What will be left in the Sea?, at 2, available at: na.oceana .org/sites/default/files/o/fileadmin/oceana/uploads/dirty_fishing/Reports/SOWF_FINAL_July07.pdf (last visited 1 July 2011), see also Review of the State of World Marine Fishery Resources, FAO Fisheries Technical Paper 457 (2005), available at: www.fao.org/docrep/009/y5852e/y5852e00.htm (last visited 1 July 2011).

[1030] Pendleton, *State Responsibility and the High Seas Marine Environment* (note 77), at 514; see also Gorina-Ysern, *World Ocean Public Trust: High Seas Fisheries after Grotius* (note 1009), at 651.

Chapter Nine

Conclusion

UNCLOS sets out the legal framework within which all activities in the oceans and seas must be carried out. It represents a compromise between the rights and duties of coastal States on the one hand, and those of the international community on the other, thereby limiting the traditional freedoms of the seas. That balance of interest is under pressure from an extensive interpretation of some of the provisions of the Convention by coastal States attempting to increase their competences with respect to ever larger areas of the sea.[1031]

Over the years, some coastal States have striven to expand their influence in the EEZ by also attempting to exercise control over non-resource related activities. There are indications that the EEZ and the continental shelf are increasingly becoming subject to claims to sovereignty over the area itself and not just to the resources.[1032] A further territorialization of the global commons can therefore not be excluded. It has rightly been pointed out that if the law of the sea is left to drift, it will undoubtedly drift in the direction of increasing coastal State restrictions on global freedoms.[1033] In this respect also landlocked States have a role to play as a kind of "watch-dog" against such tendencies, as their rights – although quite limited – have now become an integral part of the law of the sea: any further development in that field of law, also in view of continuing technological progress, cannot ignore them, if new, universally acceptable legal rules are to be devised.[1034]

It remains to be seen whether the Commission on the Limits of the Continental Shelf will resolve any doubts which may arise with respect to the delineation of the continental margin in favor of the coastal State concerned or the common heritage of mankind[1035] and whether the dispute settlement system established by UNCLOS may have a role to play in this connection. It has also

---

[1031] See Bateman, *Security and the Law of the Sea in East Asia* (note 80), at 386–389.

[1032] See also Kwiatkowska, *The 200 Miles EEZ* (note 103), at 161.

[1033] See Statement of Professor Bernard H. Oxman before the Senate Committee on Foreign Relations, 4 October 2007, at 3, available at: http://www.virginia.edu/colp/pdf/Oxman Testimony071004.pdf (last visited 1 July 2011).

[1034] Hafner, *The 'land-locked' viewpoint* (note 45), at 282.

[1035] Tuerk, *The Waning Freedom of the Seas* (note 15), at 934.

been stated that the concept of the common heritage of mankind is opposed to the freedoms of the high seas,[1036] that these are fundamental principles in conflict.[1037] There are, however, certain parallels between the legal status of the international seabed "Area" and that of the high seas, as no State can claim or exercise sovereignty or sovereign rights over any part of the "Area" or its resources, nor appropriate any part thereof.[1038] The major legal difference is that all rights to the resources of the "Area" are vested in mankind as a whole, on whose behalf the ISA is to act.[1039] With respect to these resources the exercise of individual rights by each and every member of the international community has been replaced by joint exercise through an international organization to which all States are invited to become parties. The international seabed "Area" as common heritage of mankind can in a certain way be considered *res communis*, to some degree corresponding to the approach to the freedom of the seas by Hugo Grotius, while at the same time going substantially beyond his concept.[1040]

The freedom of navigation continues to be a core element of the freedom of the seas, UNCLOS also making ample reference to it[1041] The provisions relating to innocent passage, transit passage and archipelagic sea lanes passage are reminders that the expansion of maritime zones – permitting varied degrees of national sovereignty and concurrent jurisdiction – has limited but not eliminated the freedom of navigation, even in zones of substantial coastal State authority. The rate of erosion of the freedom of the seas has, however, undoubtedly accelerated in recent years.[1042] This can be seen in measures restricting freedom of navigation in various parts of the world. As regards the EEZ it has been pointed out that it is no longer accurate to say that the freedom of navigation exists in that zone to the same extent as on the high seas.[1043] It has on the other hand also been stated that the UNCLOS regime for the EEZ and international straits makes it harder for coastal States to exercise jurisdiction over transiting ships

---

[1036] F.M. Armas Pfirter, *The Management of Seabed Living Resources in "The Area" under UNCLOS*, 11 Revista Electrónica de Estudios Internacionales, at 4 (2006), available at: www.reei.org/index.php/revista/num11/articulos/the-management-of-seabed-living-resources-in-the-area-under-unclos (last visited 1 July 2011).

[1037] See in particular Brown, *Fundamental Principles in Conflict* (note 18).

[1038] See also Oxman, *The High Seas and The International Seabed Area* (note 192), at 540.

[1039] Art. 137 (2) UNCLOS.

[1040] Tuerk, *The Waning Freedom of the Seas* (note 15), at 925.

[1041] See also Wolfrum, *Freedom of Navigation: New Challenges* (note 941), at 2.

[1042] Mapplebeck, *Management of Navigation through Vessel Traffic Services* (note 941), at 138; see also Weinstein, Regulation of Transport of Hazardous Waste (note 162), at 138.

[1043] Van Dyke, *The disappearing right to navigational freedom in the EEZ* (note 108), at 121; see also O.P. Sharma, *The Threat to Freedom of Navigation in the Exclusive Economic Zone (EEZ) – An Emerging Problem*, 18/3 Journal of Indian Ocean Studies, at 342–344 (2010).

despite the fact that any pollution incidents in these zones present an imminent risk for them, making it difficult to comply with their general obligation under UNCLOS to protect the marine environment against pollution.[1044]

There is certainly growing public pressure for more control of shipping, in particular, in the wake of a number of prominent disasters involving major pollution. Coastal States which are most at risk, are naturally concerned about those dangers, but sometimes compensatory measures go beyond the existing rules of the law of the sea.[1045] The IMO is playing an increasingly important role in striking a balance between the rights of all States to maintain the traditional freedom of navigation and the right and duty of coastal States to protect and preserve the marine environment.[1046]

The world's oceans and marine biodiversity are facing serious and multiple threats; 2010 has therefore been proclaimed the International Year of Biodiversity.[1047] Protecting the marine environment and biodiversity in waters beyond national jurisdiction has become an important priority for the international community.[1048] In this context the relationship between UNCLOS – the legal basis for all biodiversity protecting activities in that area – and the CBD will need further clarification[1049] as States hold different views in that respect.[1050] It can be assumed that freedom of navigation will continue to be impacted by ever stricter environmental regulations. Growing environmental concerns may also

---

[1044] Green Paper presented by the Commission of the European Communities, "Towards a future Maritime Policy for the Union: A European vision for the oceans and seas", EU doc .COM (2006) 275 final, Volume II, Annex (7 June 2006), at 42, available at: ec.europa.eu/ maritimeaffairs/pdf/com_2006_0275_en_part2.pdf (last visited 1 July 2011).

[1045] Mapplebeck, *Management of Navigation through Vessel Traffic Services* (note 941), at 138; see also Weinstein, *Regulation of Transport of Hazardous Waste* (note 162), at 169; see further Bateman, Rothwell & VanderZwaag, *Navigational Rights and Freedoms in the New Millennium: 20th Century Controversies and 21st Century Challenges* (note 64), at 323.

[1046] See Roberts, *Protecting Sensitive Marine Environments* (note 923), at 150. See also Art. 235 (3) UNCLOS.

[1047] See www.cbd.int/2010/welcome/ (last visited 1 July 2011). See also UN General Assembly Res. 64/71 (note 250), para. 63.

[1048] See Weinstein, *Regulation of Transport of Hazardous Waste* (note 162), at 169; see also Bateman, Rothwell & VanderZwaag, *Navigational Rights and Freedoms in the New Millennium: 20th Century Controversies and 21st Century Challenges* (note 64), at 323; see further Becker, *The Shifting Public Order of the Oceans* (note 1005), at 171. See also the Preamble of the Manado Ocean Declaration, adopted on 14 May 2009 by the World Ocean Conference held in Manado, Indonesia, which expresses concern over the degradation of the marine environment, in particular the loss of marine biodiversity, and marine ecosystems continuing to be threatened by land-based and sea-based pollution, etc., available at: ec.europa.eu/ maritimeaffairs/pdf/world_ocean_conference_declaration_en.pdf (last visited 1 July 2011).

[1049] EU Commission Green Paper "Towards a future Maritime Policy for the Union" (note 1044), at 43.

[1050] Ridgeway, *Marine Genetic Resources: Outcomes of the UN ICP* (note 260), at 321.

affect the extraction of non-living resources from the seas – within and beyond the limits of national jurisdiction.[1051] As a consequence of mining operations, damage to the seabed is practically unavoidable and the further question of whether waste material might be toxic has not yet even been considered; such operations will most probably be subjected to more stringent regulations in the future.[1052] This entire trend has also been referred to as the "greening" of the law of the sea.[1053]

Navigational freedoms may further erode if the number of States asserting a right to take measures beyond their territorial waters in order to safeguard their security continues to grow.[1054] The resurgent phenomenon of piracy, the unabated terrorist threat at sea, the danger of proliferation of weapons of mass destruction, including their transfer to non-State actors, the continuing traffic in narcotic drugs, certainly provide a strong incentive in this respect.

As long as measures resulting in infringements upon the freedom of navigation are based on multilateral agreements and/or involve competent international organizations they can certainly be considered justified. Such measures may, however, give rise to concern from the point of view of the legal framework established by UNCLOS if they are decreed bilaterally or unilaterally.[1055] The application of stringent measures for the protection of the marine environment has significant future potential but is likely to be carefully scrutinized by those in the international community who wish to limit unreasonable restrictions of navigational rights.[1056]

The freedom of fishing will undoubtedly be subject to further limitations in view of the urgency of a genuinely precautionary, long-term, eco-system approach to fisheries management in order to maintain the sustainability of fish stocks. The coverage of RFMOs could be extended, both geographically and

---

[1051] The number of seabed mining applications is a growing focus for environmentalists' concern in view of the possible damage to marine ecosystems; see Seabed Mining Risks in Pacific and Fiji Talks Agenda, BBC News Asia-Pacific, www.bbc.co.uk/news/world-asia-pacific-13663804 (last visited 1 July 2011).

[1052] See C. Sanders, *Soft Mining Technology Needed: The environmental impact of deep sea mining is still too great*, Evonik Magazine 1/2008, at 17–18, available at: corporate.evonik.com/sites/dc/Downloadcenter/Evonik/Global/en/Magazines/Evonik-Magazine/Evonik-Magazine-1-2008.pdf (last visited 1 July 2011).

[1053] Attributed to Douglas Johnston as quoted by Bateman, *The Compulsory Pilotage Regime in the Torres Strait* (note 953), at 262. It should also be noted that the regulations on prospecting and exploration for polymetallic nodules and polymetallic sulfides provide for the application by the ISA and sponsoring States of the precautionary approach, as reflected in principle 15 of the Rio Declaration; see Oceans and the law of the sea, Report of the Secretary-General (note 1020), UN doc. A/66/70/Add.1 of 11 April 2011, at 29.

[1054] Kaye, *Freedom of Navigation Post 9/11* (note 8), at 364.

[1055] See Wolfrum, *Freedom of Navigation: New Challenges* (note 941), at 2.

[1056] Roberts, *Protecting Sensitive Marine Environments*, (note 923), at 153.

by species, to eliminate unregulated fisheries. One of the results of the World Summit on Sustainable Development in 2002 was that fish stocks should be maintained or restored to levels that can produce the maximum sustainable yield on an urgent basis and where possible not later than 2015.[1057] It has to be acknowledged that flag State jurisdiction has not proven adequate for ensuring compliance, especially in the management of living resources, and some existing and new human activities, such as bioprospecting, are not subject to an international regulatory regime.[1058] Moreover, the sectoral approach by which human activities with respect to the seas are currently governed is not capable of delivering integrated ecosystem-based governance.[1059]

When considering the waning freedom of the seas, it must, however, also be borne in mind that the legal system relating to the oceans and seas based on UNCLOS needs to be further developed in order to cope with new challenges facing the international community.[1060] An enhanced protection of the environment, the conservation of resources, the safeguarding of marine biodiversity and increased security from various threats of violence at sea are in the interest of humankind as a whole. Necessary measures taken in these areas as a result of a multilateral negotiating process certainly justify further limitations of the traditional freedoms of the seas.[1061] Today, that concept needs to be understood in the context of the current range of maritime activities and in relation to all the potentially conflicting uses and interests with respect to marine spaces.[1062] The trend towards an effective overall oceans governance will in all probability increasingly transform the seas beyond the limits of national jurisdiction into a genuine *res communis*[1063] for the benefit of all nations, whether coastal or land-locked, developing or developed.

[1057] EU Commission Green Paper "Towards a future Maritime Policy for the Union" (note 1044), at 20.

[1058] P. Saunders, *Interaction of the RFMOs and the High Seas Regime*, IFLOS, 26 September 2009, presentation available at: www.iflos.org/media/42281/presentationhillipsaunders.pdf (last visited 1 July 2011); see also J. Mossop, *Protecting Marine Biodiversity on the Continental Shelf Beyond 200 Nautical Miles*, 38/3 Ocean Development and International Law, at 294 (2007).

[1059] Id., Saunders.

[1060] EU Commission Green Paper "Towards a future Maritime Policy for the Union" (note 1044), at 43.

[1061] Tuerk, *The Waning Freedom of the Seas* (note 15), at 935, 936.

[1062] Scovazzi, *Marine Protected Areas on The High Seas* (note 957), at 7.

[1063] See also Blanco-Bazán, *Freedom of Navigation – outdated?* (note 27), at 2; see further L. Henkin as quoted by Oxman, *The Territorial Temptation* (note 56), at 851; see also Rayfuse & Warner, *Securing a Sustainable Future for the Oceans Beyond National Jurisdiction* (note 17), at 410–411 and 421.

Bibliography

Adede, A.O., *The System for Settlement of Disputes under the United Nations Convention on the Law of the Sea – A Drafting History and a Commentary*, 10 Publications on Ocean Development (1987).

Alexander, Louis M., *The 'Disadvantaged' States and the Law of the Sea*, 5 Marine Policy (1981), pp. 185–193.

Anand, Ram P., *Freedom of the Seas, Past, Present and Future, in: Law of the Sea*, Hugo Caminos (ed.), Ashgate/Dartmouth/Aldershot/Burlington USA/Singapore/Sydney (2001).

Anderson, David, *Freedom of the High Seas and the Modern Law of the Sea in*: The Law of the Sea, Progress and Prospects. David Freestone, Richard Barnes, David M. Ong (eds.), Oxford University Press, Oxford/New York (2006).

——, *The Development of the Modern Law of the Sea, in: Modern Law of the Sea: Selected Essays*, Martinus Nijhoff Publishers, Leiden/Boston (2008).

Anton, Donald K., Robert A. Makgill and Cymie R. Payne, *Seabed Mining, Advisory Opinion on Responsibility and Liability*, 41/2 Environmental Law and Policy (2011), pp. 60–65.

Armas Pfirter, Frida M., *The Management of Seabed Living Resources in "The Area" under UNCLOS*, 11 Revista Electrónica de Estudios Internacionales (2006), pp. 1–29.

Arnauld, Andreas von, *Die moderne Piraterie und das Völkerrecht*, 47/4 Archiv des Völkerrechts, (2009), pp. 454–480.

Bahar, Michael, *Attaining Optimal Deterrence at Sea: A Legal and Strategic Theory for Naval Anti-Piracy Operations*, 40/1 Vanderbilt Journal of Transnational Law (2007), pp. 1–86.

Balkin, Rosalie, *The International Maritime Organization and Maritime Security*, 30/1 Tulane Maritime Law Journal, (2006), pp. 1–34.

Bantz, Vincent P., *Views from Hamburg: The Juno Trader Case or How to Make Sense of the Coastal State's Right in Light of its Duty of Prompt Release*, 24/2 University of Queensland Law Journal (2005), pp. 415–444.

Barnes, Richard, *Entitlement to Marine Living Resources in Areas Beyond National Jurisdiction, in: The International Legal regime of Areas Beyond National Jurisdiction: Current and Future Developments*, Alex G. Oude Elferink and Erik J. Molenaar (eds.), Martinus Nijhoff Publishers, Leiden/Boston (2010).

Barrios, Erik, *Note: Casting a Wider Net: Addressing the Maritime Piracy Problem in Southeast Asia*, 28/1 Boston College International and Comparative Law Review (2005), pp. 149–163.

Bateman, Sam, *Security and the Law of the Sea in East Asia: Navigational Regimes and Exclusive Economic Zones*, in: The Law of the Sea, Progress and Prospects, David Freestone, Richard Barnes, David Ong (eds.), Oxford University Press, Oxford/New York (2006).

——, *The Compulsory Pilotage Regime in the Torres Strait – A "Melting Pot" of Operational, Legal and Political Considerations*, in: Essays in Tribute to Douglas M. Johnson, Aldo Chircop, Theodore McDorman, Susan Rolston (eds.), Martinus Nijhoff Publishers, Leiden/Boston (2009).

Bateman, Sam, Donald R. Rothwell and David VanderZwaag, *Navigational Rights and Freedoms in the New Millennium: Dealing with 20th Century Controversies and 21st Century Challenges*, in: Navigational Rights and Freedoms and the New Law of the Sea, Donald R. Rothwell and Sam Bateman (eds.), Kluwer Law International, Martinus Nijhoff Publishers, The Hague/Boston/Lancaster (2000).

Bateman, Sam & Michael White, *Compulsory Pilotage in the Torres Strait: Overcoming Unacceptable Risks to a Sensitive Marine Environment*, 40/2 Ocean Development and International Law (2009), pp. 184–203.

Becker, Michael A., *The Shifting Public Order of the Oceans: Freedom of Navigation and the Interdiction of Ships at Sea*, 46/1 Harvard International Law Journal (2005), pp. 131–230.

Beckman, Robert C., *Combatting Piracy and Armed Robbery Against Ships in Southeast Asia: The Way Forward*, 33 Ocean Development and International Law (2002), pp. 317–341.

——, *Semaphore – the Newsletter of the Sea Power Centre Australia, Compulsory Pilotage in the Torres Strait*, 153 Maritime Studies (2007), pp. 23–26.

——, *PSSAs and Transit Passage: Australia's Pilotage System in the Torres Strait Challenges the IMO and UNCLOS*, 38 Ocean Development and International Law (2007), pp. 325–357.

——, *The 1988 SUA Convention and 2005 SUA Protocol: Tools to Combat Piracy, Armed Robbery and Maritime Terrorism*, in: Lloyd's MIU Handbook of Maritime Security, Rupert H. Burns, S. Bateman and P. Lehr (eds.), New York: CRC Press, Taylor and Francis Group (2009).

Beslier, Serge, *The Protection and Sustainable Exploitation of Genetic Resources of the High Seas from the European Union's Perspective*, 24/2 The International Journal of Marine and Coastal Law (2009), pp. 333–341.

Birnie, Patricia, *Law of the Sea and Ocean Resources: Implications for Marine Scientific Research*, 10/2 The International Journal Marine and Coastal Law (1995), pp. 229–251.

Blanco-Bazán, Agustín, *Freedom of Navigation – an outdated concept?, Lecture to the Summer Academy*, ITLOS Hamburg (2007).

——, *Suppressing Unlawful Acts: IMO Incursion in the Field of Criminal Law*, in: Law of the Sea, Environmental Law and Settlement of Disputes, Tafsir Malick Ndiaye, Rüdiger Wolfrum (eds.), Martinus Nijhoff Publishers, Leiden (2007).

——, *War Against Piracy?: Some Misconceptions and Oversights in the Repression of Crimes at Sea*, Il diritto marittimo, Anno CXI, Terza Serie, Fascicolo I (2009), pp. 264–270.

Boese, Wade, *Proliferation Security Initiative: A Piece of the Arms Control Puzzle*, 6 Georgetown Journal of International Affairs (2005), pp. 61–69.

Boyle, Alan E., *'Dispute Settlement and the Law of the Sea Convention: Problems of Fragmentation and Jurisdiction'*, 46/1 International Comparative Law Quarterly (1997), pp. 37–54.

——, *The International Tribunal for the Law of the Sea and the Settlement of Disputes*, in: The Changing World of International Law in the Twenty-First Century, Joseph J. Norton et al. (eds.), Kluwer Law International, The Hague/London/Boston (1998).

——, *The Environmental Jurisprudence of the International Tribunal for the Law of the Sea*, 22/3 The International Journal of Marine and Coastal Law (2007), pp. 459–466.

Brown, Edward Duncan, *Freedom of the High Seas Versus the Common Heritage of Mankind: Fundamental Principles in Conflict*, 20 San Diego Law Review 521 (1982–1983), pp. 521–560.

Burns, Rupert Herbert, Sam Bateman and Peter Lehr (eds.), *Lloyds MIU Handbook of Maritime Security*, CRC Press, London (2008).

Caflisch, Lucius C., *The Doctrine of 'Mare Clausum' and the Third United Nations Conference on the Law of the Sea*, in: International Relations in a Changing World, R. Blackhurst et al. (eds.), Sijthoff Publisher, Leiden (1977).

——, *Land-locked States and their Access to and from the Sea*, 49 British Yearbook of International Law (1978), pp. 71–100.

Caminos, Hugo, *The International Tribunal for the Law of the Sea: An Overview of its Jurisdictional Procedure*, in: New International Tribunals and New International Proceedings, A. Del Vecchio (ed.), Giuffrè Editore, Milano (2006).

Carducci, Guido, *New Developments in the Law of the Sea: The UNESCO Convention on the Protection of Underwater Cultural Heritage*, 96 American Journal of International Law (2002), pp. 419–434.

Carleton, Chris, *Article 76 of the UN Convention on the Law of the Sea – Implementation Problems from the Technical Perspective*, 21/3 International Journal of Marine and Coastal Law (2006), pp. 287–308.

Castañeda, Jorge, *Negotiations on the Exclusive Economic Zone at the Third United Nations Conference on the Law of the Sea*, in: Essays in International Law in Honour of Judge Manfred Lachs, Jerzy Makarczyk (ed.), Martinus Nijhoff Publishers, The Hague/Boston/Lancaster (1984).

Cavnar, Anna, *Accountability and the Commission on the Limits of the Continental Shelf: Deciding Who Owns the Ocean Floor*, 42/3 Cornell International Law Journal, (2009).

Chandrasekhara Rao, P., *ITLOS: The First Six Years*, in: 6 Max Planck Yearbook of United Nations Law, A. von Bogdandy and R. Wolfrum (eds.), Kluwer Law International, The Hague/London/New York (2002), pp. 183–300.

——, *ITLOS: The Conception of the Judicial Function*, in: Coexistence, Cooperation and Solidarity, Liber Amicorum Rüdiger Wolfrum, vol. II, Holger P. Hestermeyer/D. Koenig et al. (eds.), Martinus Nijhoff Publishers, Leiden/Boston (2012).

Chircop, Aldo, *The Designation of Particularly Sensitive Sea Areas: A New Layer in the Regime for Marine Environmental Protection from International Shipping*, in: The Future of Ocean Regime-building; Essays in Tribute to Douglas M. Johnston, Aldo Chircop, Ted McDorman, Susan Rolston (eds.), Martinus Nijhoff Publishers, Leiden (2009).

Chuah, Jason, *EU maritime security – protecting maritime transport from piracy*, 16/1 Journal of International Maritime Law (2010), pp. 5–6.

Churchill, Robin R., *10 Years of the UN Convention on the Law of the Sea – Towards a Global Ocean Regime? A General Appraisal*, 48 German Yearbook of International Law (2005), pp. 81–116.

——, *Some Reflections on the Operation of the Dispute Settlement System of the UN Convention on the Law of the Sea During its First Decade*, in: The Law of the Sea, Progress and Prospects, D. Freestone, R. Barnes and D.M. Ong (eds.), Oxford University Press, Oxford/New York (2006).

——, *The Jurisprudence of the International Tribunal for the Law of the Sea Relating to Fisheries: Is There Much In The Net?*, 22/3 The International Journal of Marine and Coastal Law (2007), pp. 383–424.

——, *Dispute Settlement under the UN Convention on the Law of the Sea: Survey for 2008*, 24/4 The International Journal of Marine and Coastal Law (2009), pp. 603–616.

Cogliati-Bantz, Vincent, *Views from Hamburg: The Juno Trader Case or How to Make Sense of the Coastal State's Rights in Light of its Duty of Prompt Release*, 24/2 University of Queensland Law Journal (2005).

Collins, Rosemary and Daud Hassan, *Applications and Shortcomings of the Law of the Sea in Combating Piracy: A South East Asian Perspective*, 40/1 Journal of Maritime Law and Commerce (2009), 89–113.

Costa, Antonio, *Fighting Piracy on Land and at Sea*: Testimony to the *U.S.* House of Representatives, Foreign Affairs Subcommittee on International Organizations, Human Rights and Oversight, Washington, May 14, 2009.

Cronan, David, *A Fortune on the Seabed*, UNESCO Courier (1986).

Dahlvang, Nicholas, *Thieves, Robbers and Terrorists: Piracy in the 21st Century*, 4 Regent Journal of International Law (2006), pp. 17–45.

Daley, Robert, *Commentary: New Agreement Establishing Global Port State Measures to Combat IUU Fishing*, 2/1 Australian Journal of Maritime Affairs (2010), pp. 28–31.

Danilenko, Gennady M., *The Concept of the "Common Heritage of Mankind" in International Law*, XIII Annals of Air and Space Law, Editions A. Pedone, Paris (1988), pp. 247–265.

Davidson, Scott, *The Law of the Sea and Freedom of Navigation in Asia Pacific*, in: International Law Issues in the South Pacific, Jeff Leane and Barbara Van Tigerstrom (eds.), University of Canterbury, New Zealand (2005).

DeCaro, Phil, *Safety Among Dragons: East Asia and Maritime Security*, 33 Transportation Law Journal (2005–2007), pp. 227–248.

Diaz, Leticia & Barry Hart Dubner, *On the Problem of Utilizing Unilateral Action to Prevent Acts of Sea Piracy and Terrorism: A Protective Approach to the Evolution of International Law*, 32/1 Syracuse Journal of International Law and Commerce (2005), pp. 1–50.

——, *Environmental Damage and the Destruction of Life – Problems that Add a New Balancing Dimension to International Port Access vs. Efficient Trade Under International Law*, 10 Barry Law Review (2008), pp. 1–23.

Dromgoole, Sarah, *Legal Protection for the Underwater Cultural Heritage: The Immediate Challenge and Methods of Response*, in: The Recent Developments in the Law of the Sea and China, Myron H. Nordquist, John Norton Moore and Kuen-chen Fu (eds.), Martinus Nijhoff Publishers, Leiden/Boston (2006).

Dupuy, René-Jean, *The Law of the Sea: Current Problems*, Oceana Publications Dobbs Ferry, N.Y., (1974).

——, *La mer sous compétence nationale*, in: Traité du Nouveau Droit de la Mer, René-Jean Dupuy and Daniel Vignes (eds.), Economica/Paris/Bruylant/Bruxelles (1985).

Dupuy, René-Jean and Daniel Vignes (eds.), *A Handbook on the New Law of the Sea*, Martinus Nijhoff Publishers, Dordrecht/Boston/Lancaster (1991).

Ehlers, Peter and Marian Paschke (eds.), *Meeresfreiheit und Ocean Governance – Festgabe zum 65. Geburtstag von Rainer Lagoni*, Schriftenreihe der Fakultät für Rechtswissenschaften der Universität Hamburg (2008).

Eklöf, Stefan, *Pirates in Paradise: A Modern History of Southeast Asia's Maritime Marauders*, Book Review, 7/2 WMU Journal of Maritime Affairs (2008), pp. 509–511.

Escher, Anne-Katrin, *Release of Vessels and Crews before the International Tribunal for the Law of the Sea*, 3/2 The Law and Practice of International Courts and Tribunals: A Practicioner's Journal, E. Valencia-Ospina (ed.) (2004), pp. 205–374.

Fischer-Lescano, Andreas and Lena Kreck, *Piraterie und Menschenrechte: Rechtsfragen der Bekämpfung der Piraterie im Rahmen der europäischen Operation Atalanta*, 47/4 Archiv des Völkerrechts (2009), pp. 481–524.

Franckx, Eric, *The 200 Mile Limit: Between Creeping Jurisdiction and Creeping Common Heritage?*, 39/3 George Washington International Law Review (2007), pp. 467–498.

Freestone, David, *The 1988 International Convention for the Suppression of Unlawful Acts Against the Safety of Maritime Navigation*, 3 International Journal of Estuarine and Coastal Law (1988), pp. 305–327.

——, *A Decade of the Law of the Sea Convention: Is It a Success?*, 39/3 George Washington International Law Review (2007), pp. 499–542.

——, *Advisory Opinion of the Seabed Disputes Chamber of International Tribunal for the Law of the Sea on "Responsibilities and Obligations of States Sponsoring Persons and Entities With Respect To Activities in the Area"*, 15/7 American Society of International Law, Insights, Final Thoughts (2011).

Garmon, Tina, *International Law of the Sea: Reconciling the Law of Piracy and Terrorism in the Wake of September 11th*, 27 Tulane Maritime Law Journal (2002–2003), pp. 257–276.

Gautier, Philippe, *Les affaires de 'prompte mainlevée' devant le Tribunal international du droit de la mer*, 3/d Global Community Yearbook of International Law and Jurisprudence (2003), pp. 79–106.

——, *Le Règlement Obligatoire des Différends Relatifs au Droit de la Mer et la Pratique des Etats*, The Global Community Yearbook of International Law and Jurisprudence (I) (2009), pp. 107–125.

——, *Urgent Proceedings before the International Tribunal for the Law of the Sea*, 8/1 Issues in Legal Scholarship (2009), pp. 1–20.

——, *The International Tribunal for the Law of the Sea: Activities in 2009*, 9/4 Chinese Journal of International Law (2010), pp. 783–798.

Gjerde, Kristina M., *Current Legal Developments: High Seas Marine Protected Areas*, 16/3 The International Journal of Marine and Coastal Law (2001), pp. 515–528.

Glassner, Martin I., *The Status of Developing Landlocked States since 1965*, 5/3 Lawyer of the Americas (1973), pp. 480–498.

——, *Developing Land-locked States and the Resources of the Seabed*, San Diego Law Review (1973–1974), pp. 633–655.

Goldie, L. Frederick E., *A Note on some diverse meaning of "The Common Heritage of Mankind"*, 10 Syracuse Journal International Law and Commerce (1983), pp. 69–112.

Goodwin, Joshua Michael, *Universal Jurisdiction and the Pirate: Time for an Old Couple to Part*, 39 Vanderbilt Journal of Transnational Law (2006), pp. 973–1012.

Gorina-Ysern, Montserrat, *World Ocean Public Trust: High Seas Fisheries after Grotius – Towards a New Ocean Ethos?*, 34/3 Golden Gate University Law Review (2004), pp. 645–714.

——, *An International Regime for Marine Scientific Research*, 9 Transnational Publishers, Ardsley, New York (2005).

Guilfoyle, C. Douglas, *Piracy off Somalia: UN Security Council Resolution 1816 and IMO Regional Counter Piracy Efforts*, 57 International and Comparative Law Quarterly (2008), pp. 690–699.

Guntrip, Edward, *The Common Heritage of Mankind: An Adequate Regime for Managing the Deep Seabed?*, 4/2 Melbourne Journal of International Law (2003), pp. 376–405.

Hafner, Gerhard, *Die Gruppe der Binnen- und geographisch benachteiligten Staaten auf der Dritten Seerechtskonferenz der Vereinten Nationen*, 38 Zeitschrift für ausländisches öffentliches Recht und Völkerrecht (1978), pp. 568–615.

——, *The 'land-locked' viewpoint*, 5 Marine Policy (1981), pp. 281–282.

——, *The Regulation of Marine Scientific Research Activities of Landlocked and Geographically Dis-advantaged States in the Draft Convention on the Law of the Sea*, in: The Law of the Sea in the 1980s, Proceedings of the 14th Annual Conference of the Law of the Sea Institute, October 20–23, 1980, C. Park (ed.) (1983).

——, *Bemerkungen zur Funktion und Bestimmung der Betroffenheit im Völkerrecht anhand des Binnenstaates*, 31 German Yearbook of International Law (1988), pp. 187–229.

——, *The Rights of Landlocked States in the Baltic Area*, in: The Baltic Sea: New Developments in National Policies and International Cooperation, Renate Platzöder and Philomène Verlaan (eds.), Martinus Nijhoff Publishers, The Hague/London/Boston (1996).

——, *Austria and the Law of the Sea*, in: The Law of the Sea: The European Union and its Member States, Tullio Treves and Laura Pineschi (eds.), Martinus Nijhoff Publishers, The Hague/London/Boston (1997).

Hakapää, Kari, *Foreign Ships in Vulnerable Waters: Coastal Jurisdiction over Vessel-Source Pollution with Special Reference to the Baltic Sea*, 33 International Journal of Legal Information (2005), pp. 256–266.

Halberstam, Malvina, *Terrorism on the High Seas: The Achille Lauro, Piracy and the IMO Convention on Maritime Safety*, 82/2 American Journal of International Law (1988), pp. 269–310.

Hanson, Stephanie, *Combating Maritime Piracy*, Council on Foreign Relations Publications (2010).

Harrington, Caitlin A., *Heightened Security: The need to Incorporate Articles 3bis (1) (A) and 8bis (5) (E) of the 2005 Draft SUA Protocol into Part VII of the United Nations Convention on the Law of the Sea*, 16 Pacific Rim Law and Policy Journal (2007), pp. 107–136.

Hasselmann, Cord-Georg, *Die Freiheit der Handelsschiffahrt: eine Analyse der UN – Seerechtskonven-tion*, N.P. Engel Verlag, Kehl am Rhein (1987).

Hayashi, Moritaka, *Enforcement by Non-Flag States on the High Seas under the 1995 Agreement on Straddling and Highly Migratory Fish Stocks*, 9 Georgetown International Environmental Law Review (1996–1997), pp. 1–36.

——, *Introductory Note to the Regional Cooperation Agreement on Combating Piracy and Armed Robbery Against Ships in Asia*, 44 International Legal Materials (2005), pp. 826–828.

Heim, Barbara Ellen, *Exploring the Last Frontiers for Mineral Resources: A Comparison of Interna-tional Law Regarding the Deep Seabed, Outer Space, and Antarctica*, 23 Vanderbilt Journal of Transnational Law (1990–1991), pp. 819–850.

Hinrichs, Ximena, *Die Ausschließliche Wirtschaftszone und die Praxis der lateinamerikanischen Staaten*, Lit Verlag, Hamburg (1997).

Hjalmarsson, Johanna, *Piracy and International Law*, 8/10 Shipping & Trade Law (2008), pp. 1–3.

Jesus, José Luis, *Protection of Foreign Ships against Piracy and Terrorism at Sea: Legal Aspects*, 18/3 The International Journal of Maritime and Coastal Law (2003), pp. 363–400.

Johnson, Derek S. and Erika Pladdet, *Maritime Piracy in Asia*, 32 IIAS Newsletter 45 (2003).

Joyner, Christopher C., *The Proliferation Security Initiative: Nonproliferation, Counterproliferation, and International Law*, 30 Yale Journal of International Law (2005), pp. 507–548.

Kachel, Markus J., *Particularly Sensitive Areas: the IMO's Role in Protecting Vulnerable Marine Areas*, 13 Hamburg Studies on Maritime Affairs (2008).

Kamto, Maurice, *Regard sur la jurisprudence du tribunal international du droit de la mer depuis son entrée en fonctionnement (1997–2004)*, 109/4 Revue générale de droit international public (2005), pp. 793–828.

Kaye, Stuart B., *Regulation of Navigation in the Torres Strait: Law of the Sea Issues*, in: Navigational Rights and Freedoms and the New Law of the Sea, Donald R. Rothwell and Sam Bateman (eds.), Kluwer International, The Hague (2000).

——, *Freedom of Navigation in a Post 9/11 World, Security and Creeping Jurisdiction*, in: The Law of the Sea – Progress and Prospects, David Freestone, Richard Barnes and David. M. Ong (eds.), Oxford University Press, Oxford/New York (2006).

——, *State Practice and Maritime Claims: Assessing the Normative Impact of the Law of the Sea Convention*, in: The Future of Ocean Regime-Building: Essays in Tribute to Douglas M. John-ston, Aldo Chircop, Ted L. McDorman and Susan J. Rolston (eds.), Martinus Nijhoff Pub-lishers, Leiden (2009).

Keyuan, Zou, *Governing Marine Scientific Research in China*, Singapore: East Asian Institute, National University of Singapore (2001).

——, *Law of the Sea Issues between the United States and East Asian States*, 39/1 Ocean Develop-ment and International Law (2008), pp. 69–93.

——, *The International Tribunal for the Law of the Sea: Procedures, Practices, and Asian States*, 41/2 Ocean Development and International Law (2010), pp. 131–151.

——, *Maritime Enforcement of United Nations Security Council Resolutions: Use of Force and Coercive Measures*, 26/2 The International Journal of Maritime and Coastal Law (2011), pp. 235–261.

Khalid, Nazery, *A Rush of Blood to the Head? Some Reflections on Post-9/11 Maritime Security Measures*, 21 Ocean Yearbook (2007), pp. 505–526.

Kieserman, Brad, *Preventing and Defeating Terrorism at Sea: Practical Considerations for the Imple-mentation of the Draft Protocol to the Convention for the Suppression of Unlawful Acts Against the Safety of Maritime Navigation (SUA)*, in: Recent Developments in the Law of the Sea and China, Myron H. Nordquist, John Norton Moore, and Kuen-Chen Fu (eds.), Martinus Nijhoff Publishers, Leiden/Boston (2005).

Kirsch, Philipp, *The 1988 ICAO and IMO Conferences: An International Consensus against Terrorism*, 12 Dalhousie Law Journal (1989–1990), pp. 5–33.

Kiss, Alexandre-Charles, *La notion de patrimoine commun de l'humanité, 172–II Recueil des Cours*, Collected Courses of the Hague Academy 1982, Martinus Nijhoff Publishers, The Hague/Boston/London (1983).

——, *The Common Heritage of Mankind: Utopia or Reality?*, 40 International Journal (1984–1985), pp. 423–441.

——, *Conserving the Common Heritage of Mankind*, 39 Revista Juridica Universidad de Puerto Rico (1990), pp. 773–777.

Klein, Natalie, *Dispute Settlement in the UN Convention on the Law of the Sea*, Cambridge University Press, Cambridge (2005).

——, *The Right of Visit and the 2005 Protocol on the Suppression of Unlawful Acts Against the Safety of Maritime Navigation*, 35 Denver Journal of International Law and Policy (2006–2007), pp. 287–332.

Koh, Tommy T.B., *A Constitution for the Oceans, Remarks made by the President of the Third United Nations Conference on the Law of the Sea*, in: Official Text of the United Nations Convention on the Law of the Sea with Annexes and Index (1983).

——, *The Origins of the 1982 Convention on the Law of the Sea*, 29/1 Malaya Law Review (1987), pp. 1–17.

——, *The Territorial Sea, Contiguous Zone, Straits and Archipelagoes under the 1982 Convention on the Law of the Sea*, 29/2 Malaya Law Review (1987), pp. 163–199.

König, Doris, *Die EU-Meeresverschmutzungsrichtlinie – Weiterentwicklung oder Bruch des Seevölkerrechts?*, in: Meeresfreiheit und Ocean Governance – Festgabe zum 65. Geburtstag von Rainer Lagoni, Peter Ehlers, Marian Paschke (eds.), Lit Verlag, Münster (2008).

Kontorovich, Eugene, *International Legal Responses to Piracy off the Coast of Somalia*, 13/2 American Society of International Law, Insights (2009).

——, *"A Guantanamo on the Sea": The Difficulty of Prosecuting Pirates and Terrorists*, 98 California Law Review (2010), pp. 243–276.

Korolyova, Natalya D., *International Legal Issues of Cooperation Between States in Suppressing Piracy and Terrorism: Some Aspects, Moscow Symposium on the Law of the Sea*, Thomas A. Clingan, Jr. and Anatoly L. Kolodkin (eds.), Law of the Sea Institute, University of Hawaii (1988).

Kraska, James, *The Law of the Sea Convention and the Northwest Passage*, 22/2 International Journal of Marine and Coastal Law (2007), pp. 257–281.

——, *Developing Piracy Policy for the National Strategy for Maritime Security*, in: Legal Challenges in Maritime Security, Myron H. Nordquist, Rüdiger Wolfrum, John Norton Moore and Ronán Long (eds.), Martinus Nijhoff Publishers, Leiden/Boston (2008).

——, *Coalition Strategy and the Pirates of the Gulf of Aden and the Red Sea*, 28/3 Comparative Strategy (2009), pp. 197–216.

Kraska, James & Brian Wilson, *Combating pirates of the Gulf of Aden: The Djibouti Code and the Somali Coast Guard*, 52 Ocean and Coastal Management (2009), pp. 516–520.

——, *Piracy Repression, Partnering and the Law*, 40/1 Journal of Maritime Law and Commerce, (2009), pp. 43–58.

Kullenberg, Gunnar, *The Exclusive Economic Zone: Some Perspectives*, 42/9 Ocean and Coastal Management (1999), pp. 747–765.

Kunoy, Bjørn, *The Rise of the Sun: Legal Arguments in Outer Continental Margin Delimitations*, 53/2 Netherlands International Law Review (2006), pp. 247–272.

——, *Establishment of the Outer Limits of the Continental Shelf: Is Crossing Boundaries Trespassing?*, 26/2 The International Journal of Maritime and Coastal Law (2011), pp. 313–334.

Kwiatkowska, Barbara, *The 200 Mile Exclusive Economic Zone in the New Law of the Sea*, Martinus Nijhoff Publishers, Dordrecht/Boston/London (1989).

——, *Creeping Jurisdiction beyond 200 Miles in the Light of the 1982 Law of the Sea Convention and State Practice*, 22/2 Ocean Development and International Law (1991), pp. 153–187.

La Fayette, Louise A. de, *A New Regime for the Conservation and Sustainable Use of Marine Biodiversity and Genetic Resources Beyond the Limits of National Jurisdiction*, 24/2 The International Journal of Marine and Coastal Law (2009), pp. 221–280.

——, *The Sound Management of Wastes Generated at Sea – MARPOL, not Basel*, 39/4–5 Environmental Policy and Law (2009), pp. 207–214.

——, *Principles and Objectives of the Legal Regime Governing Areas Beyond National Jurisdiction*, in: The International Legal Regime of Areas Beyond National Jurisdiction: Current and Future Developments, Alex G. Oude Elferink and Erik J. Molenaar (eds.), Martinus Nijhoff Publishers, Leiden/Boston (2010), pp. 221–280.

Lagoni, Rainer, *Marine Protected Areas in the Exclusive Economic Zone*, in: International Marine Environmental Law, Institutions, Implementations and Innovations, A. Kirchner (ed.), Kluwer Law International, The Hague/New York (2003).

——, *Festlandsockel und Ausschließliche Wirtschaftszone*, in: Handbuch des Seerechts, Wolfgang Graf Vitzthum (ed.), Verlag C.H. Beck, München (2006).

Lagoni, Rainer, and Marian Paschke, *Seehandelsrecht und Seerecht: Festschrift für Rolf Herber zum 70. Geburtstag*, Lit Verlag, Hamburg (1999).

Laly-Chevalier, Caroline, *Lutte contre la piraterie maritime et droits de l'homme*, 42/1 Revue belge de droit international (2009), pp. 5–51.

Lapidoth, Ruth, *Freedom of Navigation – its Legal History and its Normative Basis*, Journal of Maritime Law and Commerce (1975), pp. 259–272.

Lavranos, Nikolaos, *The MOX Plant judgment of the ECJ: How exclusive is the jurisdiction of the ECJ?*, 15/10 European Environmental Law Review (2006), pp. 291–296.

Lefebvre-Chalain, Hélène, *Fifteen Years of Particularly Sensitive Sea Areas: A Concept in Development*, 13/1 Ocean and Coastal Law Journal (2007), pp. 47–39.

Lehmann, Friederike, *The Legal Status of Genetic Resources of the Deep Seabed*, 11 New Zealand Journal of Environmental Law (2007), pp. 33–66.

Lelarge, Aurélia, *La Somalie entre anarchie et piraterie*, 137/2 Journal du droit international (2010), pp. 449–474.

LeSieur, François, *Commentaire sur la nouvelle loi française relative à la lutte contre la piraterie et à l'exercice des pouvoirs de police de l'état en mer*, 4/1 Journal of East Asia and International Law (2011), pp. 115–129.

Lodge, Michael W., *The International Seabed Authority and Article 82 of the UN Convention on the Law of the Sea*, 21/3 The International Journal of Marine and Coastal Law, (2006), pp. 323–333.

Logan, Samuel E., *The Proliferation Security Initiative: Navigating the Legal Challenges*, 14 Journal of Transnational Law and Policy (2004–2005), pp. 323–333.

Lowry, Thea, *Protecting the Mysteries of the Deep: Conserving Biodiversity in Marine Areas Beyond National Jurisdiction*, 16 Dalhousie Journal of Legal Studies (2007), pp. 113–134.

Lupinacci, Julio César, *The Legal Status of the Exclusive Economic Zone in the 1982 Convention on the Law of the Sea*, in: The Exclusive Economic Zone, A Latin American Perspective, Francisco Orrego-Vicuña (ed.), WestView Press, Boulder, Colorado (1984).

Mackenzie, Ruth et al., *The International Tribunal for the Law of the Sea, Manual on International Courts and Tribunals*, Oxford University Press, Oxford/New York (2010).

Mapplebeck, Graham, *Management of Navigation through Vessel Traffic Services*, in: Navigational Rights and Freedoms and the New Law of the Sea, Donald R. Rothwell and Sam Bateman (eds.), Martinus Nijhoff Publishers, The Hague/London/Boston (2000).

Martinez Guttierrez, Norman A. (ed.), *Serving the Rule of International Maritime Law, Essays in honour of Professor David Joseph Attard*, Routledge, London/NewYork (2010).

Matz-Lück, Nele, *The Concept of the Common Heritage of Mankind: Its Viability as a Management Tool for Deap-Sea Genetic Resources*, in: The International Legal Regime of Areas Beyond National Jurisdiction: Current and Future Developments, Alex G. Oude Elferink and Erik J. Molenaar (eds.), Martinus Nijhoff Publishers, Leiden/Boston (2010).

Mellor, Justin S.C., *Missing the Boat: The Legal and Practical Problems of the Prevention of Maritime Terrorism*, 18 American University International Law Review (2002–2003), pp. 341–397.

Mensah, Thomas A., *Provisional Measures in the International Tribunal for the Law of the Sea*, 62 1/2 Zeitschrift für ausländisches öffentliches Recht und Völkerrecht (2002), pp. 43–54.

——, *Suppression of Terrorism at Sea: Developments in the Wake of the Events of 11 September 2001*, in: Verhandeln für den Frieden – Negotiating for Peace, Liber Amicorum Tono Eitel, Jochen Frowein et al. (eds.), Springer, Berlin (2003).

Mingay, George, *Article 82 of the LOS Convention: Revenue Sharing – The Mining Industry's Perspective*, 21/3 The International Journal of Marine and Coastal Law (2006), pp. 335–346.

Monnier, Jean, *Right of Access to the Sea and Freedom of Transit, in*: A Handbook on the New Law of the Sea, René-Jean Dupuy and Daniel Vignes (eds.), The Hague, Martinus Nijhoff Publishers (1981).

Morita, Akio, *Piracy Jure Gentium Revisited: For Japan's Future Contribution*, 51 Japanese Yearbook of International Law (2008), pp. 76–97.

Mossop, Joanna, *Protecting Marine Biodiversity on the Continental Shelf Beyond 200 Nautical Miles*, 38/3 Ocean Development and International Law (2007), pp. 283–304.

Nelson, Dolliver M. *The New Deep Seabed Mining Regime*, 10 The International Journal of Marine and Coastal Law (1995), pp. 198–203.

——, *The Continental Shelf: Interplay of Law and Science*, in: Liber Amicorum Judge Shigeru Oda, Nisuke Ando et al. (eds.), Kluwer Law International, The Hague/London/Boston (2002).

——, *Reflections on the 1982 Convention on the Law of the Sea*, in: Law of the Sea: Progress and Prospects, David Freestone, Richard Barnes, David Ong (eds.), Oxford University Press, Oxford/New York (2006).

——, *The Settlement of Disputes Arising From Conflicting Outer Continental Shelf Claims*, 24/4 The International Journal of Marine and Coastal Law (2009), pp. 409–422.

Nicholson, Graham, *The Common Heritage of Mankind and Mining: An Analysis of the Law as to the High Seas, Outer Space, the Antarctic and World Heritage*, 6 New Zealand Journal of Environmental Law (2002), pp. 177–198.

Nöll, Hans-Heinrich, *Schifffahrtsfreiheit und Meeresumweltschutz im Seerechtsübereinkommen von 1982 – sie richtig austariert?* in: Meeresfreiheit und Ocean Governance – Festgabe zum 65. Geburtstag von Rainer Lagoni, Peter Ehlers and Marian Paschke (eds.), Schriftenreihe der Fakultät für Rechtswissenschaften der Universität Hamburg (2008).

Noyes, John E., *Compulsory Third-Party Adjudication and the 1982 United Nations Convention on the Law of the Sea*, 4 Connecticut Journal of International Law (1988–1989), pp. 675–696.

——, *The International Tribunal for the Law of the Sea*, 32 Cornell International Law Journal (1999), pp. 109–182.

——, *Judicial and Arbitral Proceedings and the Outer Limit of the Continental Shelf*, 42 Vanderbilt Journal of Transnational Law (2009), pp. 1211–1264.

Oude Elferink, Alex G., *Article 76 of the LOSC on the Definition of the Continental Shelf: Questions Concerning its Interpretation from a Legal Perspective*, 21/3 The International Journal of Marine and Coastal Law (2006), pp. 269–285.

——, *The Regime of the Area: Delineating the Scope of Application of the Common Heritage Principle and Freedom of High Seas*, 22/1 The International Journal of Marine and Coastal Law (2007), pp. 143–176.

——, *Clarifying Article 121(3) of the Law of the Sea Convention: The Limits Set By Nature Of International Legal Processes*, 6/2 IBRU, Boundary and Security Bulletin (2008), pp. 58–68.

Oxman, Bernard H., *The Regime of Warships under the United Nations Convention on the Law of the Sea*, 24 Virginia Journal of International Law (1984), pp. 809–864.

——, *The High Seas and The International Seabed Area*, 10 Michigan Journal of International Law (1989), pp. 526–542.

——, *The 1994 Agreement and the Convention*, in: Law of the Sea Forum: The 1994 Agreement on Implementation of the Seabed Provisions of the Convention on the Law of the Sea, 88 American Journal of International Law (1994), pp. 687–696.

——, *The Territorial Temptation; A Siren Song at Sea*, 100 American Journal of International Law (2006), pp. 830–851.

——, *The Barbados/Trinidad and Tobago Arbitration Award of 2006*, Belinda Macmahon (Series Editor), T.M.C. Asser Press, The Hague (2009).

Passman, Michael H., *Protections Afforded to Captured Pirates Under the Law of War and International Law*, 33/1 Tulane Maritime Law Journal (2008), pp. 1–40.

Pardo, Arvid & Carl Q. Christol, *The Common Interest: Big Tension between the Whole and Parts*, in: The Structure and Process of International Law: Essays in Legal Philosophy, Doctrine and Theory, Ronald St. J. Macdonald, Douglas M. Johnston (eds.), Martinus Nijhoff Publishers, Dordrecht/Boston/Lancaster (1986).

Pedrozo, Raul, *Encroachment on Navigational Freedom*, 84 International Legal Study Series, US Naval War College (2008), pp. 85–96.

Peet, Gerard, and Susan Gubbay, *Marine Protected Areas in the North Sea*, 5 International Journal of Estuarine and Coastal Law (1990), pp. 241–251.

Pendleton, Gregory D., *State Responsibility and the High Seas Marine Environment: A Legal Theory for the Protection of Seamounts in the Global Commons*, 14 Pacific Rim Law and Policy Journal (2005), pp. 485–514.

Peppetti, Jon D., *Building the Global Maritime Security Network: A Multinational Legal Structure to Combat Transnational Threats*, 55 Naval Law Review (2008), pp. 73–156.

Plant, Glen, *The Convention for the Suppression of Unlawful Acts Against the Safety of Maritime Navigation*, 39 International and Comparative Law Quarterly (1990), pp. 27–56.

Pulvenis, Jean François, *Le plateau continental, définition et régime*, in: Traité du nouveau droit de la mer, R.J. Dupuy and D. Vignes, (eds.), Economica, Bruylant, Paris/Bruxelles (1985).

Potts, Tavis and Clive Schofield, *Current Legal Developments: The Arctic*, 23 The International Journal of Marine and Coastal Law (2008), pp. 151–176.

Power, Jason, *Maritime Terrorism: A New Challenge for National and International Security*, 10 Barry Law Review (2008), pp. 111–134.

Proelss, Alexander, *Ausschließliche Wirtschaftszone*, in: Handbuch des Seerechts, Wolfgang Graf Vitzthum (ed.), Verlag C.H. Beck, München (2006).

——, *Marine Genetic Resources under UNCLOS and the CBD*, 51 German Yearbook of International Law (2008), pp. 417–446.

Rasband, James R., James Salzman and Mark Squillace, *Natural Resources Law and Policy*, in: Natural Resources Law and Policy, Foundation Press, New York (2004).

Rashbrooke, Gwenaele, *The International Tribunal for the Law of the Sea: A Forum for the Development of Principles of International Environmental Law*, 19/4 The International Journal of Marine and Coastal Law (2004), pp. 515–536.

Rayfuse, Rosemary, *The Future of Compulsory Dispute Settlement Under the Law of the Sea Convention*, 36 Victoria University of Wellington Law Review (2005), pp. 683–712.

Rayfuse, Rosemary and Robin Warner, *Securing a Sustainable Future for the Oceans Beyond National Jurisdiction: The Legal Basis for an Integrated Cross-Sectoral Regime for High Seas Governance for the 21st Century*, 23 The International Journal of Marine and Coastal Law (2008), pp. 399–421.

Ridgeway, Lori, *Marine Genetic Resources: Outcomes of the United Nations Informal Consultative Process (ICP)*, 24 The International Journal of Marine and Coastal Law (2009), pp. 309–331.

Roach, J. Ashley and Robert W. Smith, *United States Responses to Excessive Maritime Claims*, 2nd ed., Martinus Nijhoff Publishers, The Hague/Boston/London (1996).

Roberts, Julian, *Protecting Sensitive Marine Environments: The Role and Application of Ship's Routeing Measures*, 20/1 International Journal of Marine and Coastal Law (2005), pp. 135–159.

Roberts, Julian, Martin Tsamenyi, Tim Workman and Lindy Johnson, *The Western European PSSA proposal: "a politically sensitive sea area"*, 29 Marine Policy (2005), pp. 431–440.

Romero, Jorge et al., *The Pirates of Puntland: Practical, Legal and Policy Issues in the Fight Against Somali Piracy*, in: K&L/Gates, Maritime White Paper: Piracy, Washington, D.C. (2009).

Rosenne, Shabtai, *International Tribunal for the Law of the Sea: 1996–97 Survey*, 13/4 The International Journal of Marine and Coastal Law (1998), pp. 487–514.

Rotberg, Robert I., *Combating Maritime Piracy: A Policy Brief with Recommendations for Action*, in: World Peace Foundation, Policy Brief #11 (2010).

Rothwell, Donald R. and Sam Bateman (eds.), *Navigational Rights and Freedoms and the New Law of the Sea*, Kluwer International Law, The Hague (2000).

Rothwell, Donald R., *The International Tribunal for the Law of the Sea and Marine Environmental Protection: Expanding the Horizons of International Ocean Governance*, 17 Ocean Yearbook (2003), pp. 26–55.

Rothwell, Donald R. and Tim Stephens, *The International Law of the Sea*, Hart Publishing, Oxford and Portland, Oregon (2010).

Rubin, Alfred P., *The Law of Piracy*, 2nd ed., University Press of the Pacific, Honolulu, Hawaii (2006).

Sanders, Constanze, *Soft Mining Technology Needed: The environmental impact of deep sea mining is still too great*, 1 Evonik Magazine (2008), pp. 17–18.

Schorr, Jennifer L., *The Australian Representative System of Marine Protected Areas and the Marine Zoning System: A Model for the United States?*, 13 Pacific Rim Law and Policy Journal (2004), pp. 673–709.

Schwarze, Jürgen (ed.), *EU-Kommentar*, Nomos (2000).

Scott, Steven, *'Minerals on Land, Minerals in the Sea'* in: Geotimes – December 2002.

Shulman, Mark R., *The Proliferation Security Initiative and the Evolution of the Law on the Use of Force*, 28 Houston Journal of International Law (2006), pp. 771–828.

Scovazzi, Tullio, *Marine Protected Areas on The High Seas: Some Legal and Policy Considerations*, 19/1 The International Journal of Marine and Coastal Law (2004), pp. 1–17.

——, *The Seabed Beyond the Limits of National Jurisdiction: General and Institutional Aspects*, in: The International Legal Regime of Areas Beyond National Jurisdiction: Current and Future Developments, Alex G. Oude Elferink and Erik J. Molenaar (eds.), Martinus Nijhoff Publishers, Leiden/Boston (2010).

——, *The entry into force of the 2001 UNESCO Convention on the Protection of the Underwater Cultural Heritage*, 1 Aegean Rev Law Sea (2010), pp. 19–36.

Seymour, Jillaine, *The International Tribunal for the Law of the Sea: A Great Mistake?*, 13/1 Indiana Journal of Global Legal Studies (2006), pp. 1–35.

Sharma, O.P., *The Threat to Freedom of Navigation in the Exclusive Economic Zone (EEZ) – An Emerging Problem*, 18/3 Journal of Indian Ocean Studies (2010), pp. 325–346.

Shearer, Ivan Anthony, *Military Activities in the Exclusive Economic Zone: The Case of Aereal Surveillance*, 17 Ocean Yearbook (2003), pp. 548–562.

——, *The International Tribunal for the Law of the Sea and its Potential for Resolving Navigation Disputes*, in: Navigation Rights and Freedoms and the New Law of the Sea, Donald R. Rothwell and Sam Bateman (eds.), Martinus Nijhoff Publishers, The Hague/London/Boston (2006).

——, Piracy, Max Planck Encyclopedia of Public International Law, Max Planck Institute for Comparative Public Law and International Law, Rüdiger Wolfrum (ed.), Oxford University Press (2012).

Serdy, Andrew, *The paradoxical Success of UNCLOS Part XV: A Half-hearted Reply to Rosemary Rayfuse*, 36 Victoria University of Wellington Law Review (2005), pp. 713–722.

Silva, Mario, *Somalia: State Failure, Piracy, and the Challenge to International Law*, 50/3 Virginia Journal of International Law (2010), pp. 553–578.

Sinjela, Mpazi, *Freedom of Transit and the Right of Access for Landlocked States: The Evolution of Principle and Law*, 12 Georgia Journal of International Comparative Law (1982), pp. 31–54.

Sittnick, Tammy M., *State Responsibility and Maritime Terrorism in the Strait of Malacca: Persuading Indonesia and Malaysia to take Additional Steps to Secure the Strait*, 14 Pacific Rim Law & Policy Journal (2005), pp. 743–769.

Sohn, Louis B., *Law of the Sea Forum: International Law Implications of the 1994 Agreement*, 88 American Journal of International Law (1994), pp. 696–705.

——, *The Greek Contribution to the Development of the International Law of the Sea*, in: Greece and the Law of the Sea, Theodore C. Kariotis (ed.), Kluwer Law International (1997).

Soons, Alfred H.A., *Marine Scientific Research and the Law of the Sea*, Kluwer International, Deventer, The Netherlands (1982).

Spadi, Fabio, *Navigation in Marine Protected Areas: National and International Law*, 31/3 Ocean Development and International Law (2000), pp. 285–302.

Stracke, Nicole, and Marie Bos, *Piracy: Motivation and Tactics: The Case of Somali Piracy*, in: Gulf Research Center: Knowledge for All, Gulf Research Center (2009).

Suarez, Suzette V., *The Outer Limits of the Continental Shelf, Legal Aspects of their Establishment*, Chapter 7, Springer, Berlin/Heidelberg/New York (2008).

Taft, George, *Applying the Law of the Sea Convention and the Role of the Scientific Community Relating to Establishing the Outer Limit of the Continental Shelf Where It Extends Beyond the 200 Mile Limit*, in: Law, Science and Ocean Management, Ronán Long, Tommy H. Heidar and John Norton Moore (eds.), Martinus Nijhoff Publishers, Leiden (2007).

Tasikas, Vasilios, *The Regime of Maritime Port Access: A Relook at Contemporary International and United States Law*, 5 Loyola Maritime Law Journal (2007), pp. 1–44.

Tavernier, Paul, *Les nouveaux États sans littoral d'Europe et d'Asie et l'accès à la mer*, 97/3 Revue générale de droit international public (1993), pp. 727–744.

Thedwall, Craig, *Choosing the Right Yardarm: Establishing an International Court for Piracy*, 41/2 Georgetown Journal of International Law (2010), pp. 501–523.

Thomas, Ticy V., *The Proliferation Security Initiative: Towards Relegation of Navigational Freedom in UNCLOS? An Indian Perspective*, 8/3 Chinese Journal of International Law (2009), pp. 657–680.

Thun-Hohenstein, Christoph et al. (eds.), *Europarecht*, Manz, Wien (2008).

Tiribelli, Carlo, *Time to Update the 1988 Rome Convention for the Suppression of Unlawful Acts Against the Safety of Maritime Navigation*, 8 Oregon Review of International Law (2006), pp. 133–156.

Treves, Tullio, *The Jurisdiction of the International Tribunal for the Law of the Sea*, 37 Indian Journal of International Law (1997), pp. 396–419.

——, *The Convention for the Suppression of Unlawful Acts against the Safety of Maritime Navigation*, 2 Singapore Journal of International and Comparative Law (1998), pp. 541–556.

——, *The Exclusive Economic Zone and the Settlement of Disputes*, in: The Exclusive Economic Zone and the United Nations Convention on the Law of the Sea 1982–2000: A Preliminary Assessment of State Practice, Erik Franckx and Philippe Gautier (eds.), Bruylant, Bruxelles (2003).

——, *The European Community and the European Union and the Law of the Sea: Recent developments*, 48 Indian Journal of International Law (2008), pp. 1–20.

——, *Marine Scientific Research*, Max Planck Encyclopaedia of Public International Law, Max Planck Institute for Comparative Public Law and International Law, Rüdiger Wolfrum (ed.), Oxford University Press (2012).

——, *Piracy, Law of the Sea, and Use of Force: Developments off the Coast of Somalia*, 20/2 European Journal of International Law (2009), pp. 399–414.

Tsamenyi, Martin and Mary Ann Palma, *Long-Range Identification and Tracking Systems for Vessels: Legal and Technical Issues*, in: Lloyd's MIU Handbook of Maritime Security, Rupert H. Burns et al. (eds.), (2009).

Tuerk, Helmut, *The Landlocked States and the Law of the Sea*, 40/1 Revue Belge de Droit International, Editions Bruylant, Bruxelles (2007), pp. 91–112.

——, *The Contribution of the International Tribunal for the Law of the Sea to International Law*, 26/2 Penn State International Law Review (2007), pp. 289–316.

——, *Combating Terrorism at Sea – The Suppression of Unlawful Acts against the Safety of Maritime Navigation*, 15 University of Miami International and Comparative Law Review, Special Issue (2008), pp. 337–367; also in: Legal Challenges in Maritime Security, Myron H. Nordquist, Rüdiger Wolfrum, John Norton Moore and Ronán Long (eds.), Martinus Nijhoff Publishers, Leiden/Boston (2008).

——, *The Waning Freedom of the Seas*, in: L'évolution et l'état actuel du droit international de la mer, Mélanges de droit de la mer offerts à Daniel Vignes Casado Raigon et Giuseppe Cataldi (eds.), Bruylant, Bruxelles (2009).

——, *The Resurgence of Piracy: A Phenomenon of Modern Times*, 17/1 University of Miami International and Comparative Law Review (2009), pp. 1–42.

——, *Zwölf Jahre Internationaler Seegerichtshof*, in: Die Welt im Spannungsfeld zwischen Regionalisierung und Globalisierung – Festschrift für Heribert Franz Köck, Peter Fischer et al. (eds.), Linde Verlag, Wien (2009).

——, *The Idea of the Common Heritage of Mankind*, in: Serving the Rule of International Maritime Law, Essays in honour of Professor David Joseph Attard, N.A. Martinez Guttierrez (ed.), Routledge, London (2010).

——, *Advisory Opinions and the Law of the Sea*, in: The Challenges of Contemporary International Law and International Relations – Liber Amicorum Dr. Ernest Petrič, M. Pogačnik et al. (ed.). European Law Faculty of Nova Gorica, Nova Gorica (2011), forthcoming.

——, *The Arctic and the Modern Law of the Sea*, in: Governing Ocean Resources: Essays in Tribute to Judge Choon-Ho Park, Jin-Hyun Paik, John M. Van Dyke and Seokwoo Lee (eds.), Brill/Martinus Nijhoff Publishers, Leiden/Boston, forthcoming.

——, *The Work of the International Tribunal for the Law of the Sea*, in: 26 Ocean Yearbook, A. Chircop, S. Coffen-Smout and M. McConnel (eds.), Brill Publishers (2012), forthcoming.

Tuerk, Helmut and Gerhard Hafner, *The Landlocked Countries and the United Nations Convention on the Law of the Sea*, in: Essays on the New Law of the Sea, Budislav Vukas (ed.), Zagreb (1985).

Tyler, Zachary, *Saving Fisheries on the High Seas: The Use of Trade Sanctions to Force Compliance with Multilateral Fisheries Agreements*, 20 Tulane Environmental International Journal (2006), pp. 43–96.

United Nations Convention on the Law of the Sea 1982, A Commentary, Martinus Nijhoff Publishers, Vol. I, Myron H. Nordquist (ed.), Dordrecht/Boston/Lancaster (1985), Vol. II, Satya N. Nandan, Shabtai Rosenne, Neil R. Grandy (eds.), Dordrecht/Boston/London (1993), Vol. III, Satya N. Nandan, Shabtai Rosenne, Neil R. Grandy (eds.), The Hague/Boston/London (1995), Vol. IV, Myron H. Nordquist, Shabtai Rosenne, Alexander Yankov, Neil R. Grandy (eds.), Dordrecht/Boston/London (1991), Vol. V, Myron H. Nordquist, Shabtai Rosenne, Louis B. Sohn (eds.), Dordrecht/Boston/London (1989), Vol. VI, Satya N. Nandan, Michael W. Lodge, Shabtai Rosenne (eds.), The Hague/London/New York (2002) (cited as: "Virginia Commentary").

Ünlü, Nihan, *Particularly Sensitive Areas: Past, Present and Future*, 3/2 WMU Journal of Maritime Affairs (2004), pp. 159–169.

Van Dyke, Jon M., *Sharing Ocean Resources – in a Time of Scarcity and Selfishness*, in: Law of the Sea, the Common Heritage and Emerging Challenges, Harry N. Scheiber (ed.), Martinus Nijhoff Publishers, The Hague/London/Boston, (2000).

——, *The Disappearing Right to Navigational Freedom in the Exclusive Economic Zone*, 29/2 Marine Policy Law Review (2005), pp. 107–121.

Vasciannie, Stephen, *Landlocked and Geographically Disadvantaged States and the Question of the Outer Limit of the Continental Shelf*, 58 British Yearbook of International Law (1987), pp. 271–302.

——, *Land-Locked and Geographically Disadvantaged States in the International Law of the Sea*, Clarendon Press, Oxford (1990).

——, *Landlocked and Geographically Disadvantaged States*, 31 Commonwealth Law Bulletin (2005), pp. 59–70.

Verlaan, Philomène A., *Experimental activities that internationally perturb the marine environment: Implications for the marine environmental protection and marine scientific research provisions of the 1982 United Nations Convention of the Law of the Sea*, 31/2 Marine Policy (2007), pp. 210–216.

Vitzthum, Wolfgang Graf, *Die Bemühungen um ein Regime des Tiefseebodens*, 38 Zeitschrift für ausländisches öffentliches Recht und Völkerrecht (1978), pp. 745–800.

——, *Die Europäische Gemeinschaft und das Internationale Seerecht*, 111 Archiv des Öffentlichen Rechts (1986), pp. 33–62.

Vukas, Budislav, *The Law of the Sea*, Selected Writings, Chapter 10: The New Law of the Sea and Navigation: A View from the Mediterranean, Martinus Nijhoff Publishers, Leiden/Boston (2004).

Weinstein, Elaine B., *The Impact of Regulation of Transport of Hazardous Waste on Freedom of Navigation*, 9 International Journal of Marine and Coastal Law (1994), pp. 135–172.

Weckel, Philippe, *Les premieres applications de l'article 290 de la Convention sur le droit de la mer relatif a la prescription de mesures conservatoires*, 109/4 Revue générale de droit international public (2005), pp. 829–858.

White, Mary Victoria, *The Common Heritage of Mankind: An Assessment*, 14 Case Western Reserve Journal of International Law (1982), pp. 509–542.

Winn, John and Kevin H. Govern, *Maritime Pirates, Sea Robbers, and Terrorists: New Approaches to Emerging Threats*, 2 Homeland Security Review (2008), pp. 131–156.

Witschel, Georg, *Mare Liberum and Maritime Security: Contradiction or Complementarity?, Keynote address*, in: Legal Challenges in Maritime Security, Myron H. Nordquist, Rüdiger Wolfrum, John Norton Moore and Ronán Long (eds.), Martinus Nijhoff Publishers, Leiden/Boston (2008).

Wolfrum, Rüdiger, *The Principle of the Common Heritage of Mankind*, 43 Zeitschrift für ausländisches öffentliches Recht und Völkerrecht (1983), pp. 312–337.

——, *Common Heritage of Mankind*, in: Encyclopedia of Public International Law, Vol. I, Rudolf Bernhardt (ed.), (1992).

——, *Verfahren zur Freigabe von Schiffen vor dem Internationalen Seegerichtshof*, in: Seehandelsrecht und Seerecht: Festschrift für Rolf Herber zum 70. Geburtstag, R. Lagoni and M. Paschke (eds.) Lit Verlag, Hamburg (1999).

——, *Der Internationale Seegerichtshof*, in: Handbuch des Seerechts, Wolfgang Graf Vitzthum (ed.), Verlag C.H. Beck München (2006).

——, *The Tenth Anniversary of the International Tribunal for the Law of the Sea*, 2/3 Romanian Journal of International Law (2006), pp. 66–78.

——, *Fighting Terrorism at Sea: Options and Limitations Under International Law*, in: Legal Challenges in Maritime Security, Myron H. Nordquist, Rüdiger Wolfrum, John Norton Moore and Ronán Long (eds.), Martinus Nijhoff Publishers, Leiden/Boston (2008).

——, *The Settlement of Disputes Before the International Tribunal for the Law of the Sea, A Progressive Development of International Law or Relying on Traditional Mechanism?*, 51 Japanese Yearbook of International Law (2008), pp. 140–163.

——, *The Delimitation of the Outer Continental Shelf: Procedural Considerations*, in: Le procès international – Liber amicorum Jean-Pierre Cot, R. Badinter (Président du Comité d'Honneur), Bruylant, Bruxelles (2009).

——, *Freedom of Navigation: New Challenges*, in: Freedom of Seas, Passage Rights and the 1982 Law of the Sea Convention, Myron H. Nordquist, Tommy T.B. Koh and John Norton Moore (eds.), Martinus Nijhoff Publishers, Leiden (2009).

——, *The Obligation to Cooperate in the Fight Against Piracy – Legal Considerations*, 116 3/4 Chuo Law Review (2009), pp. 81–98.

Wood, Michael, *The International Tribunal for the Law of the Sea and General International Law*, 22/3 International Journal of Marine and Coastal Law (2007), pp. 351–367.

Young, Christopher, *Balancing Maritime Security and Freedom of Navigation on the High Seas: A Study of the Multilateral Negotiation Process in Action*, 24/2 University of Queensland Law Journal (2005), pp. 355–414.

Index

www.ingramcontent.com/pod-product-compliance
Lightning Source LLC
Chambersburg PA
CBHW061210220326
41599CB00025B/4596